Resource Therapy

Names used in therapeutic examples in this book

are not the

names of actual patients.

Gordon Emmerson, PhD

Copyright Gordon Emmerson 2014

Old Golden Point Press

Blackwood, Victoria: Australia

ISBN-10: 0992499518X

ISBN-13: 978-0-9924995-1-8

This book is Dedicated to those who look outward,

experience what they see and feel,

and live honestly and openly with each breath.

Foreword

Leaving myself out of this book to provide a more objective work was a conscious decision, but one that gives me some pause. This foreword is where I allow myself the license to speak of what is important to me.

The metaphor of a primary school playground is one I like to use to better understand and relate meanings in life. For example, when people are being petty or disparaging, I say, 'That is not a part of the playground I want to play in'. Or, when people are being mean, I see that as a grimy part of the playground that I prefer to stay away from.

Using that metaphor of a school playground, probably one of the saddest places to be would be standing alone with no one to play or talk with. Only slightly better would be to be spoken to with a low level of honesty or connection. It would feel best if others would share their honest feelings, and if they would share them feeling they could get something valuable in return. As therapists, this is our place. We have an amazing profession where we are sought out by people who trust us, who tell us what is in them, and who seek help from us. We should only be in this profession if this is something we honor as valuable.

I feel extremely lucky to be in such a profession, and I truly believe the best way to help clients get what they want is to find their personality part that needs change. There is no doubt that we have parts. One part of us can do something that another part regrets. One part can even block another part from stopping it, leaving us only later to wish we had not done that. It just makes sense to work with the part that is upset, that feels rejected, that has learned behavior that is unwanted, or that is in conflict. There is little value in working with the part that wants the change, when it is not the part that needs the change. This therapy is effective, and the reason I took the time to write this book and the Primer is to provide our clients with something that goes beyond merely lessening the symptoms.

There is no reason we and our clients cannot have internal Resource Parts that get along with each other, that feel safe, and that can enjoy living. It is an amazing world we have to live in, and we should not have to experience it through the filter of pathological personality parts. We should be able to experience it, and we should be able to help our clients experience it, with a united group of healthy Resources. It is good when we can place the best resource forward at any given time.

Why smell a rose with the Resource State that does taxes? Why play a sport with the Resource that wants to win, but that is not the player? Why attempt to give a speech with a Resource that feels unable? We have many Resources and I want more therapists to be able to offer their clients the ability to move their pathological Resources to normality and to learn how to engage with the best part for each endeavor.

It is an honorable profession we have chosen. I ask of you to read this book, the ideas presented, and the techniques for change with an open mind and heart. I consistently hear back from those who do, that their stuck clients have moved more than they had thought possible. I want more people to feel safe to experience the world unfiltered by pathological states. It is a place worth experiencing. Thank you for bearing my soapbox.

Resource Therapy: Brief – Powerful – Lasting

The purpose of Resource Therapy is twofold:

1. To attend to pathology expressed as Unwanted Feelings, Behaviors, or Conflicts, and
2. To ensure that the preferred Resources are available.

What does Resource Therapy provide the therapist?

Personality Theory	It provides a clear personality theory that allows the therapist understanding about how and why techniques work.
Diagnosis	It provides a straightforward way to diagnose each presenting issue so the therapist can understand the therapeutic direction to take.
Treatment	It provides clear therapy regimens for each diagnosis.

This is a book of theory, diagnosis, technique regimens, and therapeutic case examples.

Prologue

Resource Therapy (RT) is a new, brief Psychodynamic Therapy. It provides detailed and clear regimens to respond to the causal factors that result in pathology.

The Psychodynamic movement of the early 1900's was based on the contention that traumatic events that occurred earlier in life resulted in later psychological distress. This movement was led by Sigmund Freud, and while the later movements of Phenomenology and Cognitive Behavioralism did not deny this cause and effect relationship, they evolved because the psychodynamic techniques failed to address the underlying issues initiated by earlier distressing events. The Psychodynamic movement had succeeded in contributing a theoretical understanding of the causes of pathology, but it failed in devising ways to address these causes to eliminate their symptoms.

It was because the psychodynamic therapists did not have effective techniques to address the causes of pathology, that cognitive behaviorists attempted another type of intervention. They determined to leave the past alone and aim the focus of therapy toward homework and reframing. The goal was symptom relief, not a resolution of what was taken on from the past. This was helpful, but the problem with this approach was that the unresolved emotions remained in the psyche. These unresolved emotions would return when situational issues brought them out, plus the client often maintained a continued awareness of an unresolved issue still pending. The cause of psychological distress was left unresolved, while the therapeutic focus was on attending to the symptoms.

What is needed is

1. a theory of personality that accurately recognises the causes of psychological stress, and
2. a clear intervention strategy to enable therapists to locate and to resolve these causes.

When the causes of pathology are resolved the symptoms related to that pathology are also resolved. It is important to understand the precise parts of the personality that relate to specific types of pathological symptoms.

Personality parts are Resources and when a Resource becomes pathological the result is distress. It is my contention that some personality parts carry negative affect (Vaded States), some carry out unwanted behavior (Retro States), and some are conflicted with other states (Conflicted States). The precise condition of each pathological state can be diagnosed to understand the dynamic role it has assumed within the personality. This book will assist in the understanding of the etiology of issues including, but not limited to, OCD, depression, eating disorders, addictions, and PTSD.

Technique regimens for working directly with the different Pathological States are clearly presented and illustrated. These techniques will enable therapists to gain direct access to the personality parts that hold pathology and to assist in resolution. Resolving the pathology of the Resource States alleviates the causes of psychological distress, and frees Personality Resources to resume positive functions.

Contents

List of Tables

Table of Case Examples

Vaded with Fear

Vaded with Rejection

Vaded with Disappointment

Vaded with Confusion

Retro Original

Retro Avoiding

Conflicted States

Dissonant State

(*) Transcribed Cases

All client's names have been changed

RT techniques sometimes work best when the client allows his or eyes to close. Shading is used in this text to designate when clients have their eyes closed.

Unit 1: Etiology

Chapter 1
Resource Therapy Preview

The personality is made up of different parts, or Resources. The part that brings the client to therapy is usually non-pathological.

It is better to work directly with pathological parts than to spend extended session time talking with the personality part that brought the client to therapy. There are four types of pathological Resource States, as illustrated in Assumption 4 below.

Table 1: Assumptions of Resource Therapy

1. The personality is composed of parts
2. Clients react differently from different personality parts
3. Parts can be healthy or pathological

4. Pathological parts can be
    • Vaded: Carry unwanted emotions
    • Retro: Do unwanted behavior
    • Conflicted: Parts are in conflict to the point of anxiety
    • Dissonant: The wrong part is holding the Conscious

5. Pathological parts can be brought back to normality

Vaded States: These states are personality parts that carry unresolved feelings that can result in psychological distress. They can cause issues for clients when they come into the Conscious or when they are avoided with some type of avoiding behavior (see the table below).

Vaded States can be Problematic

Vaded States can be problematic in two ways	Symptoms
Vaded Conscious State: Brings its negative feelings into the Conscious	Phobia, panic, anxiety, fear, sense of worthlessness or incompetence, guilt, rumination, or depression
Vaded Avoided State: The negative feelings are avoided by Retro State Avoiding behavior	Addictions, OCD, self-harming, obsessive behavior (shopping, eating, work)

Retro States: Retro States carry out unwanted behavior. There are two types of Retro States. Retro Avoiding States carry out behavior so the client will not have to experience the feelings of a Vaded State. Retro Original States carry out unwanted behavior that was originally learned in childhood. This is not avoiding behavior, but behavior that was originally learned to cope with the challenging situations in childhood. Examples of this behavior include, anti-social behavior, pouting, passive aggressive behavior, personality disorders, and rage. Both Retro Original States and Retro Avoiding States benefit from Retro State Negotiation, although avoiding behavior will most usually return unless the underlying Vaded State is first resolved. In other words, it is difficult for a gambler to stop gambling as long as the anxiety that fuels that behavior continues.

Conflicted States: Clients will sometimes present due to Conflicted States. These personality parts are in conflict to the point of emotional distress. A client with Conflicted Resource States will present with an inner struggle such as procrastination, sleep difficulties, or anxiety over decision-making. Statements such as, "I wish I didn't do that," or, "I hate myself when I am like that," are indicative of either Retro Behavior or Conflicted Resource States.

Dissonant States: These are otherwise Normal States that come into the Conscious at the wrong time. They feel uncomfortable when they are Dissonant, and they result in below par performance for the client. Clients with Dissonant States will be disappointed in the way they cope or with their ability in a sport, task, or relationship.

All personality parts originated to help with coping. They are our resources. Resource Therapy facilitates a precise diagnosis of pathological Resource States. Once the correct classification is made a clear treatment regimen can begin. It is the goal of this therapy to ensure that all states are positive Resources within the personality.

Resource Therapy is straightforward and powerful. The therapist can focus on four steps (ACAR) to attend to the issues presented.

Table 2: Resource Therapy Process (ACAR)

Aim	Determine what the client is ready to change.
Classify	Diagnose the Pathological Resource State into a category.
Actions	Follow the prescribed RT Actions for the Classification.
Review	Debrief with the client.

There are 12 core RT Actions that are the basis of most treatment. The first of these is Diagnosis, and the prescription of the next Actions is directed by the diagnosis. There are treatment variations specific to pathological concerns which are detailed later in this book.

This book is divided into two units:

- **Unit I Aetiology:** Explains personality dynamics
- **Unit II Diagnosis and Treatment:** Presents diagnostic criteria and treatment regimens, case examples and transcripts

Chapter 2
Resource Personality Theory

It is important to understand Resources to understand the techniques that facilitate them to change.

The different parts of the personality are termed Resources. These Resources may be 'Normal' and non-pathological, or pathological. They may be **Surface** (conscious or observing), or **Underlying** (unconscious of the present). Resource States together make a federation of personality, much like the states of a federated country, with each state being different from the next and each state being part of the whole personality. Both well-functioning and pathological parts are termed Resources because a pathological personality part can return to a positive function with the appropriate intervention.

Resource: A personality part that was created by the repetition of returning over and over again to a coping skill. It is a physiological part of the nervous system created by axon and dendrite growth and trained synaptic firings. Each Resource manifests the traits of the coping skill that formed it. Each will have its own level of emotion, intellect, and abilities. Whenever a person is Conscious there is a Resource State holding the Conscious.

When a Resource is 'Conscious' it is out and it has control of the personality. For example, when a person is currently in a joking, light hearted mood, that Resource State is referred to as the 'Conscious' state. Other personality parts that may be fragile, reactive, intellectual, or reflective do not at that time hold the Consciousness. A person will not experience the symptoms of a pathology unless a state related to that pathology is 'Conscious'. The 'subconscious' is the collection of Underlying Resource States that are not currently conscious or observing.

Conscious: The awareness of self. The Conscious is held by the Resource State that is currently experiencing, aware, and behaving. When a different Resource State takes over the Conscious, sense of self, emotions, behavior and abilities change. The Conscious awareness may change from intellectual and reflective, to reactive and emotional with a change of Resource State.

The client suffering from OCD, while doing checking behavior, will have a checking Resource in the Conscious as he or she feels and thinks, "I have to check these locks," but when another Resource becomes Conscious he or she will likely detest that checking Resource and wish it was not there. Those two Resources are conflicted. A person who says, "I hate myself when I am like that," is expressing from one Resource about another Resource, and this type of statement is endemic of **Conflicted States**. In Resource Personality Theory the terms Resource and Resource State are synonymous.

Paul Federn, a contemporary of Freud, first defined the personality as composed of parts. He saw distinct states that individuals moved into and out of, and noted that as they do, no matter which state individuals operated from their ego was present. Federn called these personality parts Ego States (Federn, 1953). These personality parts are termed Resources in Resource Personality Theory. Federn's, and later Weiss' (1950), conception of the personality has been interpreted within a number of therapeutic orientations, including Resource Personality Theory, Ego State Personality Theory (Watkins, 1978), and Transactional Analysis (Berne, 1957). Federn's and Weiss' work has also influenced the theories of Guntrip (1961), Jacobson (1964), Kernberg (1976), Kohut (1977), Winnicott (1965), and Watkins and Watkins (1997). Differences between Resource Therapy and other Ego State Therapy are detailed in Appendix 1.

The Origin of Resources

Resources are personality parts that first developed as coping mechanisms for the client. When a coping skill was developed, especially early in life, and returned to over and over again, the repetitive behavior caused specific axon and dendrite growth, and trained synaptic connections. This repetitive training creates a personality part that can be returned to when its function is needed.

The formulation of the personality and the formulation of the Resources coincide. Most Resources develop during childhood and early adolescence, although it is possible for new Resources to develop in adulthood given sufficient training. Resource development is a physiological development.

Animal studies have made it clear that the brain develops according to stimulation. Animals that have been exposed to enhanced activity had enhanced brain growth. Their brains grow more and weigh more. Axon and dendrite growth and the development of synaptic connections vary both according to the amount of stimulation and according to the type of stimulation. Schrott (1997) overviewed a number of studies, both animal and human that indicate the brain develops 'profoundly' in relation to the stimulation it receives.

Muir, Dalhousie, and Mitchell (1975) demonstrated how the brains of kittens develop in early life in relation to vision. During the first four months of life the vision of kittens was confined to contours of a single orientation (using special lenses), either vertical or horizontal. Kittens that were raised where they could only view a vertical orientation of their surroundings during their first four months were later less able to see horizontal shapes, and kittens that were raised where they could only view a horizontal orientation of their surroundings during their first four months were later less able to see vertical shapes. Numerous other animal studies confirm that the brain develops according to the particular type of stimulation it receives (Levin, 2010; Wilkinson & Frances, 1995; Blakemore, 1987; Wark, Peck, & Carol, 1982; Buisseret, Gary-Bobo, & Imbery, 1982).

Not only do brains grow according to stimulation, but existing synapses fire more easily with repetitive practice. The first time something is attempted, whether it is a physical activity or mental learning task, ability is normally low, but with repetition the same activity or task may become easy and commonplace (Brych & Fisher, 2011).

Resource Personality Theory is based on the evidence that the brain is formed, and is trained through repetition. During early childhood, if the child is nurturing to a parent and receives positive feedback for this nurturing behavior, the child may return over and over again to this nurturing behavior to receive the positive feedback. This repetition of nurturance can create a nurturing Resource; that is, a neural pathway made by axon and dendrite connections and trained synaptic firing that may be activated in the future when the person wants positive feedback. Physiological brain growth and training from repeated practice creates this neural pathway, this Resource. When this Resource comes into the Conscious it brings with it its particular level of feelings, intellect and the skills it has learned during the repetitive behavior that formed it.

For example, a child who wanted attention (unmet need) might attempt to gain that attention by telling a joke or by doing something funny (coping skill). If that child got the wanted attention from this behavior and returned repeatedly to that behavior over and over again that child would develop a joking Resource. Later in life, when that child needs attention, he or she may tell a joke or do something funny, because the joking Resource is activated.

The brain grows and develops according to stimulation. A different child, who found attempts at being funny unsuccessful, would not develop a joking Resource. Therefore, each individual has his or her own Resource map. This Resource map is what defines personality (Emmerson, 2011). Each person has a number of Resources, and those Resources will be in one of the five conditions above, Normal, Conflicted, Vaded, Dissonant, or Retro, (Emmerson, 2006).

If the child learns, in a family where there is a lot of yelling and screaming, that withdrawing and being quiet results in 'Keeping out of trouble', and if this withdrawing occurs repetitively to the benefit of the child then a withdrawing Resource may develop. In childhood, and later in life, when this person is confronted with anger or loudness, this withdrawing Resource may emerge, giving the person the feelings of being frightened and having to be quiet. When a client feels inner conflict in relation to this behavior the withdrawing Resource becomes a Retro Original State, a Resource whose behavior is not wanted by other states.

Resource States, therefore, are physiological. They are a result of normal brain development. They are a result of axon and dendrite development and of synaptic training. They become a part of the personality. Each person has an undetermined number of Resource State neural pathways, numbering at least in double digits. Resources can be divided roughly into two types, Surface (used often) and Underlying (rarely used), and the state a person is experiencing life from at any time is called the Conscious state.

Memory and its Therapeutic Importance

We often think of memory as only intellectual memory, our ability to intellectually and verbally revisit a past event. I propose that along with our Intellectual Memory we also have a Sensory Experience Memory (SEM) that is the emotional re-experiencing of an event. Because SEM is core to many psychological issues and also key to resolving many psychological issues it is important to gain a good understanding of it.

Sensory Experience Memory (SEM)

Sensory Experience Memory (Emmerson, 2014) is the emotional re-experiencing of the emotions of a past event. It may, or may not, be connected to an Intellectual Memory. For example, if a person witnesses a car accident, during the immediate re-telling of that event the person will often experience the SEM related to the accident. Here, the Intellectual Memory and the SEM are directly connected, and the person will feel the emotions experienced when retelling the accident that was witnessed. But, the SEM may become dissociated from the Intellectual Memory. For example, a person may experience a trauma in childhood, and if left unprocessed, that person can later re-experience the SEM associated to that trauma in adulthood in the form of anxiety, fear, feelings of unworthiness, or panic, without knowing where the unwanted emotions are coming from.

A SEM normally diminishes over time. As long as the person is able to talk about what was experienced, gain a perspective about it, and feel comfortable in moving forward, the Sensory Experience Memory of the accident will lessen over time and the person will become better able to recall the Intellectual Memory without feeling emotionally out of control. Therefore, a trait of a SEM is that it naturally diminishes over time, when there has been conversations that help the person feel understood, so fears, anger, and other negative emotions can diminish.

The nature of Sensory Experience Memories:

- They are the non-intellectual, emotional recall of an event

- They may or may not be connected to the Intellectual Memory (i.e., the person may not know where the feeling is coming from)

- They may be positive or negative

- They tend to extinguish over time, unless left unprocessed

- They are the negative experiences of Vaded States

- They may be used in therapy to achieve understanding and change

- In order to experience a SEM the Resource that originally experienced it must hold the conscious

Examples of Sensory Experience Memories:

- Fears associated with Phobias

- Panic Attacks

- Anxiety that expresses beyond the current situation

- Feelings of low self-worth

- Depression

- Feelings of Confusion and Rumination

SEMs may be negative or positive, but sadly the negative SEMs last longer because they are the ones that require processing. It is probable that following a negative experience, SEMs are held so the person can learn something before letting go of what was experienced. It is problematic that a negative SEM can be held for a lifetime, re-emerging, causing the person to re-experience the negative feelings even when they are no longer associated with the original event.

How SEMs can be used in Therapy

Later in this book it will be shown how the negative emotions experienced during a SEM can guide the therapist and client to the initial sensitizing event that caused that emotion. This both creates an intellectual understanding of where that emotion comes from and it provides an opportunity to process the emotion so the client can become empowered, safe and supported in relation to the event. The negative SEM is therefore extinguished and the client is left with their intellectual understanding of the event. This is how Vaded States are brought back to a state of Normality.

SEMs are also useful in helping clients with a number of other issues. When there is confusion relating to a present or past relationship, that confusion is most often the result of a sense of 'unknowing' about how another person may feel. When the therapist has a client to speak with the Introject of the other person (living or dead) in an empty chair, then asks the client to go to that chair and reply as the other person, a SEM is created. The SEM is the emotional experience of being the Introject. When clients return from an Introject's chair they return with a SEM of the feelings of the Introject. This SEM is more important than what the client said as the Introject while they were speaking from the Introject's chair. It is the client's experience of the SEM of the Introject that can provide a cathartic increase in understanding about the relationship. More succinctly, it is not as much what the Introject has said, as what the Introject felt that allows the client to experience a catharsis in understanding. A number of therapeutic examples of this are presented in this text. Remember, an Introject is an internal impression. It is not the other person that causes a client to hold anxiety over a relationship, it is the Introject of that person (that the client holds). The other person is not in the therapy room, but the Introject is. Therefore, there is real change power in the client gaining an understanding of the feelings of the Introject.

Conflicted Resource States are states that do not understand and appreciate the value of each other, e.g., a work state and a rest state. They can achieve an understanding of the value of each other with the use of SEMs. In the same way a client can gain a better understanding of another person with the use of properly directed empty chair work, Resource States can gain an appreciation and understanding of each other when they return to their chair holding the SEM of the state that just spoke from the other chair. SEMs often extinguish quickly, but they are still strong during the process of switching from one chair to the next. That means a state that has just spoken about needing rest and the importance of recharging the body can be felt by the state that wants to work constantly when the client moves to that chair. When states learn that each are important and each needs time, an inner peace can develop and states can respect each other and compromise so each can help appropriately.

Resource Conditions: Normal and Pathological

Normal states

Resources in the Normal condition exhibit psychological health. They function well externally and within the personality. They are not conflicted with other states and they do not hold psychological distress.

Conflicted States

Resources in a conflicted condition are in a level of conflict with another Resource to the extent that the individual experiences psychological distress. While it is common and appropriate that Resources hold different opinions ['I would really like the car', and 'there's no way I can afford a new car'] conflicted states acquire a level of conflict that becomes stressful to the client. A 'work state' and a 'rest state' may be in conflict over the activity of the client, which is the case when a client presents with procrastination. A state that wants to sleep and a state that wants to think can be in conflict, which can result in insomnia.

Dissonant States

Resources that would otherwise be normal, except the Dissonant State is not the preferred state to hold the Conscious. The Dissonant state is uncomfortable in the Conscious, and it would prefer another state to take over. Examples of this is having the wrong state out when testing, when playing a sport, or when dealing with a boss, a partner, or a child.

Vaded States

Vaded States are Resource States that have become overwhelmed by negative emotion to the point where they can no longer carry out their normal functions, and when they come to the Conscious they bring their negative emotions (a SEM) with them, resulting in the client feeling upset and out-of-control. When a Vaded State becomes conscious the client feels bad emotionally, and this can be experienced as anxiety, fear, frustration, panic, or even an undefined negative feeling. There is most often an Initial Sensitizing Event that relates to when a Normal State became Vaded, and helping the Vaded State reframe the Introjects it holds around this event can return it to a state of normality. Vaded States are the origin of a number of psychological issues that will be detailed in this book.

All Vaded States have in common the fact that they were Normal functioning Resources that were developed to fulfill a function prior to the time they became Vaded. Once Vaded, these states are no longer able to fulfill their normal function, until they become resolved.

Traumatic incidents do not always vade Resources. Following a traumatic incident, if the individual gets support and understanding, is able to talk about what happened, and is able to gain some perspective then the Resource will not be Vaded. This underlines the importance of crisis intervention therapy. It is often family or friends who are able to offer understanding and support.

Most Resources that become Vaded are vaded in childhood. Children often feel unable to ask for help or support, and may not have the experience to do so. Sometimes they feel they would get into trouble if they tried to talk to someone about their issues. A state is Vaded when it experiences something outside of its ability to deal with emotionally, and does not gain a resolution.

Table 3: Stage of Development when Normal states become Vaded

	Vaded with Fear	Vaded with Rejection	Vaded with Confusion	Vaded with Disappointment
Childhood	Predominately	Predominately	Occasionally	Occasionally
Adulthood	Occasionally	Occasionally	Predominately	Predominately

Adults may also have experiences outside their ability to cope, and when this happens without proper crisis intervention they too may experience the vading of a Resource. Adult onset PTSD is an example of this. PTSD is the result of a Resource that has experienced a life-threatening situation and has not received proper emotional resolution.

Resources may be Vaded in four ways. They may be

- **Vaded with Fear**: (Phobias, PTSD, Panic, situational fear),
- **Vaded with Rejection**: (Feeling worthless or unlovable, high need for approval),
- **Vaded with Confusion**: (Rumination, confusion), or
- **Vaded with Disappointment**: (Depression, Despair).

Each of these types of Vaded States may result in an array of psychological disturbance. The following sections will detail the types of disturbance that can be attributed to each type of Vaded State.

Vaded States cause psychological issues in two ways:

- **Vaded Conscious:** These states come into the Conscious giving the client the negative feelings they hold, along with a feeling of being out of control. This state may feel emotionality, anxiety, or have feelings of worthlessness, confusion or despair. Examples include, PTSD, Depression, Panic Disorders, Phobias and others. States Vaded with Disappointment or

Confusion will manifest as Vaded Conscious States, while states Vaded with Fear or Rejection may manifest as Vaded Conscious States or they may be avoided by Retro State Avoiding behavior.

- **Vaded Avoided States:** These Vaded States come into or near the surface then are driven from the surface by avoidance behavior. It is the behavior of a Retro Avoiding State (described below) that directs the Vaded State away from surface consciousness in order to avoid the negative feelings of the Vaded State. Examples include, Addictions, OCD, Eating Disorders, Anti-Social Behaviors, and others. These states may be Vaded with Fear or Rejection.

Table 4: Pathological Manifestation of Vaded States

	Vaded with Fear	Vaded with Rejection	Vaded with Confusion	Vaded with Disappointment
When Vaded Conscious States	Phobias, PTSD, Panic, situational fear	Feeling worthless or unlovable, high need for approval	Rumination, confusion	Depression, Despair
When Vaded Avoided States (are driven from the Consciousness by Retro Avoiding States**)**	Addictions, Drug Taking, OCD, Withdrawal, Anger	Eating Disorders, Work/relationship avoidance, Shopping Addiction, 'Perfectionistic' behavior	Sleeplessness, Inability to concentrate, can't let go.	Withdrawal, Anti-Depressant Medication

Retro states

Retro states, when conscious, act in ways that other Resources (and usually other people) find problematic. The two types of Retro States, **Retro Original States** and **Retro Avoiding States** are described below.

- **Retro Original States** are states that have learned a functional coping skill in childhood that is no longer wanted by the client. Much antisocial behavior is a result of **Retro Original States** and examples include passive aggressive behavior and rage. These Retro States will continue to see their role as important, until they can be negotiated with to take on an altered or lesser role.

- **Retro Avoiding States** learn to hold the Consciousness to avoid the experience of a Vaded State. In problem gambling, the state that gambles is a Retro Avoiding State. It has learned to protect the client from a painful Vaded emotion filled state by filling the Consciousness with gambling activity. Other Resources will dislike this gambling Resource, but the Retro state believes its role in saving the client from the negative emotions of the Vaded State is more important than the disapproval it endures. Other examples of Retro Avoiding States include the states that cause a client to feel numb, states that act out OCD behavior, self-harming behavior, and states that are involved with eating disorder activities and addictions. These states will hold a strong compulsion to maintain their "helping" behavior until the feelings of the Vaded State are resolved.

Table 5: Pathological Manifestations of Retro States by Type

Retro Original State Behaviors	Retro Avoiding State Behaviors	
Pouting, Anti-Social Behavior, Rage, Personality Disorders, Passive Aggressive Behavior	Addictions, Drug Taking, OCD, Withdrawal, Anger Eating Disorders, Work/relationship avoidance, Shopping Addiction, 'Perfectionistic' behavior, Self-Harming behavior.	**Retro Original Behavior** is learned in childhood as a coping mechanism during the development of the Resource State. **Retro Avoiding Behavior** is used as an escape mechanism to assist the personality to avoid the traumatic feelings of a State Vaded with Fear or Rejection.

Table 6 Stage of Development when states begin Retro Behavior

	Retro Original States	**Retro Avoiding States**	Behavior becomes Retro when other States wish it would not happen. A behavior that all states view as OK is not Retro Behavior.
Childhood	Predominately	Occasionally	
Adulthood	Occasionally	Predominately	

Dissonant States

A Dissonant State is a state that is holding the Conscious at a time when a different Resource State would be preferred. The Dissonant State does not want to hold the Conscious, so it is a rather straightforward process to find a more preferred Resource State and negotiate with states for a better outcome. These techniques are included with other treatment regimens.

When a Dissonant State holds the Conscious the following symptoms may be evident:

- Frustration in Coping Ability

- Feelings of ineptitude

- Inability to be real self

- Writers block

- Sporting slumps

- Below par performance

A more detailed analysis of Dissonant States can be found in Chapter 12 Treatment for Dissonant States, page 335. This chapter also has case examples of assisting clients to ensure the preferred state is available for challenging situations.

Introjects

It is the impressions Resources hold of Introjects that give them fear and feelings of low value.

Introjects are our internalized impressions of another person, an animal, or even an inanimate, like a flood, a fire, a storm, or a fictional character. We will have an Introject, an internalized impression, of every person we know. It is **Introjects** that Vaded States internally fear, feel rejected by, feel disappointed by, or feel confusion about. While a Resource is a physiological part of the brain that has developed with axon and dendrite growth during the repetition of a useful coping skill, an Introject is merely an impression that a Resource holds. While an Introject may be feared by a resource, the only power it has is the power that is given it by the Resource that has introjected it. The person that an Introject represents may be real, but an Introject is merely a memory fragment.

A central feature in assisting a Vaded State to return to normality is a process of providing it with the understanding that the Introject it has feared, felt rejected by, been disappointed by, or felt confusion about is not real. It may be appropriate for the client to fear a real person, but there is no utility in fearing an Introject, a memory fragment.

Introject: A Resource State's internalized impression of another person, an animal, or an inanimate. Most Introjects are experienced as emotionally positive, but Vaded States hold Introjects from which they have experienced negative emotion. These Introjects have only the power given them by the Resource States that hold them.

Introjects are Resource State specific. That means that one Resource may hold an Introject of the person, John, and another Resource may hold a different Introject (impression) of the same person. One Resource may see John as an important friend, while another Resource may distrust, or dislike John. A battered client may have a Resource that hates their battering partner, Terry, but when another Resource is Conscious that same client may love and need Terry.

This state dependent introjection is most evident with people suffering from DID, multiple personality disorder. One alter may know an individual well, while another alter may not know the same person at all.

The fact that Resources have their own **Introjects** means that one Resource may hold an unfulfilled need to gain love from a parent, while another Resource may either know it has that love, or may not be interested in having that love at all. A Vaded childhood Resource may fear an older, bigger cousin, while the adult Resource may hold no fear of that cousin.

Figure 1: Illustration of one Client's three Resources (Playful, Work, and Homemaker) holding different Introjects of the same persons.

Child **Playful** State's
Introjects

Adult **Work**
State's Introjects

Adult **Homemaker**
State's Introjects

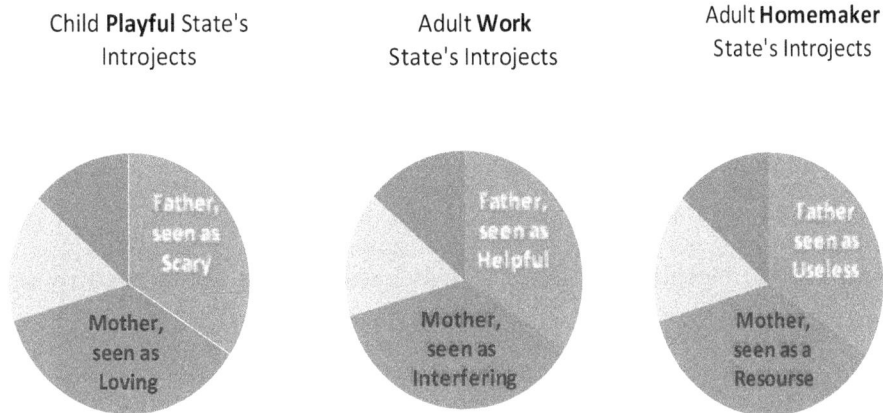

The understanding that clients have a number of Resources, each holding their own Introjects, is very important when working in therapy, because clients often respond to the therapist from a mature, intellectual, talkative Resource State. This intellectual Resource State will have different feelings about, for example, a parent, than will other underlying Resources that may have been vaded by that parent. The most powerful therapeutic interventions work directly with the Resource States that are pathological.

Resource States are the real personality parts. Introjects are merely the impressions they hold.

Outline of Resource Personality Theory regarding Pathology

Resources: Neuro-physical personality states created by the repetition of returning to the same coping behavior numerous times. Most of these states are formed during childhood or early adolescence when varied coping behaviors are needed.

Resource conditions:

Normal states: Healthy Resources with behavior that is appreciated by other Resources.

Vaded States: Resources that hold negative, unprocessed emotions from the past. These states may be Vaded in four ways:

- Vaded with Fear: (Phobias, PTSD, Panic, situational fear)

- Vaded with Rejection: (Feeling worthless or unlovable, high need for approval)

- Vaded with Confusion: (Rumination, confusion, guilt)

- Vaded with Disappointment: (Depression, Despair)

Vaded States cause psychological issues in two ways, as being:

- Vaded Conscious States: The state surfaces with its feelings of angst causing the person to feel emotionality, anxiety, or have feelings of worthlessness, confusion or despair.

- Vaded Avoided States: Vaded States that come into or near the surface then are driven from the surface by avoidance behavior. This behavior is often regretted by the person.

Retro States: Resources that carry out learned behavior that the person regrets.

There are two types of Retro States:

- **Retro Original States:** These states learned in childhood how to benefit the person in a way that other states find offensive. (Pouting, Anti-Social behavior, Rage, Passive-Aggressive behavior)

- **Retro Avoiding States:** These states carry out the behavior that protects the person from the feelings of the Vaded Avoided States. (Addictive behavior, OCD behavior, self-harming behavior, eating disorder behavior)

Conflicted States: Resources that demonstrate or advocate behavior that other states do not agree with to the point the inner conflict causes anxiety to the person.

Dissonant States: Resources that come into the Conscious at the wrong time. They do not want to be in the Conscious, and they feel uncomfortable and often incompetent.

The movement toward Mental Health is the movement for **Vaded States**, **Retro States**, **Conflicted States** and **Dissonant States** to achieve a **Normal Resource Condition.** Chapters 5 through 12 present treatment regimens for Resource States from each pathological type and for clients who have not learned how to access their best Resource.

How SEMs relate to each pathological state

- Vaded States: It is the unresolved negative SEMs that Vaded States experience when they hold the Conscious. These states need help processing the negative SEMs so they can move back to a state of Normality.

- Retro States: Retro Avoiding States are using avoiding behaviour to escape the unwanted SEMs that Vaded States hold. When these SEMs are processed the Retro Avoiding States will no longer have a need to escape them. Both Retro Original and Retro Avoiding States can better learn new, preferred behavior when they have experienced the SEMs of other states showing appreciation to them for taking on the new behavior. I.e., a Rage state may have not been liked by other states. The therapist can ask the state that decided to come to therapy if it will like the Rage State if it will only come out during life threatening instances. This state will be able to express approval and appreciation of the Rage State if it takes on this limited behavior. Then, by immediately returning to the Rage State while the SEM proves evidence of appreciation, this Rage State can realise what if feels like being liked. This feeling of actually being liked is so compelling to it, it will agree to take on a more limited role so it can be internally appreciated.

- Conflicted States: As discussed earlier in this chapter, states that have been in conflict can learn to understand and appreciate each other by experiencing the SEM of each other during directed switching in therapy. This can help end issues such as procrastination and insomnia for many clients.

- Dissonant States: A state that has been uncomfortable holding the Conscious becomes pleased to allow a different state to hold the Conscious once it has experienced the SEM of that state desiring to help with the skills that are needed.

Pathologies associated with Resource State by Type

The Tables below lists pathologies and the Type of Pathological Resource States that are directly associated with them. These lists can help guide the therapist to the correct treatment regimens when clients present with one of these pathologies. The first RT Action in the next Chapter helps the therapist diagnose each presenting concern into one type of Resource State Pathology.

Table 7: Resources Vaded with Fear can cause these Pathologies

• Nightmares and sleep terror • Specific Phobia • Panic attack • PTSD • Agoraphobia • Self-harming behavior • Generalized Anxiety Disorder • Dissociative Identity Disorders	• Pathological Gambling • Addictions • Workaholism • OCD (or may Vaded with Rejection) • Social Phobia (or may Vaded with Rejection) • Business Phobia (or may Vaded with Rejection)	• Compulsive Shopping (or more often is Vaded with Rejection) • Antisocial (or may be Retro or Vaded with Rejection) • Crisis reaction (benefitting from crisis intervention)

See   Chapter 5 Treatment of states Vaded with Fear 161

Table 8: Resources Vaded with Rejection can cause these Pathologies

- Social Phobia (or may be Vaded with Fear)
- Business Phobia (or may be Vaded with Fear)
- Narcissism
- Anorexia Nervosa
- Bulimia Nervosa
- Antisocial (or may be Vaded with Fear)
- Feeling Unlovable
- Business Phobia (or may be Vaded with Fear)
- Compulsive Shopping (or may be Vaded with Fear)
- Over competiveness

See Chapter 6 Treatment of States Vaded with Rejection 207

Table 9: Resources Vaded with Disappointment cause these Pathologies

- Depression
- Relationship blame
- Prolonged and intense feelings of loss

See Chapter 7 Treatment for states Vaded with Disappointment 241

Table 10: Resources Vaded with Confusion can cause these Pathologies

- Complicated Bereavement
- Rumination (over the welfare of others, death, or an event)
- Guilt or Shame
- Existential angst
- Deep confusion over the breakdown of a relationship

See Chapter 8 Treatment of states Vaded with Confusion ……. . 269

Table 11: Retro Original States can cause these Pathologies

- Anti-Social Behavior
- Withdrawal
- Pouting
- Rage
- Personality Disorders
- Passive Aggressive Behavior

See Chapter 9 Treatment of Retro Original States ……………… 289

Table 12: Retro Avoiding States can cause these Pathologies

- Addictions	- Anger or Rage as a means to act out
- OCD	- Eating Disorders
- Self-harming behavior	- Work/relationship avoidance
- Obsessive behavior (shopping, eating, work)	- Shopping Addiction
	- 'Perfectionistic' behavior
- Drug Taking	- Self-Harming behavior

See Chapter 10: Treatment of Retro Avoiding States …………… 301

Table 13: Conflicted States can cause these Pathologies

- Procrastination
- Sleep Disturbance
- Chronic Fatigue
- Cognitive Dissonance

See   Chapter 11 Treatment of Conflicted States 321

Table 14: Dissonant States can cause these Pathologies

- Frustration in Coping Ability
- Feelings of ineptitude
- Inability to be real self
- Writers block
- Sporting slumps
- Below par performance

See   Chapter 12 Treatment for Dissonant States 335

Chapter 3
Etiology of Pathological Resource States

There are eight pathological state types and each one relates to specific DSM categories.

States Vaded with Fear

A Resource Vaded with Fear is characterized by one of the following feelings, when that feeling does not fit the situation at hand.

- General Anxiety
- Fear
- Panic
- Inability to be alone
- A feeling of being out of control
- Feeling Fragile
- A feeling that the focus of anxiety is bigger than the client

Resources may be Vaded by dramatic events or by minor incidents. Sometimes the determining factor on whether a Resource becomes Vaded is the resilience of the person at the time. If the person is tired, if the person already feels in a weakened emotional state, or the person is fragile, minor incidents may vade a Resource. In the following sections I will detail examples of how each of the four types of Vaded States can be vaded.

How is a Resource Vaded with Fear Pathological?	Normal State
A Resource Vaded with Fear is stuck in a past event. It actually believes it is still happening. When it comes to the surface it brings with it fear that interferes with the ability of the client to respond to life's current challenges.	Normal States hold no fear from the past. They can appropriately fear something present that could hurt them, but they no longer harbor fear from events that come from the past. They are able to make wise decisions based on current realities.

Resources that have been vaded have in common the fact that they carry with them an illusion that the past is still happening. They are stuck in a past event and continue to experience it as the present. They are stuck in the emotion or the confusion of the past event and they cannot move beyond it. In order to help understand the context of Vaded States it is important to understand **Introjects**, because it is the impression states hold of **Introjects** that vade Resources.

Initial sensitizing events may vade a Resource with fear

Resources may be Vaded with Fear following exposure to something dramatic and horrible, or they may be Vaded with Fear following exposure to what would seem to be a minor event but is one that the Resource is not able to understand or process. For example, a Resource may be Vaded with Fear following a life-threatening event, or a Resource may be Vaded with Fear merely after calling out for a parent repeatedly and getting no response.

A number of factors determine if a state becomes vaded by an event.

- **Nature:** Genealogy is a factor. Some people are naturally more resilient than others, and some people are naturally more sensitive than others. Two people experiencing the same event will be stressed by it at different levels. This is probably due both to nature and nurture.

- **Nurture:** Resilience is also a factor in relation to nurture. Some children are more protected than others. Those who have been overly protected may find some situations overwhelming while those who have had more exposure may find the same situations commonplace.

- **Love and support:** Resilience is also affected by the amount of support that is experienced. Children who know they are loved and know they can talk about things with a loving family member are more resilient. Some children have a compromised level of resilience because they are not sure they are loved.

- **Safety:** When people feel unsafe they are more vulnerable. This can be the case for a child walking to school, child at school, or even a soldier in war. Living with a chronic concern for safety weakens resilience.

- **Crisis intervention:** When a person experiences something as traumatic, there is a need to gain an understanding of what was experienced and feel support. Being able to talk about an experience that was perceived as traumatic is very important. Even extremely traumatic incidents may not vade Resources when there is an ability to gain understanding, feel support, and feel safe.

- **Type of incident:** As stated above, a Resource may be vaded by a relatively minor incident, but the level of drama in an incident is directly related to Resources becoming vaded. Incidents that are experienced as overwhelming are the type that most commonly vade Resources. An incident that vades a Resource is referred to as the initial sensitizing event, ISE (Boswell, 1987; Ritzman, 1992).

Case Illustrations of how a Resource can become Vaded with Fear

These examples will demonstrate the nature of Vaded States, how they were **Normal States** before becoming overwhelmed by a negative experience (during an ISE), and how they became stuck in that experience until a resolution was found.

Jane had PANIC ATTACKS

In "Ego State Therapy" (Emmerson, 2003, 2007, 2010), I wrote about a woman who was suffering from panic attacks (the transcript is in that book). She did not know why she had the panic attacks, but when she had one she felt as if she was being choked, and she felt that she needed to break away and run for her life.

In therapy, the Resource that was vaded with this feeling was brought to the surface and a bridging technique allowed the woman to revisit the initial sensitizing event. She bridged to being a 10 year old girl swimming in the ocean. She was caught in a rip tide and a smaller cousin was hanging onto her neck. While she had not previously connected this event to her panic attacks, it was her cousin trying to hang onto her neck that caused her to want to rip something away from her neck during her panic attacks. At ten, in that rip tide she thought she might drown and was terrified.

She had been swimming, having a good time, experiencing consciousness in a resource that enjoyed, among other things, swimming. When the near drowning experience happened the Resource State that held the Conscious at the time became Vaded with that experience and could not come to the Conscious without experiencing feelings of panic.

Following the incident she was afraid to tell her parents. She was afraid she might be in trouble. Had she been able to talk with her parents, and had she been able to get love and support and understanding it is likely that she would not have developed panic attacks. As a 10-year-old, she lived through a life-threatening, terrifying event, and talked to no one about it. The Resource State that experienced that event became extremely upset and was left in that condition.

It became overwhelmed by experiencing an event that it did not fully understand. From that time on, whenever this Resource State was brought to the surface, usually by life incidents that reminded it in some way of the near drowning experience, it would relive this unresolved feeling. It is interesting that it would not bring with it the memories of this experience, but it did bring the emotions of the experience. She did remember the almost drowning, but she did not intellectually connect it to her panic attacks. When Resources are Vaded, the experience they have when they become Conscious, and the adjectives that are used to describe their bad feelings directly describe the initial sensitizing event.

Table 15: Vaded State emotions come from the unresolved feelings during the ISE

Jane's description of her experience during panic attack.	What Jane experienced during the initial sensitizing event.
She said she would have trouble breathing.	Her head would dip into the water making it hard to breathe.
She had a need to get away or felt she might die if she couldn't.	She knew she had to get out of the water or she would die.
She saw the color, 'blue but black', and	When her head would dip into the water she would see 'blue but black'.
She had a need to pull something away from her throat.	Her little cousin was hanging onto her throat making it harder to breathe and stay afloat.

An added benefit of resolving the negative feelings of Vaded States is that the state that had been Vaded can return to its original role. Often clients report feeling more free and playful following this kind of resolution. It is much better to resolve the negative feelings of a Vaded State, leaving that state feeling safe, supported and cared for, than to merely teach a coping skill that would not resolve and free that personality part.

Jane's attacks were the direct result of a Vaded State that held onto the feelings of panic, and it would periodically come into the Conscious, bringing with it those feelings. When Conscious, it felt it was still in danger, because those feelings had not been resolved or contextualized. Those were the occasions she would experience a panic attack.

Once that Vaded State was brought into the Conscious in therapy and was able to

- understand that the Introject of her experience (the ocean) could not now hurt that child state,

- feel safe, and

- feel supported and cared for by another Resource State of the client,

then it no longer held onto the terrified feelings. It was relieved of them. At that point the Vaded State returned to a Normal condition, holding a feeling of understanding and support. That personality segment (Resource) was freed to again be available to Jane.

Luke could not speak to a group

Luke came to see me with the issue that he had never been able to speak in front of a group. He was in the early stages of a higher degree and would have to make group presentations in order to finish his degree. He said that it was totally impossible for him to speak in front of a group, with any effort being met by an extreme fear and a loss of being able to speak.

I asked him to allow his eyes to close and imagine sitting in a group, knowing that in a few moments he would be called to go to the front of the group and speak. He actually found even this activity challenging, and when I asked him to hear his name being called, that it was his turn to walk to the front of the room and speak, he became even more nervous.

I asked him to imagine standing up so he could move to the front of the room. At this point he showed a high level of nervousness, indicating that the Vaded State had moved into the Conscious.

The imagery of standing in a group to move to the front and speak had brought the Vaded State into consciousness. With the Vaded State Conscious, it was possible to bridge to the original sensitizing event. I used Bridging techniques that will be later described in this book to assist him into the imagery of the initial sensitizing event.

He showed evidence of being emotionally upset and related to me that he was in a field working with his father. The ISE occurred when he was eight years old, when his father was upset at him because he was not doing his work correctly. His father kept yelling at him, telling him that he could not do anything right, and that he was worthless. He did not talk to anyone about this later and the negative feelings that this Resource experienced stayed with it, making it a Vaded State.

This eight-year-old Resource State that had been attempting to do his best at work was overwhelmed with a feeling of being judged and of being worthless. The client's other Resources were not affected. While he had no difficulty working later in life, any time he attempted to move to the front of a group and speak, this Vaded Resource would come into the Conscious causing him to feel judged, incompetent and worthless.

Both of these examples, Jane and Luke, demonstrate Resources that experienced negative events and were not able to understand and incorporate those events. Resources may be Vaded with Fear by events such as, the first day of kindergarten, being lost in a crowd, feeling frightened and calling for a parent and no one comes, feeling frightened on the street or at school, feeling humiliated in a classroom, experiencing a dangerous traumatic event, being physically or sexually abused, or by any of many other causes.

The common feature of Resource States that are Vaded with Fear is that they give power to the **Introjects** of which they are afraid. **Introjects** are powerless, but the Vaded Resource holds an illusion that they still have power. **Introjects** are not real, as they are merely memory fragments.

A memory fragment has no power. It cannot reach out and hit, it cannot yell or hurt in anyway. The client is sitting on the therapy chair in the therapy room and there is nothing in that room that is harmful to the client. Good therapeutic techniques can bring the Vaded State to consciousness where it can become empowered over the **Introjects** that have been previously feared. This is what moves the Resource State from a Vaded condition to a Normal condition.

Jane, who had experienced a life-threatening, near drowning initial sensitizing event, had a Vaded State that continued to give power to the inanimate

Introject, the deep ocean. The ocean was not in the therapy room so it was an illusion that the Vaded State held that it was in danger. While the ocean may be dangerous and should be respected there is no reason to fear the ocean when it is not present.

Luke, who feared speaking in front of a group, had a Vaded State that feared his yelling father. The client's eight-year-old Vaded State feared the yelling father that had been present when Luke was eight years old. Luke, as an adult, maintained a loving relationship with his father. Here, two separate Resource States had different **Introjects** of the same father.

Introjects are Resource specific. It was important for the eight-year-old Vaded Resource to become empowered in relation to the Introject it held of his father. This therapeutic work did not focus on and did not impact upon the relationship Luke's mature Resources had with his father. Therapeutically, the process to move a Vaded State to normality is to work specifically with that Vaded State. What other mature Resource States do is up to them, and will not impact upon the health of the underlying Vaded State.

The client who returns to an abuser as an adult and confronts that abuser has every right to do so, but will often report that the experience somehow left them feeling empty and unfulfilled. The factor that is most important for their therapeutic resolution is that the underlying Vaded State becomes empowered, supported, and gains the sense of being valued. This has to do with working with the Introject from the past, not with confronting the older person of the present.

Chapter 4 of this book will detail treatment regimens to recognize Vaded States, and to move them to Normality.

States Vaded with Rejection

A Resource Vaded with Rejection is characterized by:

- Feeling not good enough
- Feels positive when the client has pleased another person, but feels terrible when the client has disappointed another person
- Feelings of worth are based on the impressions of others
- Feels like a fake, and feels that if others saw the real person they would be disappointed
- Is unsure if it is loved

Initial sensitizing events may vade a Resource with Rejection

States Vaded with Rejection are almost always vaded in childhood. While clients may remember times in adulthood when they felt rejection, their memories tend to be of times when the Vaded State has come to the surface, not of when it was originally vaded. Good bridging techniques can assist the client to locate the initial sensitizing event. It is imperative that the initial sensitizing event is located, as it is the images around this event that fuels the feelings of rejection. It is not possible to find the ISE by asking the client when he or she first had these feelings, as most often an intellectual state does not know. Good bridging techniques will connect the emotion of the Vaded State directly with the incident where that emotion was first experienced.

How is a Resource Vaded with Rejection Pathological?	Normal State
A Resource Vaded with Rejection believes it is unlovable, or not good enough. This can keep the client from engaging, and can cause the client to question personal value.	Normal States have positive feelings about themselves. They enjoy the time they have in the Conscious and feel they have something to offer.

Children have an innate need for unconditional love and acceptance. They seek this, especially from a parent or Guardian, and the child is more susceptible to becoming Vaded with Rejection when there is a sustained period of time when love is doubted. This resulting fragility makes it easier for an initial sensitizing event to cause a Resource State to feel overwhelmed with rejection.

Some parents seem naturally gifted at demonstrating unconditional love. There appears to be no relationship between the demonstration of unconditional love and boundaries. It is possible for parents to set clear and strict boundaries and still demonstrate unconditional love.

Some parents confuse power with a demonstration of love. It is difficult for them to show unconditional love, because they fear that if they do so they will lose power. They see their child seeking love and attempting to get it, and they use this as a means to exert control. It is the children of parents who exercise this dynamic that are most susceptible to having Resources that are Vaded with Rejection.

Other parents can have so much difficulty in living their own lives that they do not have the energy or the ability to show unconditional love. They can see their child as, "just too demanding," or they may even make statements such as, "I just don't have time for them." Sometimes they will say that they should never have had children.

Because children need unconditional love, and look for it, it is easy for them to recognize when it is not there. The normal reaction of these children is to think there is something wrong with them. After being weakened in resilience, by a lack of display of unconditional love, it does not take a big incident to vade a Resource State with Rejection.

Resources may be Vaded with Rejection even when parents are making their best efforts. Their lives may be so busy and difficult that they do not have the time and energy to share appropriate love with their child.

Case Illustrations of how a Resource can become Vaded with Rejection

The following two examples will illustrate how Resources can be Vaded with Rejection.

Mary had an inability to feel loved by her husband

Mary presented with complaints about her marital relationship. She did not feel emotionally connected to her husband and she felt he was incapable of knowing and understanding her. She had children in the relationship and was reluctant to leave, and she was struggling with the decision whether to leave or not.

When asked to describe the feelings that she was having, and when she was having them, she related incidents that, to an outside observer, would appear that her husband was trying to be understanding. At these times, she was still feeling a lack of connection.

Of course, this dynamic could be caused by a number of different things, and it would not necessarily have anything to do with a State Vaded with Rejection. A positive aspect about this kind of work is that the therapist does not have to jump to conclusions. Bringing to the surface the troubling emotions is the first step to determine where these emotions are based.

In Mary's case, it could have been that she and her husband were not well suited, or that he was incapable of providing her with a kind of connection with which she could be happy. This was not to prove to be the case.

Mary related that her husband had rang her after work saying that he had to pick something up on the way home and this would cause him to be 30 minutes to an hour late. Upon hearing this, Mary became very emotional and felt like he did not love her.

An emotional reaction that does not fit the current situation is indicative of a Vaded State.

A client can be experiencing life from a Normal Resource and when a Vaded State comes into the Conscious, bringing with it its unresolved emotions, the Normal Resource State cannot respond to the life situation in the way it would like. Mary's Normal Resource State that answered the phone could not respond in a way that it would have liked because it was forced out of the Conscious by a Resource State Vaded with Rejection.

I like to use the metaphor, a Normal Resource is walking down the road doing normal things when it is confronted by a large bear that is frightening and forces it from the road. The normal state cannot stay on the road because the large bear is so powerful. The large bear is the Vaded Resource State. When it comes to the surface it forces a Normal Resource State out of the Conscious and it takes over with its negative feelings. It is not a choice the client has the ability to make. In this way the client is out of control.

When Mary heard that her husband would be home late, her Resource Vaded with Rejection took over her Conscious. She could not control or help the feelings that she had.

It was necessary in therapy to have Mary relate in detail the experience of her husband calling and the feelings that she had at that time. It was important that she relate this from a first person perspective.

She was instructed to describe in detail where she was when she received the call, what she was wearing, what time it was, and even how she was holding the phone. It is important to revivify the setting in detail and ask questions such as,

"Now that he is telling you this on the phone, exactly how are you feeling? Where do you feel this in your body?" Questions such as these help bring the Vaded Resource back into the Conscious so that Bridging can occur.

During Bridging (see RT Action 3, Chapter 4), Mary said she felt like a three-year-old child while having these feelings of rejection. She was in the kitchen while her mother was feeding her baby sister. Her mother was upset with Mary, telling her that she did not have time for her and that she would have to take care of herself. Mary's frustration overcame her and she threw her cup. At this time Mary's mother yelled at her with frustration and sent her to her room.

There was no sense of understanding achieved after the event. Mary, having already felt chronic rejection due to the introduction of a baby sister, felt overwhelmed by her inability to feel the connection she desired with her mother.

The Resource that was in the Conscious at the time of the incident became Vaded with Rejection. From that point on, throughout Mary's life, when an incident would occur, especially when she was feeling tired, that would cause her to feel some rejection, Mary would become very emotional and have a deep sense of not being loved. She could not control this feeling.

Mary had felt loved for the first three years of her life. She was accustomed to getting a lot of attention and love, and she felt this love was unconditional. Then, her baby sister was born. Mary's mother, who was already busy, had the additional pressure of taking care of a newborn baby. She saw Mary as old enough to take care of herself in many ways. She would often show frustration over Mary's continued demands for attention.

Mary saw the attention and time that her mother gave her new sister and she began to feel unloved compared to the way that she had previously been. This dynamic had made Mary fragile, had reduced her resilience, and had made it easier for a resource to become Vaded with Rejection.

The only way to resolve this three-year-old Resource that would come to the surface causing Mary to feel unloved was to bring it to the surface, bridge to the original sensitizing event, help it gain understanding, and help it to experience unconditional love from one of her loving Resources. Techniques are described in Chapter 6 that helps the Resource Vaded with Rejection let go of the feeling of being unlovable, and learn that it is lovable.

Here is what is important for the Vaded Resource to understand:

- It was the parent at that time who was not able to show unconditional love.
- It was not the Vaded State that was unlovable.

This is a profound shift in understanding. Of course, we do not know what the actual history of the family was, but we are able to understand that the Resource Vaded with Rejection did not get the feeling of unconditional love. All children deserve to feel unconditionally loved, and if they do not feel that, it is not good if they blame themselves.

Another part of the process of assisting a Resource Vaded with Rejection to a Normal Condition is to ask for a Resource that enjoys offering support to a child to join the Vaded State so it can get unconditional love always, internally. When this process is completed, the Resource that had felt upset and rejected gains a feeling of understanding, and the experience of being loved, and is left with a feeling of being supported and cared for. Therefore, two things are important in this process, 1) that the state learn it was not its fault that it did not feel the love it needed, and 2) that it is lovable and can always have love internally from a nurturing Resource State.

Following the resolution of Mary's Vaded State, it was able to return to a Normal Resource Condition. It was no longer upset and waiting to take over the Conscious with feelings of rejection. Mary reported feeling closer to her husband, and having more understanding. She no longer felt a need to consider leaving the relationship.

Jason could not allow himself to commit in a relationship

Jason was a 34-year-old client and he was in a relationship that he hoped to continue. He came to therapy because he had started having doubts, something that had happened in all of his previous relationships. He had a history of entering into a relationship believing that, "This is going to be the right one." He would stay in the relationship until a real closeness began to develop, then he would start thinking about all the reasons the relationship would not work. He would even feel himself get physically nauseous when he thought about continuing with the relationship.

This pattern had manifested itself so many times that Jason was afraid it would happen in his current relationship. He felt really lucky to be with the woman he was with, and he was afraid he would flee this relationship, as he had his previous ones. He was already starting to have doubts.

Upon further questioning, he indicated more precisely exactly when his doubts and feelings of nausea would occur. Interestingly, they would occur shortly after his feeling that he really loved the person.

This is an example of a Vaded Resource. A Vaded Resource is evident when the client experiences emotions that do not fit the situation that they are experiencing. Feelings of doubt and the physical sensations of nauseousness do not fit the situation of feeling love for another person. This indicates that a tender spot in Jason's psyche was being touched; a Resource vaded with unresolved emotions was coming to the surface.

In order to help Jason find the origin of these unresolved emotions I, with imagery, took him to an incident when he had experienced them. I had him to describe the image in a multisensory fashion while using present tense language (see RT Action 2). I find it easier for the client to build these images with their eyes closed. I had him to describe immediately what had led up to his feelings of doubt and nauseousness, and I had him to describe the time of day, where in the room he was, where the light was coming in, what he was wearing, what he was experiencing being in that room, and what he was experiencing in his body. For example, "Right now, sitting on Melanie's couch with her sitting next to you, what is the lighting like in the room around you?"

The physical/sensory information is gathered in this present tense (right now) fashion until emotion is noticed in the client's voice or body language. Immediately, when emotion is noticed, the client is asked, "Where in your body are you experiencing this feeling right now?" When the client exhibits an emotion this reveals that the Vaded State has come to the surface and into the Conscious. Asking the question about where this experience is most felt in the body helps the client to focus more intently on the feelings of the Vaded State. This helps to bring the state out more and helps to isolate it away from other states so it may speak. Questions continue about the experience in the body in great detail prior to Bridging. It is imperative that the Vaded State is clearly in the Conscious before Bridging can occur.

Bridging steps helped Jason enter into the imagery of the initial sensitizing event. He was six years old at the time of the initial sensitizing event.

Jason's mother was leaving his father. She had fallen in love with another man. She and Jason had been very close. He had felt comfortable in his loving relationship with her. He had not developed the concept that she might go away. His focus was not on why she was leaving, it just felt to him that something he loved and felt comfortable with was leaving 'him'. During the original sensitizing event his mother was telling him that she would be leaving, and that he would stay with his father. He could not comprehend what he was hearing. He begged her not to go and she told him it was something that she had to do. He had the feeling that he could convince her to stay, but he was not able to do that, and she left. He felt alone, unloved, and unlovable.

Jason's Normal, healthy, Resource that was good at feeling love, and was comfortable with being loved, experienced this traumatic event that left it with the message, "If you love you get hurt." Each time after that, when Jason would begin feeling really close to someone he would have an unexplained need to pull away. When he felt close to someone, this hurt Vaded Resource would come to the surface with its pain. It was so painful that it would cause him to feel physically nauseous when it came to the surface. It was easier for Jason to find faults in relationships, to pull away, and leave someone that he might love than to feel this pain. He had never given himself a chance to really be connected with a woman. He had begun to think that he was emotionally incapable to do so.

While Jason was emotionally within the image of the initial sensitizing event, feeling like a six year old, I asked him if I could call this part of him, 'Hurt'. Getting a name for the Resource helps keep it in the Conscious, and provides an easy way to speak with it again. I encouraged 'Hurt' to say everything he wanted to say to the Introject of his mother who was about to leave. It is important to allow the client full expression because that is empowering to the Vaded State. When the Vaded State is able to fully express it learns that it can say anything it wants without anything bad happening. It learns it has power to speak.

Next, I told Jason that I wanted to speak directly with his mother, and I wanted him to be like a great actor fitting into her skin. I said great actors forget who they are and take on the nature of person who they are being. Then, I spoke to the Introject of his mother directly. "Mom, Jason has just told you how much he loves you and how he doesn't want you to leave. How does this make you feel, mom?"

It is important to the Resource Vaded with Rejection to take on the Introject of the person who they felt rejected by. This way the client can begin to understand that the problem is not that they are unlovable, but the problem is that, at that time it was not possible for the Introject to give them the love they deserved. This is a major shift in understanding.

The Introject of Jason's mother said that she loved Jason but that she had to leave. I asked her to tell Jason out loud directly how she felt. I asked her if she wanted to apologize to Jason for leaving, and she did. By Jason experiencing the feelings of his own introjected mother he would be better able to understand and incorporate the initial sensitizing event. I thanked her for speaking with me and for being honest and I asked to speak again to Jason's Vaded State, "Hurt."

"Hurt, I just spoke with your mother and she said that she does love you, but that she has to go. Hurt, do you love your mother, or not?" He said he did and I asked him to tell her that out loud, directly. Then I said, "Hurt, I can see that you are really good at loving, and I can see that right now you're able to be there for your mother, and she is not able to be there for you. It is impressive to me that you are able to be there for her, and I'm sorry that at this time she is not able to give you what you need and what every child deserves. Every child deserves to be unconditionally loved, and I want to make sure that you get what every child deserves. In the meantime, do you want this inner image of your mother in your inner space, or do you want your space clear?"

It does not matter how the client answers this question. The Vaded State, having the choice of whether the Introject can stay in their space or not, is empowered by owning the choice. It would be fine if he had said that she could stay, and it would be equally fine if he had said, "No, I don't want her here."

Next, I asked, "Jason, if you saw a six-year-old child who you love, crying and upset because he had lost something, what would you do?" This question is asked to bring to the surface a Resource that would like to help a six-year-old child (Jason had been six when his state was vaded). When Jason answered this question I asked him what I could call this part of him that would like to help. Then I spoke directly to that part and asked it if it would be willing to go to Jason's Resource, "Hurt," put its arms around him and let him know that it will always be there with him on the inside, giving love and safety. I told that state that it can do this, as well as everything else it does, and that the more it does the more powerful it becomes.

Next, I asked, "Hurt," how it was feeling and I told this previously Vaded State that it could also give the helping part a hug back. I said that the feeling can be like two logs in a fire glowing brighter as they are next to each other. When I saw the body language of the client reveal relief and positivity, I asked, "How are you feeling now?" He said he was feeling much better. I then asked him what term would better describe how he is feeling now, and he told me, "Loved." I told him that was a beautiful name, and that from now on I will call this part of him, "Loved." At this point the Resource that had been vaded had returned to a Normal, healthy, Resource Condition.

The time when Jason's mother left would always be a sad memory, but there was no longer a state vaded with the illusion that his mother had left because he was unlovable. More steps were followed, but the core work of changing the inner experience held by the previously Vaded Resource had been done. The state that had been named "Hurt" had changed its name to "Loved". It was at peace and was internally being taken care of by a mature, loving Resource that enjoyed taking care of it. Its experience had been changed from feeling rejected and unlovable to feeling understanding and lovable. This State, because it was no longer hanging onto the pain of being left by his mother, because it felt loved and lovable, would not again cause Jason to feel nauseous with the need to flee a relationship when he began to feel close.

Emotional reactions that do not fit the situation come from a Vaded State. There is a cause for everything. When the client has an emotional reaction that comes from left field, there is a cause. That cause is a Vaded Resource that is holding onto unresolved negative emotion.

States Vaded with Disappointment

A Resource Vaded with Disappointment is characterized by:

- Very low energy
- Difficulty relating to a time when things were good
- A reluctance to re-engage
- A lack of permission for other Resources to take up positive engagement

Resources Vaded with Fear or Rejection are almost always vaded in childhood. Resources may be Vaded with Disappointment during any time in life. It is Resources that have been Vaded with Disappointment that are the cause of psychological depression.

How is a Resource Vaded with Disappointment Pathological?	Normal State
A Resource Vaded with Disappointment carries a level of sorrow, which1) causes it to feel upset, and2) causes it to not want other Resource States to feel happy. It blocks energy from the personality.	Normal States enjoy what they do, and they are happy when other Normal States also help the personality by enjoying what they do.

Initial sensitizing events may vade a Resource with Disappointment

Any event can vade a Resource with Disappointment, if it is perceived by that Resource as being important and outside of an acceptable reality. Examples include, loss of a loved one, loss of a pet, discovery of an illness, aging, loss of a job, poor academic results, physical impairment, loss of hair, loss of a relationship, and that list goes on.

Clients who have Resources Vaded with Fear or Rejection often do not know how those Resources became Vaded, prior to Bridging. Often, clients who have Resources Vaded with Disappointment will know how their Resource became vaded. This is not always the case. Occasionally, the client will feel generally depressed without knowing the reason why. Even with these clients, it is easy to bring the Vaded State into the Conscious, by merely asking the client to describe exactly what he or she is feeling. The Resource Vaded with Disappointment is in or near the Conscious almost all of the time. It has to be, in order to block other Resources from enjoying living.

Case Illustrations of how a Resource can become Vaded with Disappointment

In the examples below Kylie discovered that her husband was having an affair, and Sarah discovered that she had genital herpes. In both cases what was expected and hoped did not match the reality that confronted these clients.

Kylie's husband had an affair

Kylie found that her husband had an affair. She came to therapy because she reported not being able to move forward in life. She felt extreme disappointment with what he had done, and she felt that he deserved no forgiveness.

It is my view that there is a difference between forgiveness and letting go. For many people, forgiveness means offering something to another person, while letting go means deciding to move forward in life while no longer hanging onto the old and destructive feelings.

Therapeutically, the Vaded State can decide to clear its inner space of the Introject of another person without offering that person forgiveness. It is not that I am against forgiveness, as I see it is a high ideal, but I do not believe it is therapeutically necessary to forgive in order for Vaded States to move to a Normal and healthy condition. It is necessary for them to let go of, and remove from their space offending **Introjects**. Once removed, the Resource will have no feelings at all for those **Introjects**, because they will be gone from its space. If the Resource wants to hold on to blame, hate, or any other emotion toward that person then it cannot let that person go, it cannot clear its space of the offending Introject.

Kylie was not ready to stop blaming her husband. She felt that if she were to stop blaming him, then that would condone his actions. I explained to her that she could intellectually maintain the understanding that what he did was wrong, but if she wanted to hang onto her emotional blame then his past actions would continue to interfere with her ability to live a light and healthy life.

She was not one of my therapeutic successes. While she saw me, I was unable to build a vision that she accepted of letting go of her blame. At the end of our therapy she maintained a resource Vaded with Disappointment that blocked her other Resources from being able to enjoy life.

It is often easier for a client to stop blaming than to offer forgiveness. Releasing blame can be accomplished when the vaded Resource clears its space of the offending Introject. This is done in the Removal Phase of the resolution, as explained in Chapter 4.

Blame is a negative and heavy emotion. The client who holds onto blame is holding on to something that will interfere in his or her ability to have positive mental health. Letting go of blame does not mean that an action is condoned. An intellectual state can maintain the understanding that what was done was wrong, and that it cannot be condoned. That is healthy and different than hanging on to the emotional blame.

Sarah became depressed when she discovered she had genital herpes

Psychological Depression is caused by a Resource taking on so much disappointment that it will not allow other Resources to have enjoyment. There is a Resource that is Vaded with Disappointment, i.e., a part of the personality is overwhelmed with the negative feelings of disappointment.

When Sarah came to therapy she was emotionally distraught. As a 27-year-old woman she was looking forward to her version of a fairy-tale future. She thought of herself as sexually conservative and she held a contention that people with venereal disease were dirty and, to some level, "Ruined."

Upon receiving her doctor's report that she tested positive for Type II Herpes, Sarah was devastated. Her reality did not match her expectations. She felt overwhelmed. Her Resource that became Vaded with Disappointment refused to allow any of her other states to enjoy the things that they had previously enjoyed. She did not want to go out. She could not imagine entering into an intimate relationship in the future. She felt like her life was over.

It is important to show an empathetic understanding to the State Vaded with Disappointment. Statements such as, "I can understand that this is really hard for you," are much more effective than statements such as, "This is not such a big thing." Empathetic statements help the Vaded State to feel understood, respected, and help prepare it to want to cooperate in a therapeutic resolution.

Helping a person with a Resource Vaded with Disappointment is a two-step process.

- It entails finding two Resources that will be willing to re-engage in positive activities that they have done previously, and getting permission from the Vaded State for them to take on these positive activities.
- It entails working with the Resource that has been Vaded with Disappointment (in a respectful way) in order to find it a new role that will be beneficial to the client. Resources Vaded with Disappointment cannot see a positive future. Therefore, they need to be able to have a vision where they have some level of positive involvement.

I listened to Sarah's story, and I was empathetic in relation to the loss that she felt. I did not try to make an intellectual case against her feelings. This helps the Vaded State feel understood and respected.

While talking with Sarah about her deep disappointment, it was possible to see that her Vaded Resource was in the Conscious. She was showing low levels of energy and speaking in a forlorn fashion. I asked her what I could call her, as she felt so bad. I asked her what name or term went with the way this part felt.

She said, "Shocked." It is important to get a name for the Resource that you're working with. This way you can address it directly, and you can ask to speak with it later after speaking with the different states. Continuing to use the name of a Resource while addressing it helps it to stay in the Conscious, e.g., "Shocked, thank you for talking with me", or "What is important to you, Shocked?"

I told 'Shocked' that I would want to speak with it again a bit later, but that I wanted to speak with some other states first. I wanted to find two states that would be willing to take on positive roles, states that already had practice in positive roles.

Next, I asked Sarah to tell me about something that she had liked to do in the past, before she found out about the herpes diagnosis. It took her awhile to remember something she liked to do. A depressed person often sees their whole life as being depressed.

I asked her to allow her eyes to close and to search her memory for something that she used to have fun doing. She said she used to enjoy finding new recipes on the Internet, recipes for food that she had never eaten before, and then making that food. A depressed person will show a low level of affect when first relating something that they previously enjoyed doing, but if you have them to go into detail (re-vivify) a time they enjoyed it, their affect will change as that Resource comes into the Conscious.

I revivified the time with her when she was cooking a recipe that she had found on the Internet. I had her to tell me what was in the kitchen at that time, what she was using from the fridge, what the lighting was like in the room, and what she was wearing. As she did this her affect improved, and I could see that her cooking Resource was Conscious. I asked this Resource, what I could call it, this part of Sarah that enjoyed cooking creatively, and it replied, "Cook."

I asked 'Cook' if it would be willing to come out occasionally, cook, and help Sarah feel better, if I could get permission for it to come out and enjoy cooking again. It said it would. At this time I had one Resource that had contracted to come out and help Sarah feel better.

I then asked Sarah to tell me about something else that she had liked to do in the past. She said that she had enjoyed jogging, but that she had stopped doing that since she had become upset, and since her energy was so low.

I assisted bringing this state to the Conscious by revivifying, and upon seeing it out with energy I asked what would be a good term for it. The name it gave was 'Jogger'. It, also, agreed that it would occasionally come out and help Sarah enjoy jogging, if I could get permission for it to do so. Then, I said thank you to

'Jogger' telling her that I would like to talk to her later, but, "Right now I want to talk to 'Shocked' again."

Upon noticing Sarah's body language change to a depressed level of energy, I said, "'Shocked', I know you don't feel very well right now, and I know you are upset about the herpes, but I was just talking to two other parts, 'Cook' and 'Jogger'. I know you heard me talking with them. They both said that they would help Sarah feel better by cooking and jogging if you would give them permission to do that. I know you are upset, and I want to continue to talk with you about what you are upset about, but in the meantime, 'Shocked', can I get your permission for 'Cook' and 'Jogger' to have some time out and enjoy it?"

When a Resource that has been Vaded with Disappointment is treated with respect and understanding it will almost always give permission for other states to come out and have some time they can enjoy. If the depressed state feels misunderstood (by hearing statements such as, "It's not that bad") it will not give permission for other states to have the Conscious.

'Shocked' said it would give permission for the two Resources to occasionally come out and enjoy what they had done in the past. I had 'Shocked' to speak out loud to each and give verbal permission for them to have some time to enjoy their time out. This agreement between states works best if there is a direct communication between the states, rather than each just talking with the therapist.

Because of the slow response nature of clients suffering from depression, this is normally all that can be accomplished in a single session. It often takes some time to find states that have enjoyed activities in the past, time to revivify until they are in the Conscious, and time to negotiate.

The next step, usually in the following session, is to work with the Resource Vaded with Disappointment to find something that it feels is important, that it would like to contribute.

Like all Vaded States, states Vaded with Disappointment were in the Normal Resource Condition prior to becoming vaded. It is important to find out how the State Vaded with Disappointment has helped the person in the past so you can discover its purpose. It will need to keep its purpose, but it can change the way it accomplishes that purpose. For example, a Resource that previously applied makeup and liked to make the face pretty might become depressed if there was a bad burn on the face, and it felt it could never again make the face pretty.

The purpose of that state was to create something beautiful. It had skills in art and appreciated beauty. This would be a great state to take up some kind of artwork that it can design and create.

Often Resources that are Vaded with Disappointment can be negotiated with to take up a smaller role in the future, but one that is seen as important. The importance of their new role should always be stressed.

In later sessions with Sarah, and in conversations with her Vaded Resource, 'Shocked', I discovered that the purpose of this state had been to help Sarah 'do things right'. It felt that it knew what was right, and what was not right, and it gave Sarah guidance to do what it felt was right. When Sarah contracted herpes that state had felt so badly, believing it had failed, that it wanted all states to experience the failure.

I praised the state, and told it how important its role was, and told it that it would be good if everyone had a state that could help make careful decisions. I also told it that while it was important and while it needed to do its job, that Sarah had other Resources that are also talented. I found a Resource that Sarah called, 'Understanding'. It was able to look at other people's shortcomings and be understanding of them. It was not a judgmental state. I asked if it would be willing to share its skills, and work directly with 'Shocked. '

Sarah's understanding Resource was able to help her Shocked Resource feel better about itself, and 'Shocked' decided it would be appropriate to change its name to 'Guidance' with the agreement that it would continue to work with 'Understanding,' because the two of them could work together in a balanced way.

This type of intervention for Resources Vaded with Disappointment has some similarity to a cognitive behavioral intervention for depression. Cognitive Behavioralists often give behavioral assignments to clients with depression in an attempt to get them out to do something that requires energy.

The type of intervention that has just been described starts out in the same way, by getting two Resources committing to help the person do something that is enjoyed, and that takes energy. A difference is, when these two Resources are talked with directly and agree to help the client, and when permission is gained from the Resource that has been Vaded with Disappointment, it is most normally not difficult for the client to take on these new roles. There is no coercion involved.

The cognitive behavioral intervention often results in the client returning with the story that the behavioral assignment was not completed. There had been no permission from the depressed state, so there was an internal fight between the state that wanted to follow the therapist's instructions and the state that felt depressed.

The first two additional elements of the Resource Therapy intervention are, 1) specific states that can enjoy activities are directly spoken with and are contracted with to take up positive activities, and 2) permission is obtained from the depressed state for them to have some time to take up those activities.

A third additional element is that the depressed state is worked with in an empathetic manner to understand its purpose, and find a new role so it can continue to fulfill that purpose.

Work with clients suffering from depression necessarily goes slower than for many other presenting concerns. Depression physically affects the body and it will take at least a few weeks for the body to recover. You will not have a client who walks in with chronically low levels of energy walk out feeling well. 1) Finding states that are willing to engage, 2) getting permission for them to engage, and 3) working with the Vaded State with Disappointment, can immediately begin the process of recuperation.

States Vaded with Confusion

A Resource Vaded with Confusion is characterized by:

- Rumination
- Feelings of Guilt or Shame
- Feelings that something was not handled properly by the client or by someone else
- An inability to let go of concern about another person
- An inability to understand another's actions

Resources Vaded with Confusion have experienced an initial sensitizing event that they cannot incorporate into their understanding. This Resource is left with a fundamental and profound level of confusion, and the response to this lack of ability to understand, is a profoundly uncomfortable unknowing. While Resources Vaded with Disappointment hold a distinctly negative emotion, Resources Vaded with Confusion appear to exhibit angst about what is not known. Like Resources Vaded with Disappointment, they may affect the energy of other Resources, but when they do, this is at a much lower level. They may exhibit symptoms of rumination, existential angst, complicated bereavement, or withdrawal following breakdown of a relationship, losing a job, or other losses. Clients with these types of Resources report being unable to stop ruminating about what they do not know.

How is a Resource Vaded with Confusion Pathological?	Normal State
A Resource Vaded with Confusion cannot let something go. It ruminates to the point of obsession. The client cannot settle, sometimes for months or years.	Normal States can accept things as they are. There may be hard times, but Normal States can let hard times go within a typical timeframe.

Initial sensitizing events that vade a Resource with Confusion

The mother who places a child up for adoption and then comes to therapy 20 years later with a deep yearning to know about her child has a Resource Vaded with Confusion. Her initial sensitizing event may have occurred at, or before, the time she placed her child up for adoption, or it may have occurred days, weeks, months, or years later. If she has a Resource Vaded with Confusion there would have been a time when the question of her child's life and well-being became profound for her. Bridging can locate this time, but with Vaded States suffering from Confusion other therapeutic techniques can offer a solution.

The woman who lost a fetus in miscarriage and can't stop thinking about the child, and what that child might think of her, has a Resource Vaded with Confusion. Just as the woman who put her child up for adoption, this woman may have had an existential moment at the time of the miscarriage, or any time thereafter.

The young man who wants to be straight and consistently has sexual fantasies about other men has a Resource Vaded with Confusion. It is not unusual for young men who have sexual fantasies of other men, to have no concerns about this for many years. If they develop a Vaded State of Confusion there will be a moment in time when the question of their sexual identity becomes profound to them.

The devout religious person whose religion does not make intellectual sense to him has a resource Vaded with Confusion. The devout religious person who questions his or her belief can have an initial sensitizing event when one Resource realizes this belief does not make sense, while another Resource is confused and not ready to accept a new way of thinking.

The woman whose partner committed suicide, and cannot stop wondering 'why', has a Resource State Vaded with Confusion. It is often the case that clients will get a Resource State Vaded with Confusion following profound events where they would like an understanding, but do not have one.

These states are very easy to bring to the Conscious. All the therapist has to do is to talk with the client about their confusion, and about how this confusion makes them feel. It is good to get a name for this confused Resource. Techniques will be described later in detail, but it is important for the Vaded State to be able to speak directly with **Introjects** that can bring peace to their confusion.

Case Illustrations of how a Resource can become Vaded with Confusion

Andrew did not want to think he might be gay

Andrew had been raised in a small country town. He had come to the city to go to university. His friends at the University were also from his town. He shared accommodation with them.

During the first therapy session, it took Andrew several minutes to feel comfortable enough to tell me why he had come to see me. He finally told me that his problem was he could not get crazy thoughts out of his head. I ask him what crazy thoughts he was having, and he told me that he was looking at his roommates and having sexual fantasies.

He told me that he was not gay, that he had been out with females. He told me that he could not be gay because his father and his friends hated gays.

I told him that was too bad, because I did not feel it was right to hate any group. I asked him to tell me more about the confusion he was having. I told him that it seemed to me that he was having a lot of deeply confusing feelings, and I wanted to hear more about them.

He told me that when his friends would walk through the house with just a towel wrapped around them that he couldn't get sexual thoughts out of his head. He said he wished they would not do that, and that his friends would hate him if they knew what he was thinking.

The first session went very slowly, with Andrew making a lot of testing statements to see how I would respond. At one point Andrew asked me, "You don't think I could be gay, do you?" I did not feel that he was ready for a direct response. I said, "I don't really care at all if you wind up deciding you are not gay or if you wind up deciding you are gay. It doesn't make any difference to me at all. I just want you to be able to be comfortable with yourself and to be happy with who you are." I told him there was no clock ticking, there was no rush to make any determination, and that I would be happy to talk with him until he was comfortable in whatever he decided. I told him that I knew it was difficult for him to talk about this, and that I felt honored that he was willing to share something so difficult with me. This was as far as we got at the end of the first session.

It appeared that Andrew needed time to incorporate the idea of his sexual orientation. His father, especially, was a person who made it difficult for Andrew to accept that he might be gay. Here is an example of both an Introject from the past being an issue, and the current person being an issue. Andrew held within him the Introject of his father (from the past) who was homophobic, and he also knew when he travelled home he would have future encounters with his father, who he expected would still be homophobic.

Andrew told me that he had never had a sexual fantasy about a female, and while all his sexual fantasies were about males, and always had been, he constantly tried to get those images out of his head. He couldn't.

It appeared that, at some level, Andrew knew he was gay, but it was difficult for him to accept this. According to Andrew, I was the first person he had talked with who made him feel comfortable about gays. He said there was a boy in his school, in his home town, who others believed was gay and they had made his life hell. Andrew feared this would be his fate.

At the point in therapy where it appeared to me that Andrew was more ready to accept the notion that he might be gay, I told him we could experiment with a pretend conversation with his father that might help bring some clarity. I said this would be safe to do, because we know that his father is not in the therapy room, therefore anything can be said to the image of the person who's not really here. I told him we could have two pretend conversations with his father, one where he was not gay, and one where he was. Andrew said he would be willing to do this.

I told him we will first have the two pretend conversations, and then we can talk about it. I brought an empty chair and sat it in front of Andrew and asked him to invite the essence of his father into the empty chair. I then instructed Andrew to tell his father that he was not gay and to tell him anything else that he might want to say about gay people. After he did this, I had Andrew to rise and move over to his father's chair, and as he was sitting down I said, "Dad, your son just told you that he wasn't gay. I wonder how that makes you feel, Dad?" He said he felt relieved, but at the same time had a level of distrust about what Andrew said.

Then, I had Andrew move to his original chair; to speak to his father again and tell him that he was gay. I instructed Andrew to tell him his exact feelings about this, and his fears about not being accepted.

Andrew spoke to his father with authenticity. He was quite emotional. When I had him to go to his father's chair and reply, the father was confused and did not know how to handle the situation. He did report that he had wondered about this.

Then, I had Andrew to return to his chair and tell me how he had felt each time he had spoken to his father. He looked at me, and said, "I am gay."

I asked him how he felt when he said that, and he said, "Relieved."

We talked about how he had no responsibility to tell anyone, anything, unless he wanted to. We continued with sessions while Andrew became more accustomed to his sexual identity and restructured his life. He changed accommodation, because he knew the friends he had lived with would not be able to accept his sexual identity. He found new friends who he felt comfortable with, and even made the decision that he would not be returning to the small town to live. He surrounded himself with the life that allowed him to be who he was, a life that respected him.

Here, it was important for Andrew to face the Introject he most feared. The fear of his father, especially, had held him in a constant state of confusion about his sexual identity. He had not been able to accept who he was. By being able to have an open and honest conversation with the Introject of his father and feel his own authenticity when he told him that he was gay, Andrew's Resource that had been Vaded with Confusion gained clarity. He discovered, with the use of the empty chair, that the sky did not fall when he spoke with authenticity.

Andrew's Resource that had been Vaded with Confusion was no longer confused, or vaded. When it spoke with the Introject of his father, it let go if it's fear of that Introject, and became empowered. It was able to let go of its confusion and accept what it had known for some time.

Elizabeth's son was murdered

Elizabeth came to therapy because the bereavement of her son, Landon, was complicated by her inability to stop thinking about how he had died. Sadly, he had been brutally murdered. It serves no purpose to go into detail here, but his death had not been quick and had likely been very painful.

Elizabeth ruminated about how he had died. She found it impossible to grieve his loss because of her ruminations. She exhibited great emotional pain.

I responded with empathetic care and with an understanding that her pain must be very deep. She was allowed to and encouraged to express what she had been feeling. She was not encouraged to go into any detail surrounding her son's death.

As with all work to bring clarity to States Vaded with Confusion, I placed an empty chair in front of Elizabeth. I told her that it was clear to me that she loved her son very much, and that I wanted her to be able to express her feelings directly to the essence of her son in the empty chair. I asked her to tell me what kinds of things she would like her son to know, and after she did that, I asked her to speak directly to the essence of her son in the empty chair to tell him.

Upon focusing on the chair, Elizabeth spoke with great emotion and told her son how much she loved him, how sorry she was about what had happened, and about how concerned she was about him.

I asked her to stand, move to the other chair, and as she sat down I said, "Landon, it is clear that your mother loves you very much. How does that make you feel?" It is good, when speaking with an Introject, to first call it by name, and ask it to express its feelings about something. That helps the client to respond from his or her internalized impression of the Introject.

Landon said that it made him feel good that his mother loved him as she did. He said he loved her too, and that he did not want her to suffer. I asked him to tell her that directly (by speaking to her chair), and he did, and I also asked him to tell me how he was feeling now. He said he felt good, and was at peace. I asked him to tell his mother that also, and he did.

Then, I said, "Stand up, (pause) move over to the other chair", and as she sat down I said, "Elizabeth, Landon just said that he loves you very much and that he would like for you to be at peace. He said that he is at peace. How does that make you feel?" She responded with a completely different affect. She had felt peace while she was speaking from the Introject of her son. She carried this feeling of peace back with her when she sat down in her own chair.

There is something very powerful about a Resource speaking from the Introject of another person. They come away with a core understanding that they did not have before. They do not get this understanding unless they sit in the chair of the Introject and speak directly back to the Resource of the client.

Elizabeth had felt peace when she spoke from the Introject of Landon. The confusion that she had about the terror that he had been through was replaced with the peace she felt when she spoke from his Introject. She stopped ruminating about how her son had died. This, in no way, made everything okay, but it cleared confusion of the state that had been vaded. It allowed her to continue with her process of grieving in a more natural way.

Retro Original States

A Retro Original State is characterized by:

- Statements by a personality Resource State indicating a disapproval of this state's behavior.
- An indication that during this behavior the client is dismissive of attempts to cease the behavior, even though after the behavior the client is regretful.
- An indication that this behavior has been evident since childhood.
- No indication that this behavior relates to an Addiction.

Resource States form mostly in early childhood. They form according to coping needs. When a behavior is found that assists the person to cope, that behavior will be returned to over and over again, hence the neurology of the brain is trained and formed into a Resource State.

How is a Retro Original State Pathological?	Normal State
A Retro Original State carries out behavior learned in childhood that becomes unwanted by other personality states. This causes the client to feel regret and a lack of personal control.	Normal States carry out behavior that other states appreciate. Normal states feel at peace with each other.

Retro Original States form as new Resources in early childhood. At that time they assist the child to cope with the challenges that are present. A child may find that by withdrawing it is easier to cope in an angry household. A child may find that by becoming enraged, its needs are better met, in terms of getting what is wanted or at least in getting more attention. A child may find when acting in an anti-social way benefits are forthcoming from a sibling or a parent, or a child may find that passive-aggressive behavior pays off. When these behaviors become repetitively trained a Retro Original State is born.

The only difference in a Retro Original State and a Normal Resource State is that at some point in the person's life the behavior of the Retro State became unwanted by other states of the person. Therefore, a Retro Original State is a Resource State whose behavior formed in childhood, and whose behavior is not liked by other states.

Often the behavior of Retro Original States will not be liked by other people too, but that is not what defines them. A person may have a Resource State that has behavior other people may find very annoying, but if all Resource States of the person are pleased with it, then it is considered a Normal part of the personality. The person who is at ease with self, who is not conflicted, may be mentally healthy even if that person is terribly annoying to others.

For a case example of a Retro Original State therapeutic intervention see, Grant, page 291.

Retro Avoiding States

A Retro Avoiding State is characterized by:

- Statements by a personality Resource State indicating a disapproval of this state's behavior.
- An indication that during this behavior the client is dismissive of attempts to cease the behavior, even though after the behavior the client is regretful.
- No indication that this behavior has been evident since childhood.
- An indication that without this behavior anxiety is consistently experienced (usually with a feeling of fear or low self-esteem).
- An indication that sincere efforts to cease this behavior are met with frustration and failure.
- An indication that this behavior relates to an addiction, OCD, or Self-Harm.

Retro Avoiding States are helping states whose behavior is not liked by other states. All Resource States would like to be liked, but Retro Avoiding States will accept not being liked because they see their behavior as important. They were Normal States but found that by repeating certain behavior the personality was saved from deeply negative feelings.

How is a Retro Avoiding State Pathological?	Normal State
A Retro Avoiding State carries out (addictive) behavior unwanted by other states so the personality does not have to experience the angst of a Vaded State.	Normal States carry out behavior that other states appreciate. Normal states feel at peace with each other.

For instance, the Resource State that can concentrate on walking through the house checking all the locks, making sure everything is securely fastened may find that when doing this 'concentrating' activity the night-time anxiety of a Vaded State is not felt. It may not take long for this 'concentrating' checking state to learn that it can be very useful in helping the person zone out and feel more peace. While it holds the Conscious it is protecting the personality from the negative feelings of a Vaded State. Later, other states may become very annoyed that it wastes so much time Checking, but it will accept their disapproval because it sees its role as important.

A Resource State may find that when it ingests a certain drug a Vaded State with negative feelings is chemically blocked from the Conscious. This drug can be returned to again to save the personality from the negative feelings of the Vaded State. Other people and other personality parts may want the person to stop taking the drug, but the Retro Avoiding State has found a way it can help and it will attempt to do so.

Retro Avoiding States attempt to save the personality in many ways. Workaholism, shopaholism, OCD behavior, illicit or unhealthy drug behavior, self-harm, and any addictive behavior are just a few ways Retro States attempt to help. With the exception of the drug behavior Retro States normally cause the client to feel somewhat zoned out. When a Retro State is in the Conscious it feels focused.

It is often the case that when a Retro State is in the Conscious that other Resource States are refused access. Consider the person who comes home from work, tired, to an empty house. A sense of uncontrolled anxiety begins to surface, a Vaded State, then a Retro Avoiding State assumes the Conscious and moves to the refrigerator. This state is single-minded and will allow no other Resource State to consider whether this activity is positive or not. The person may eat for the next 45 minutes before another Resource State comes into the Conscious, feeling bad about what has just happened. The person may not have been hungry at all, but the Retro Avoiding State had found a helping behavior to assist the personality to avoid the anxiety of coming home to an empty house.

For a case example of a Retro Avoiding State therapeutic intervention, see Meagan's father was not good at showing love, page 310.

The Conflicted State

Conflicted States are characterized by at least one of the following:

- Two states wanting to be out at the same time.
- One state disliking or disrespecting another State.
- The client may report being bothered by an unhappy voice, "e.g., You should be working."
- Procrastination.
- Inability to decide on a major life decision.
- Lack of ability to rest or sleep.

Resource States in Conflict will prevent a client from consistently experiencing a feeling of being internally settled, an internal peace. For two Resource States to be Conflicted they must experience a level of conflict that is anxiety producing for the client.

Table 16 Pathology of Conflicted States

How are Conflicted States Pathological?	Normal State
Conflicted States cause anxiety because they do not respect and understand each other. They each want different things and they hold negative feelings about the state with which they are conflicted.	Normal States respect each other and they feel thankful that other Normal States are there to do the things they do not want to do, or do not have the abilities to do.

Resources often disagree or have different opinions. We use those different opinions in decision making, to weigh up different options. If we are considering buying a new car we want to consider the 'fun' state that wants something new, that enjoys driving, and we also want to consider the more 'serious' State that understands the bank account.

Resource States can often respect each other and come up with a decision made of wise compromise. It is when states do not understand the value of each other or do not respect each other that compromise is not forthcoming. Here are some examples.

- A work state may think of a rest state as lazy. This work state may constantly tell the rest state it should be doing something, making it impossible to rest. When this dynamic is evident, the rest state will often think of the work state as a slave driver, and wish it would just leave it alone. It is possible for work states to resent a rest state so much that almost no time is allowed for resting, and this can result in Chronic Fatigue, due to the prolonged and intense stress put on the body. Here, both the rest state and work state want the Conscious at the same time.

- A state that wants to sleep may be bothered by a state that wants to think. There may be a thinking/planning Resource State that really wants time to review the past day and plan for the next. This planning state may not have been allocated any time during the day to plan, so it determines that bedtime is a time it can review and plan. This is in conflict with a state that wants to sleep and get a good night's rest. Here again, two Resource States want to be out at the same time.

- One state may want to leave a relationship and another state may want to stay. This is an example of two states with different opinions when they cannot come to an agreement. The person can feel torn between two courses of action to the point of anxiety.

It is the key feature of Conflicted States that gives direction to their resolution. They do not understand the value of each other. When a work state resents rest, it does not understand that rest is necessary to gain energy and maintain wellness. It does not understand that it is in its own best interest for a rest state to have some unbothered time so the work state can have a body that is sharp and ready for good work. The techniques for working with Conflicted States are designed for each state in conflict to gain an understanding of the other states, and to gain an ability to communicate and compromise.

Retro Avoiding States will always be in conflict with other states because they do behavior that other states do not like. When a Retro Avoiding State ceases its unwanted behavior, the conflict it had with other States also ceases. This is obvious because the behavior that caused that conflict no longer happens. Therefore, it will be necessary to recognize the difference between Retro Avoiding behavior and Conflicted States. This difference will be made clear in the next chapter.

Similarly, a Vaded State can also be in conflict because another state may not like it coming to the surface with bad feelings that interfere with the person's ability to function. Here, again, when the Vaded State returns to normality there is no more conflict.

It is when two states, which would otherwise be Normal States, do not respect each other that Conflicted State Negotiation is appropriate. Chapter 4, RT Action 1, will make clear how to distinguish states that can benefit from Conflicted State Negotiation.

For a case example of Conflicted States therapeutic intervention, see Stewart could not sleep*, page 325.

The Dissonant State

A Dissonant State is characterized by:

- A feeling of discomfort when doing an activity.
- Performance that is below normal for the person.
- Feelings of frustration with self in the way a situation is being handled.
- A feeling of frustration that an activity has to be done.

A Dissonant State is a state that is holding the Conscious at the wrong time. The client feels a disharmony. When a Dissonant State is conscious the client feels a bit like he or she is in the wrong skin.

Table 17 Pathology of Conflicted States

How are Dissonant States Pathological?	Normal State
Dissonant States can cause the client to feel like performance is below par, can cause the client to feel like, 'I know I can do better', or can cause the client to feel frustrated with self.	When a Normal State is Conscious it feels like it is the best part to be out. It feels good to hold the Conscious and feels like it has the opportunity to make a contribution.

While Conflicted States often are in conflict over which will be able to hold the Conscious, a Dissonant State does not want to hold the conscious. It has an understanding that it is not the best state for the present time, but if feels stuck to have to deal with what is happening. Examples include how a sportsperson feels when in a slump, how a student feels when taking an exam without being able to remember what was learned, or how a parent feels when attempting to talk with a son or daughter and feeling clumsy and incapable.

Unit 2: Diagnosis and Treatment

The structure of a Resource Therapy Session is straightforward. A clear aim is the primary goal of the start of the session, then RT Actions facilitate the diagnosis and treatment part of the session, followed by a debrief near the end.

Resource Therapy Process (ACAR)		Found in Chapter 4
Aim	Determine what the client is ready to change.	Session Start
Classify	Diagnose the Pathological Resource State into a category.	RT Action 1
Actions	Follow the prescribed RT Actions for the Classification.	Specified RT Actions
Review	Debrief with the client.	Session End

The RT Actions are covered in Chapter 4. Chapters 5to 12 indicate exactly how these Actions are used for specific pathologies, such as Addiction, Depression, or Anorexia.

Chapter 4
Resource Therapy (RT) Actions

This chapter will begin with some important aspects of how sessions are started and ended, then each RT Actions will be defined.

Starting and Ending Sessions

Session Start: The therapeutic aspect of beginning each session is to determine precisely what the client is most ready to change. This gives direction to the therapy session. The process of starting the session differs, depending on whether it is a first session, or a following session.

First Session

Following introductions, seating, and generic information, I like the question:

- "What are you ready to change today?"

It is nearly impossible to change what the client is not ready to change, regardless of the skill of the therapist.

Questions like:

- "What do you want to talk about today?"
- "What brings you in today" or
- "What do you want to change?"

merely give direction to a topic with the implicit message being, "We can talk about it" or "We will explore what you want." These questions fall short of finding out exactly what the client is actually ready to change.

When clients are asked what they are ready to change they will often look a bit surprised. They may have not really been prepared to contract for a change. They will sometimes say something like, "Oh, what am I ready for?"

The response to the "READY TO CHANGE" question does not mean that clients will get everything they want, but it does mean that the therapy session will be focused on what clients have the most readiness to change at that time. That is a big help to the therapist. When a client answers the "READY TO CHANGE" question, a verbal contract is made that what is nominated is something he or she is prepared to work toward.

Too often therapists do a long history and make a decision from that history on what should be worked on during the session. This work may well miss the cause of the issue that brought the client to therapy. The therapist leads the client and the client may well abscond responsibility for contributing to their own improvement.

The session does not have to be limited to the issue that the client nominates at the beginning of the session, but it is good to begin the session responding to the direction set by the client.

Following Sessions

Near the end of a therapy session I will often jot down a couple of things that we may want to attend to in later sessions, but the first thing I ask when the client returns on a later session is, **"Since our last session, what have you noticed that you are ready to change today?"**

It is important to say, "Since our last session" as occasionally clients will not have had the opportunity to trial the resolutions from the last session. For example, if the client had wanted to change an ability to ride in an elevator and work was done with the Vaded State that had feared elevators, the next time the client returned if there had been no opportunity to test the resolution, then the client might again present this as an issue. It might no longer be an issue for the client, so it is best to always focus on what the client has experienced since the last session.

When I have jotted down possible things to work on in future sessions, I can always present them to clients as considerations for what they may be ready to change, but it is important to allow the client to define the direction of the session. The client will be more ready for change during the session.

The Change Question

Some clients will attempt to steer the therapist away from the issue they have presented by talking about many other things. This is a defense mechanism where a protector state is afraid to tackle what the client wants to change. The therapist should remain focused on the issue the client has elected to change. Long diatribes should be stopped so the issue can remain in focus.

Of course, if a larger issue presents itself during the therapy session, and there is a desire to work on the larger issue the therapist should be flexible enough to refocus. The important thing is that the issue that is being worked on is one the client is energized to change.

I like to say that beginnings and endings are fragile things. The beginning of a session needs to align the client's and therapist's purpose for the session, and the end of the session needs to provide awareness that the session may have facilitated change.

Clients will sometimes nominate what they believe causes their problem. I find they are usually wrong when they do this. A good thing about RT is that when the Resource State that is central to the issue is brought in to the Conscious, what is related to the issue can become evident. For instance, there is no need to talk about sexual abuse if the Initial Sensitizing Event was an embarrassment in a school class. The Bridging techniques of RT allow the therapist and the client to become clear in relation to what the client may be carrying from the past that is still causing a problem.

Session Ending: The therapeutic aspect of ending each session is to debrief with the client and set a tone of optimism. It is important that the client feel attended to, with Resources that have been spoken with acknowledged, and reminded of changes that have been made.

Following completion of the relevant Actions relating to the present issue, it is good to summarize the session to the client, highlighting any changes that have been made, regarding the Resources. I like to get a name for each Resource State (see Naming the Resource State, page 151) and thank it, by name and make a short statement regarding the changes in which it will be taking part, e. g., following work on an issue with procrastination, "I want to thank the 'Work' state and the 'Rest' state each for acknowledging the value of the other, and for agreeing to continue to compromise with one another, so each can have their own time."

It is sometimes the case that a client will have a cautious Resource State that comes to the Conscious right at the end of the session. This state may wonder how much change to expect. I do not like to specifically quantify expectations to the client, as this can create a paradigm of judgment and measurement. No therapist can know the exact improvement a client will have following a session. Therefore, if a client asks about what to expect, I usually say something like,

"I'm not exactly sure how you will experience this. Sometimes it is nice just to be surprised."

This statement leaves the connotation that the intervention may work quite well. While the real power is in the intervention, subtle phrasing like this can also be helpful. It is also an example of refusing to tell the client what will happen in the future. Of course, we really don't know what the future holds, and I have found that some clients have a tendency to want to prove the therapist wrong if a prediction is made.

By giving the honest answer that we don't really know what will happen, and then by adding 'sometimes it's nice to be surprised', the message is given that they may do very well. This message is given without creating an internal resistance where a part could want to prove the therapist wrong.

RT Actions

These Actions are a core part of this book. Actions in this chapter are referred to from other Chapters of this book, as they are required in different treatment regimens. Some of these Actions are used quite often, depending on the Pathology Condition. Therefore, rather than repeat these Actions a number of times in later chapters, reference will be made to the appropriate treatment Actions in this chapter.

Action 1: Diagnosis of Resource Pathology

Purpose: Following the presentation of the issue, it is necessary to determine the precise Resource State that is related to the presenting issue. The power of Resource Therapy is focusing therapy on the correct state. It is by determining the precise pathological condition of the Resource that the correct therapeutic regimen can be undertaken. A separate chapter is devoted to the appropriate therapeutic regimen for each diagnostic classification. The process of pathology diagnosis, below, is different from DSM diagnosis, and does not include or preclude it. DSM diagnosis places the client into a category. RT diagnosis places each issue into a category. Sometimes a number of different issues may be worked with in a single session.

Process: The presentation of the presenting concern points to the Resource that needs change. By discussing the presenting concern with the client and using the Diagnostic Criteria below, the therapist will be able to determine if the pathological state(s) is(are) in one of the following conditions; Vaded Rejection, Vaded Fear, Vaded Confusion, Vaded Disappointment, Retro Original, Retro Avoiding, Conflicted, or Dissonant.

Clients will often say their problem is another person, and therapists must understand that the therapy is for the person in the room. Therapy cannot benefit someone who is not in the room.

The same thing is true with Resources. It is common for an intellectual Resource to talk about the problem of another Resource. The best way to help the troubled Resource is to work with it directly. That is probably the only way to help it. It is preferable to resolve the issues of a trouble state than to teach coping skills that the client can use, without attending to the causal issues. When a trouble state is left troubled, it leaves the client feeling unsettled and it is always there to come out in the future with the negative feelings that it holds. Therefore, it is important to find out the precise Resource that is pathological.

Table 18 (Gordon Emmerson, 2014) is a quick flowchart indicating the different classification. Further elaboration will follow to help therapists diagnose each presenting issue.

Table 18: RT Classification Flowchart

1. What is the presenting concern?	2. The Resource might be:	3. When Conscious it feels?	4. Has been noticed since Childhood?	5. Diagnostic Classification
Unwanted Behavior	Retro Original	Feels competent	Yes →	Retro Original
	Retro Avoiding		No →	Retro Avoiding
	Dissonant	Feels incompetent →		Dissonant
Unwanted Emotion (Vaded)	Fear	Fear →		V/ Fear
	Rejection	Not good enough →		V/Rejection
	Disappointment	Low Energy →		V/Disappointment
	Confusion	Ruminates →		V/Confusion
Internal Conflict	Conflicted	In conflict with another state →		Conflicted

Table 19 is a synopsis of the RT Treatment Actions associated with each diagnosis.

Table 19: Pathological States and associated Treatment Actions

Client Presents with:	Type of Pathology	Classification	Treatment Actions
Unwanted Feelings →	**Vaded State**(with)		
	Frightened →	Fear	2-4, 6-8, 12
	Not good enough →	Rejection	2-8, 12
	Rumination or guilt →	Confusion	2, 9, 12
	Depression →	Disappointment	8, 8, 10
Unwanted Behavior →	Retro State		
	Lifelong Behavior →	Retro Original	2, 8, 10, 12
	Escape Behavior →	Retro Avoiding	2-7, 10, 12
Two states either want to be Conscious at the same time or are in Decision Conflict →	Here, two states want to be out at the same time, or they are in disagreement.	Conflicted States	2, 11, 12
Failure to meet needs of the situation, but not unjustifiably distressed. The Conscious state does not want to be out. →	(a non-preferred state holds the Conscious)	Dissonant State	2, 8, 12

Diagnostic Criteria

Vaded State: Unwanted Feelings or Anxiety

Vaded States feel bad. Vaded Avoided States must be resolved prior to work with a Retro Avoiding State otherwise the Retro Avoiding State will return to its old avoiding behavior to save the personality from the negative feelings of a Resource State Vaded with Fear or Rejection.

Most clients have issues that relate to Vaded States. Vaded States manifest themselves by the client feeling emotions that are unwanted, and to some level, that are uncontrollable. Vaded States can be thought of as being a tender spot in the psyche, and when exposed, the client experiences negative emotions in the form of anxiety, fear, confusion, depression, or rejection. The client who is reactive in an argument or a discussion is demonstrating a Vaded State. The client who feels compelled to compete is demonstrating a Vaded State that has feelings of low self-worth. When the client reveals emotion or anxiety, and there is nothing in the immediate situation that is emotional, a Vaded State is being revealed. These states are the holders of unresolved emotion. When clients learn to avoid the experience of Vaded States by unconsciously and artificially creating safe havens, such as addictions, OCD, self-harming behaviors, and others, the resolution of these Vaded States negate the need to escape from them into these unwanted behaviors.

Vaded with Fear:

These states carry a feeling of fear or panic. When this Resource State is Conscious it will feel out of control. It may also fail to reach the Consciousness when a Retro Avoiding State takes over the Conscious to save the client from these negative feelings.

Pathological examples of Resources Vaded with Fear include, Specific Phobia, Panic attack, PTSD, Agoraphobia, Self-harming behavior, Generalized Anxiety Disorder, Dissociative Identity Disorders, Pathological Gambling, Addictions, Workaholism, OCD (or may be Vaded with Rejection), Social Phobia (or may be Vaded with Rejection), Business Phobia (or may be Vaded with Rejection), Compulsive Shopping (or more often is Vaded with Rejection), Antisocial (or may be Retro or Vaded with Rejection), and Crisis reaction.

A Resource Vaded with Fear is characterized by one of the following feelings, when that feeling does not fit the situation at hand.

- General Anxiety
- Fear
- Panic
- Inability to be alone
- A feeling of being out of control
- Feeling Fragile
- A feeling that the focus of anxiety is bigger than the client

---

Vaded with Rejection:

These states carry a feeling of 'not being good enough'. They can be debilitating to the client and they can prevent the client from feeling autonomy in their choices. Clients with a Resource Vaded with Rejection may feel their choices are made to please others.

Pathological examples of Resources Vaded with Rejection include, Social Phobia (or may be Vaded with Fear), Business Phobia (or may be Vaded with Fear), Narcissism, Anorexia Nervosa, Bulimia Nervosa, Feeling Unlovable, Business Phobia (or may be Vaded with Fear), Compulsive Shopping (or may be Vaded with Fear), and Over-Competiveness.

A Resource Vaded with Rejection is characterized by:

- Feeling not good enough
- Feels positive when the client has pleased another person, but feels terrible when the client has disappointed another person
- Feelings of worth are based on the impressions of others
- Feels like a fake, and feels that if others saw the real person they would be disappointed
- Is unsure if it is loved

Vaded with Confusion:

Their most evident indication is rumination. The client with a Resource State Vaded with Confusion will report not being able to stop thinking about the issue that confuses them. They may report thinking about it many times during the day, and may report not being able to sleep due to these thoughts.

Pathological examples of Resources Vaded with Confusion include, Complicated Bereavement, Rumination (over the welfare of others, over a death, or over an event), Guilt or Shame, Existential angst, and a Deep confusion over the breakdown of a relationship.

A Resource Vaded with Confusion is characterized by:

- Rumination
- Feelings of Guilt or Shame
- Feelings that something was not handled properly by the client or by someone else
- An inability to let go of concern about another person
- An inability to understand another's action

Vaded with Disappointment:

These are the states that are depressed or states that prevent other states from engaging in positive experiences or in a positive relationship. They are blocking states. They are so disappointed they take over the ability of other states to enjoy living, or to enjoy a relationship. Just as a Resource State that has found a partner has been unfaithful may block other states from enjoying the relationship, a Resource State Vaded with Disappointment can block all other states from engaging in any enjoyable activity. They have noticed or experienced something that falls well short of expectation or desire and this results in them refusing to allow other Resource States enjoyment.

Pathological examples of Resources Vaded with Disappointment include, Depression, relationship blame, and prolonged and intense feelings of loss.

A Resource Vaded with Disappointment is characterized by:

- Very low energy
- Difficulty relating to a time when things were good
- A reluctance to re-engage
- A lack of permission for other Resources to take up positive engagement

---

Retro State: Unwanted Behavior

Retro States are states that conduct behavior that other states do not like. When a Retro State is Conscious it feels it is doing its job. While a Vaded State will feel a lack of control while it is Conscious, a Retro State will feel that it is doing 'what it does' and it will feel that what it does is important. When a different Resource State of the client is reflecting on the behavior of a Retro State, it will often report that the client was out of control (e.g., a Rage State), but the Retro State itself feels it is doing the right thing.

Retro Original:

This behavior started in childhood as a coping skill when the Resource State was first formed. Although this behavior started in childhood it only became Retro when other states began to disapprove of the behavior.

Pathological examples of this behavior include Pouting, Anti-Social Behavior, Withdrawal, Rage, Personality Disorders, and Passive Aggressive Behavior.

A Retro Original State is characterized by:

- Statements by a personality Resource State indicating a disapproval of this state's behavior
- An indication that during this behavior the client is dismissive of attempts to cease the behavior, even though after the behavior the client is regretful
- An indication that this behavior has been evident since childhood
- No indication that this behavior relates to an Addiction

Retro Avoiding:

This behavior normally started sometime after childhood as a coping mechanism to avoid the negative feelings of a State Vaded with Fear or Rejection.

Pathological examples of this behavior include Addictions, uncontrolled drug taking, OCD, Withdrawal, Anger, Eating Disorders, Work/Relationship avoidance, Shopping Addiction, 'Perfectionistic' behavior, Self-Harming behavior.

It is possible for some ego states to have poor communication between them. Occasionally, a person may have read a couple of pages, and then upon switching states may have no memory of what was just read. Ego states that have poor communication are said to be more dissociated from each other.

A Retro Avoiding State is characterized by:

- Statements by a personality Resource State indicating a disapproval of this state's behavior
- An indication that during this behavior the client is dismissive of attempts to cease the behavior, even though after the behavior the client is regretful
- No indication that this behavior has been evident since childhood
- An indication that without this behavior anxiety is consistently experienced (usually with a feeling of fear or low self-esteem)
- An indication that sincere efforts to cease this behavior are met with frustration and failure
- An indication that this behavior relates to an addiction, OCD, or Self-Harm

---

Conflicted:

Conflicted States may otherwise be Normal (healthy), Retro or Vaded. All Retro States are conflicted, by definition. The definition of a Retro State is one that has behavior that another state regrets, but Retro State Negotiation ends unwanted behavior and conflict. A Vaded State may also be in conflict with other states. An intellectual state may wish an emotionally laden Vaded State would just go away.

There is often an effort to push the feelings of a Vaded State away by the states that they bother. A person who feels nervous when talking in front of a group will often try and push these nervous feelings away. This natural and understandable reaction does not help the Vaded State, as the attempt to push it away results in it feeling more upset. When Vaded States gain resolution the conflict between them and other states cease, so as with Retro States, no further attention is required to resolve the conflicts caused by Vaded States. When the person no longer gets nervous when talking to a group, conflict between the states no longer exists.

Often states are conflicted without being either Retro or Vaded, and these states do require an intervention to resolve their conflict.

Pathological examples of Resources that are Conflicted with each other include, Procrastination, Inability to rest or sleep, Chronic Fatigue, Insomnia, and Anxiety over decision making.

Conflicted States are characterized by at least one of the following:

- Two states wanting to be out at the same time.
- One state disliking or disrespecting another State
- The client may report being bothered by an unhappy voice, e.g., "You should be working."
- Procrastination
- Inability to decide on a major life decision
- Lack of ability to rest or sleep

Dissonant State:

A Dissonant Resource State is merely not the most preferred state to be holding the Conscious. It is out at the wrong time. When a boss is difficult it may be normal to feel frustrated.

Examples of a Dissonant State includes being in a sporting slump, feeling discontented with responses to others, writer's block, feeling frustrated at having to do a normal activity such as cleaning or driving, feeling a difficulty in being able to learn a particular subject of study, or feeling unable to appropriately respond to a child or boss.

A Dissonant State is characterized by:

- A feeling of discomfort when doing an activity
- Performance that is below normal for the person
- Feelings of frustration with self in the way a situation is being handled
- A feeling of frustration that an activity has to be done

Action 2: Vivify Specific

Purpose: This is an Action that is used to bring a resource to the surface, into consciousness, so it can be worked with directly, or to facilitate Bridging to the Initial Sensitising Event.

This is one of the most commonly used Actions in Resource Therapy. The central advantage of Resource Therapy is that it enables the therapist to work directly with the part of the personality that can most benefit from change. Most other therapies engage an intellectual, talkative personality part that does not need to change.

The Vivify Specific Action brings to the surface, to consciousness, the Resource that needs change, by encouraging the client to build a detailed image of one specific time when it was previously in the Conscious. If this Action is not learned, or is not administered appropriately the whole therapeutic endeavor loses its foundation.

The Action requires the therapist to have the patience to ensure that a specific time is located when the unwanted emotion was evident. For example, if the client presents feeling anxiety when talking in front of a group, a specific time that this anxiety was felt needs to be defined by the client.

Often clients will attempt to stay general rather than define a specific instance. Clients may say something like, "It's every time I want to talk in front of a group," or, "It's mainly when I'm talking to larger groups at a conference."

When a client attempts to stay general in presenting when the undesired emotion was present the therapist must require a single, specific presentation of when the state was out. It is only by getting a specific time the state was out, and vivifying in detail that time that the appropriate Resource is brought into the Conscious.

Vivify Specific means specific. The therapist can say something like, "I need to know one precise time you have felt this way; one point in time. Tell me exactly where you were in one single instance when you had these feelings." Some clients will continue to give general responses, and when this occurs the therapist must be tenacious, never give up, and make sure a specific time is presented.

The next step is to vivify this specific time until it is evident that the Resource with the unwanted feelings is present. This is noticed by some exhibition of emotion, such as, breaking voice, tears, obvious discomfort, an exhibition of fear, or speaking with a reduced level of confidence or authority. When this action is used to locate a needed Resource State, such as an assertive state, the therapist will be able to notice a change in voice tone that signifies the preferred state has entered the Conscious.

Notes:

An important aspect of the Vivify Specific Action is the notes that are taken. The therapist should take detailed notes containing verbatim statements identifying the specific time the unwanted emotional reaction occurred. Especially, any statement relating to feelings should be written down. These notes will be necessary for the **Imagery Check Action** near the end of the therapy session.

Steps:

The steps of the Vivify Specific Action:

1. Gain an understanding about which Resource State is needed in the Conscious.

2. Be tenacious in ensuring that the client gives a specific time when this state has previously been Conscious.

3. Vivify this time specifically requiring the client to describe things like, what was worn, time of day, lighting in the room, who else was there, if anyone, the expressions on their faces, the temperature, or anything else that seems pertinent.

4. As soon as the client begins telling about a specific place it is important to begin using present tense language. This helps bring the wanted state to the surface.

5. Take detailed verbatim notes of what the client says.

6. Continue this process until it is evident that the desired Resource is Conscious.

7. Ask the state directly, "What can I call you. What term or name fits you as you experience this place and time (See Naming, page 151)?"

If the emotions that the client describes during the Vivify Specific Action seem to be an appropriate response for the moment presented, then it is unlikely that the Resource State you are speaking with is vaded.

Table 20: Examples of Vivify Specific Language

Initial Information gathering	When exactly have you experienced this feeling before? What time of day was it?
Move to present tense language until you see the state is out.	"Right now, as you are sitting on the couch looking at his face, what are you experiencing?"
When you see the state is out, get a name for the state.	"As you are feeling this sense of being unable to have a voice, what name or term fits you?"

Example:

John presented in therapy indicating that when he was criticized by his partner, or any other woman, he would become very emotional, feel angry, and be unable to speak. This is an obvious example of a Vaded State, because he was describing an emotional reaction that did not fit the situation at hand, thus indicating the emotions were coming from an unresolved Resource.

The first step in helping to resolve the Vaded State is to make sure that state is in the Conscious, therefore the Vivify Specific Action was used to bring the Vaded State into the Conscious.

I chose this example because it demonstrates a session when there was difficulty in getting the client to define a specific time when the unwanted emotions were experienced. This is not unusual.

Therapist: John, help me out by describing to me one specific time that you felt this emotional reaction.

John: It pretty much happens any time a woman criticizes me.

Therapist: I understand that. What I really need is to hear you tell me about one specific time that it happened.

John: It often happens when Nancy gets on to me about something.

Therapist: When is the last time you can remember that happening when it really bothered you?

John: It pretty much bothers me every time she gets on to me.

Therapist: Tell me an exact place and time this happened. I need to know if you are at home, or someplace else. I just want one precise time.

John: It can happen at home. It often does.

Therapist: I want you to tell me about one single incident. What room are you in, in one single incident, the kitchen, living room, the bedroom, or any other room at one time that it happened?

John: Well, I was in the kitchen getting ready to go to work and she told me I should not be wearing the shirt I had on.

Therapist: What were you doing in the kitchen when she complained about your shirt?

John: I was just eating some cereal.

Therapist: What time was it in the morning?

John: It was just before 7 AM.

Therapist: What color shirt are you wearing?

John: It was a blue shirt I got in Bali. I guess it was a bit bright, but it really upset me when she told me I shouldn't be wearing it.

John has finally started telling about a specific time, therefore it is time for the therapist to begin using present tense language. This helps the client connect with the feelings of the State.

> **Therapist:** So you are sitting, having cereal. Is she standing, or sitting, and what is the expression on her face?
>
> **John:** She was standing over me, and she just looked disgusted. She looked like she thought I was stupid.
>
> **Therapist:** John, just allow your eyes to close so you can get a better sense of what is happening. You are sitting having some cereal. Nancy is standing over you telling you she does not like the shirt you have on. She's looking disgusted at you. What does her look make you feel like?
>
> **John:** I just want to crawl into a hole and hide. It just really bothers me. I just hate her when she looks at me like that.
>
> **Therapist:** Wanting to crawl into a hole, right now, what name or term fits you? What can I call you as you have these feelings?
>
> **John:** "In Trouble".

John's comments revealed emotion. This indicates that a Vaded Resource has been brought to the surface. It is carrying with it the unresolved feelings it holds from the past. The Vivify Specific Action has been used to bring the Resource that needs work to the surface.

In the present example it is evident that John's Vaded State has been Vaded with Fear or Rejection, therefore a Bridging Action can begin.

Remember, it is important to take detailed notes during the Vivify Specific Action. These notes will be used again near the end of the session to help determine if the intervention has been successful. They will be used in the **Imagery Check Action**.

Action 3: Bridging

Purpose: The purpose of Bridging is to move the client to a present tense awareness of the initial sensitising event, so that the Vaded State can become resolved and assume a Normal Resource Condition.

Bridge to the initial sensitizing event

It is only possible to consistently bridge to the initial sensitizing event when the Vaded State associated with that event is in the Conscious. In the last section we saw how to bring to the Conscious the Vaded State that is associated to the presenting concern of the client. The process of Bridging is to use the 'out-of-control' negative emotions of the Vaded State to connect it to the image of the event that originally caused those emotions.

Table 21: The Three Steps in Bridging:

Vivify Specific, Action 2:	Ensure that the Vaded State is truly in the Conscious.
Find out how old the Vaded State feels when it is in the Conscious.	This is the age of the Vaded State at the time of the initial sensitizing event.
Connect the age and feeling of the Vaded State to the ISE.	Funnel the focus of the client into the initial sensitizing event using prescribed questions.

Bring the Vaded State into the Conscious

Once we have identified the Vaded State associated to the presenting issue (see Action 1: Identify the Resource with Pathology) we are ready to bring that state into the Conscious to a level that Bridging can occur. Bridging should never be attempted before the emotion of the Vaded State is noticed by the therapist. This is an indication that it is in the Conscious.

Often, clients will describe their issues from an intellectual, non-emotional state. When this is the case, detailed revivification of a time when the Vaded State was conscious is a good way to bring it back into the Conscious (see the **Vivify Specific Action**).

Get the age of the Vaded State at the initial sensitizing event

It is important to get the age of the Vaded State at the time of the initial sensitizing event. You are actually getting how old the Vaded State feels like any time it is out. It may, however, be difficult for a client just to answer the question, "How old are you feeling right now?" A more intellectual state may want to hang on to the reality of the present age, and report that. It is still possible to bridge without getting the age, by going straight to an image, but getting the age helps make bridging more precise.

Occasionally, during therapy, the client will begin crying and begin sounding like a child. When this happens, all you may need to do is make a statement like, "It sounds to me like right now I'm hearing a voice that's not really the voice of an adult. If this were the voice of a child, how old would that child be?"

Notice, I asked about the voice, not the client. If I were to ask, "How old do you feel right now," it would be easy for an intellectual part of the client to think about how old the client is before the question is answered. But, by asking about the age of the voice, the client is better able to focus on the Resource that that voice belongs to.

Most often, clients do not gift the therapist with a youthful sounding Vaded State voice early in the process. Therefore, below are some questions that can help to get the age of the Resource at the time of the ISE.

These should be asked only AFTER you see that the Vaded State is in the Conscious, and you know this by noticing that the client is currently experiencing emotion. These questions should only be asked after you have the client to close his or her eyes. I normally just say, "You can just allow your eyes to close right now."

> **Therapist:** Where in the body are you feeling this (e.g., need to run away) right now?

> **Client:** In my chest.

Therapist: How big an area in your chest does this feeling cover, an area the size of a golf ball, a tennis ball, a football?

Client: Almost as big as a football.

Therapist: Are the edges of that area distinct and smooth, or muffled and unclear?

Client: They are unclear.

Therapist: Is there a shade of lightness or darkness inside that area, where you feel like you want to run away?

Client: It's dark.

Therapist: Is there a color in that area?

Client: It's sort of dark red.

Therapist: Does that darkness go all the way across, or is it darker in the middle?

Client: It's more intense in the middle.

Therapist: What would it feel like to stand in the middle of that, e.g., dark red area?

Client: I wouldn't like it. I would feel trapped.

Anytime you notice the voice of the client sounding like that of a child, you can say something like, "It sounds like I am hearing the voice of a child right now. How old a child do you feel?" At that point you can begin with the next step in Bridging, which is to vivify the initial sensitizing event. Otherwise continue with this line of questioning.

Therapist: Right now imagine sitting on the edge of the upset area, with feet dangling inside that, e.g., dark red, thick stuff, pushing back and forth. What do those feet feel like in that stuff?

Client: They feel funny. It is hard to push.

Therapist: Look down into that red stuff and tell me what they look like, down in that stuff. How big are they?

Client: They are not very big. They look little.

Therapist: If those little feet are yours, and you are a child, about how old are you?

Client: I don't know. Maybe, about seven.

The whole reason for getting the age of the client at the time of the initial sensitizing event is to make it easier to funnel the focus of the client into that image. By returning to the image of the initial sensitizing event, by returning to precisely where the negative emotions came from, it will be possible to assist the Vaded State back to a Normal Resource Condition.

Funnel the focus of the client into the initial sensitizing event

Once the Vaded State has indicated how old it feels, it is usually not difficult to bring it to the image of the initial sensitizing event. I have had a number of clients say, intellectually, they kept wanting to go to a different memory, but the image of the initial sensitizing event was just too strong.

The questions that are most normally effective in funneling the Vaded State into the image of the initial sensitizing event help determine if, at the time of the ISE, the client was Inside or Outside, if the client was Alone or With Someone Else, and then asks the client to report on the image that is forthcoming. These questions can be asked immediately following the establishment of the age the Vaded State feels.

> **Therapist:** Being, e.g., seven right now, feeling, e.g. , like you just want to run away, does it feel like you're more inside a building or outside a building, having these feelings right now?
>
> **Client:** Inside.
>
> **Therapist:** Does it feel more like you are alone or is someone else there with you?
>
> **Client:** Someone else is here.
>
> **Therapist:** Tell me what's happening, right there for you are right now.

Immediately following the location of the ISE the Expression Action can begin.

The client does not have to give any level of detail about what is happening where they are. What will be important is that they become empowered, gain a sense of safety and continued support. This can easily happen without them going into any detail about their initial sensitizing event. It is important that they return to that event so they can gain the understanding that they have more power than the **Introjects** in that event, that they are now safe, and that they will in the future be supported, cared for and safe. Bridging is the most artful part of Resource Therapy. Clients are all different and will respond to questions in different ways.

There is no cookbook recipe that can lead the therapist with exact chronological steps to Bridge that will work with every client.

What is important is that the therapist understands the core concepts:

- The Vaded State must be in the Conscious,
- It is best to get an age that relates to the Vaded State, and
- Funnel the client into the image of the ISE using the perceived age and the expressed affect of the Vaded State (Being, e.g., seven right now, feeling, e.g., like you just want to run away, does it feel like you're more inside a building or outside a building?).

Occasionally, the therapist may need to be creative. Even if the client is unable to gain a clear image of the ISE (i.e., I just see myself surrounded by blackness) the next Actions can be used. None of the images used in therapy are real, weighable, concrete objects. They are metaphorical connections to unresolved emotion, therefore non-specific, metaphorical images may be used in the resolution process (see Actions 4-7) if Bridging does not provide a clear ISE, although the resolution does proceed better with a clear ISE. A brush can be used if you do not have a roller.

Bridging using the unwanted emotions that brought the client to therapy is the best way to locate the emotional core of the issue (the ISE). Bridging can go to the wrong place, and if that happens resolving the issue of one Vaded State will likely have no impact on the issue of the causal Vaded State. Therefore, at the end of the resolution phase it is good to use RT Action 12, Imagery Check, in order to check that the client no longer experiences the unwanted emotional reaction that was originally presented in therapy. If the unwanted emotional reaction is still evident, a second Bridging is normally straightforward, and takes minimal time.

Action 4: Expression

Purpose: Expression is the most important step in the process of bringing the Vaded State to a Normal Resource Condition. It is the step that is most useful in empowering the Resource, and in helping it to understand that the Introject is merely an internalized perception, an illusion, that has no power.

The desired result is that the Resource becomes empowered over the Introject. This result can be accomplished by making it safe for the Resource to say absolutely anything and everything it would like to say to the Introject. When the Vaded State is able to do this it realizes that the Introject has no power, because the Resource can express fully with no repercussions. It further proves it holds the power when it is given the choice of deciding whether or not the offending Introject can stay in its space (RT Action 6). It is only after the Vaded Resource State realizes that it has the power to say anything it chooses to the Introject, with no repercussions, that the Vaded State also understands it has the power to remove the offending Introject from its space, or to allow it to stay.

How to make it safe for the Vaded State to Express completely to the Introject

Depending on how upset the Resource State is within the image of the initial sensitizing event, it may at first have difficulty expressing itself to the Introject. Because the therapist understands that the Introject is not real, understands it is only an image, an illusion of the Resource; it is possible for the therapist to calmly and consistently provide safe opportunities for the Resource to express. Here are some examples of what the therapist can do to make it safe and easy for a Vaded State to express.

> **Therapist:** We know he is not really here right now, as we are sitting in a therapy room, so since he is not even here you can say absolutely anything you want to him. Go ahead and tell him exactly how you feel.

On the surface, it sounds like this would take the client out of the image of the initial sensitizing event. It actually does the opposite. It makes it safe enough for the client to engage inside the image of the initial sensitizing event.

> **Therapist:** Let's just shrink him down to 1 inch tall. He has a squeaky little voice. Please be careful not to step on him, because I want you to be able to tell him everything you want to say.

Often when I say this, clients will exhibit a relieving laugh, and later say how funny that person looked with their squeaky little voice. It is more powerful to say, "Please don't step on him," than to say, "You have more power than he does. (The truth of this latter statement may be questioned.)"

> **Therapist:** Would you like me to say something to him first?

When a client appears too frightened, or too rejected to speak, it can be good to offer the Vaded State an opportunity to hear you speak to the Introject first. It will be important for the Vaded State to express itself, afterward. It is through its Expression that it achieves a feeling of empowerment. When the client prefers me to speak first, I will usually ask the client to describe the expression the Introject has on his face, then I will say something like:

> **Therapist:** Get that stupid look off your face. You think you're something, don't you? You're not even here right now. You don't have any power, and you're just showing how stupid you are with that silly expression... (Then to the client) Now, you tell him. Tell him exactly how you feel.

The purpose is for the client to learn that there is nothing from the initial sensitizing event that can hurt him or her. Therefore, the more emotions the client can express to the Introject the greater the understanding that, "There's nothing here that can hurt me."

If what is feared is not a person:

If the initial sensitizing event relates to an animal or an inanimate, such as a flood, fire, water, or something else, it is still good to assist the client to express. Shrinking the animal or inanimate first is a good step.

> **Therapist:** We know that dog is not really in the room with us now, we are just talking with an image, so let's just shrink it down to one inch tall. It is tiny. Don't step on it, because I want you to be able to tell it exactly what you think of it. Tell it exactly how you feel now. You can say anything.

Or

> **Therapist:** We know that fire is not really in the room with us now, we are just talking with an image, so let's just shrink it down to one inch tall. It is tiny, like a small candle. Don't blow it out yet, because I want you to be able to tell it exactly what you think of it. Tell it exactly how you feel now. You can say anything.

I cannot overemphasize the importance for Vaded States to be in the Conscious (you need to consistently call the Vaded Resource State by name to ensure it maintains the Conscious), and to express fully. This is the most important Action that changes the Resource State from holding the image of powerlessness to feeling empowered.

The Vaded State should be encouraged to say things like, "You should have been there for me," or "What you did is not right." These statements are made to the Introject of the Vaded State, not to an adult state's Introject of the person, i.e., if the Vaded State is 7 years old the Expression needs to be to the Introject, as it was when the client was 7, not to the Introject as it would be now. For example, a child State holding the Introject of the mother, would hold the mother Introject at the age she was when the client was still a child. That same mother, would have changed in many ways over the years, may even have died, but the Introject we work with will remain, as that of the mother, as she was at the time of the initial sensitizing event.

Action 5: Introject Speak

Purpose: The purpose of the Introject Speak Action is for a resource to gain a deeper understanding by experiencing the perspectives and emotions of the Introject that the Resource holds of another person, by speaking as that person. For example, by taking on the persona of 'John' and speaking as John, then the Resource can gain an emotional perspective of John. There is often a cathartic change in perspective following the Introject Speak Action.

Usage: This Action is most often used during the resolution phase for a State Vaded with Rejection. When the Resource that has been Vaded with Rejection gains an understanding that the rejecting person was not able to show unconditional acceptance, there is a change in perspective from, "I am unlovable," to, "That other person was not able to show me unconditional love at that time." This switch from being, 'Unlovable,' to, 'That other person was not unconditionally loving' helps move a Vaded Rejection State to a Normal State.

This Action is also useful with grief issues to help Vaded States gain better understandings of lost loved ones, human or pet. It is also helpful when working with Resources Vaded with Confusion to assist them to gain clarity with relationships, where they feel confusion.

Process: The Introject Speak Action can be accomplished either using two chairs, or using one chair with the client's eyes closed. If it is used using two chairs, after the Resource has spoken the client is directed to stand up, move over to the other chair, and sit down. As the client is moving down to the chair the name of the Introject is called out clearly, and the Introject is spoken to by the Therapist: e.g., "Dad, your son just said several things about how he feels. How does that make you feel?" This helps the client speak from the perspective of the Introject.

It is very important that this Action be conducted keeping some vital points in mind.

The present tense should always be used (even when talking about something that happened long ago), e.g., "Your Dad is right in front of you, and now is a safe time for you to tell him exactly how you feel. Go ahead and say everything you feel now."

The Resource should speak first, prior to the Introject speaking.

The Resource should be instructed to speak directly to the Introject. An, "I want him to know that…," should be stopped with, "No, say it directly to him," like, "Dad, I want YOU to know …"

After the Resource has said everything it has to say, the Introject should be, 1) called clearly by name, and 2) asked how it feels about what was just said.

The purpose of Introject Speak is not to change the Introject in any way. The Resource State has a clear impression of the Introject, and to try to make the Introject into something that the Resource State knows it wasn't will seem inauthentic. (I.e., If a Resource State has a history of Dad as being disinterested, and non-caring, the therapist cannot transform that impression the Resource State has of his dad into being one of a loving and caring father).We are not attempting to change history, but to get a better understanding of it.

The purpose of Introject Speak is to help the Resource State get a better understanding of the Introject. By becoming the Introject, and speaking as the Introject, the Resource State can better understand that life was hard for the Introject and that the Introject was not able to give the unconditional love that all children deserve. Moving the understanding of the Resource State from, "**I am unlovable**" to, "**The Introject had a hard life and was not able to show love unconditionally,** "is a goal of the Introject Speak Action. To see a case example refer to, Meagan could not stop buying clothes*, page 304.

Action 6: Removal

Purpose: The purpose of the Removal step is to empower and to help the previously Vaded State feel safe. Following the empowering step of Expression the client will feel stronger than the Introject, and will therefore be able to decide if the Introject can stay within the space of the previously Vaded State. Being able to make this decision is empowering to the Resource, and if the Resource wants a space clear of the Introject, the space may feel safer. If the Resource decides to allow the Introject to remain within its space, then in does so only at its own discretion. Either way, the Resource becomes aware that it has the power of making this 'stay or go' decision, and this clarifies to the Resource that it is in control.

Process: The removal step is simple, quick, and easy, but important. This is one step that must go in the correct chronological order, as it is impossible for the Vaded State to ask an Introject to leave, if it appears to the Vaded State that the Introject has more power than it does. Following the empowering expression step, the Resource is then able to decide whether or not it would like the Introject to remain in its inner space.

Remember, **Introjects** are Resource specific. When a previously Vaded Resource tells an Introject to leave its space, that does not have an impact on the **Introjects** of other Resources. In other words, it will not have any direct impact on adult Resources that currently have a relationship with the father, if a childhood Vaded Resource asked the Introject of an abusive father to leave its space.

Resolving the Vaded State will have an impact on the life of the client, as the Vaded State will no longer jump into the Conscious causing the client to feel negative and out-of-control, as the Resource will no longer be vaded. Therefore, when a childhood Resource State becomes empowered that will allow adult Resources to stay in the Conscious and have better relationships.

Here's how to give the Vaded Resource the choice of removal:

> **Therapist:** That was really good, what you told him. You really told him exactly how you feel, and you told him that you're never going to let him do that again. Now, I want to get another part to come in and stay with you and make sure you feel safe and comfortable. In the meantime, do you want your dad to stay in the space you're in right now, or do you want him to leave? It's totally up to you.

> **Client:** I don't want him here.

> **Therapist:** That's fine. Just tell him to go. (**Or**, depending on the response) He can stay.

> **Therapist:** Now, I want to bring in another state to make sure you get the love and support that you should always have had.

Remember, it does not matter how this question is answered, but it does matter that it is asked, and answered. When the Resource understands that it has the power to have the Introject leave, or that it has the power to allow the Introject to stay, it realizes it has 'The power'. This is a big difference from the experience of being powerless and out-of-control.

The final Action in the resolution of States Vaded with Fear or Rejection is to bring in nurturing Resource that can make sure that the previously Vaded State gets everything it needs. This step may not be entirely necessary, but it is a nice "icing on the cake." It leaves the Resource feeling very comfortable and content. This Relief Action follows.

Action 7: Relief

Purpose: Relief is a process of bringing in a more mature, nurturing Resource of the client to the previously Vaded State so it can help it feel safe, protected, and nurtured, following the Expression and Release steps.

How to find a Resource that wants to help

A few years ago I would ask to speak with a resource that would like to help this child state to feel safe. I would say, "I want to talk with a nurturing part of this person. When that state is ready, just say, I'm here." I no longer do that. I found that, occasionally, a client would have difficulty locating a state that wanted to help. Now, I will build an imaginary scene that describes a child the age of the previously Vaded State, lonely and upset, and I will ask the client what he or she would do upon seeing a child like this. When I get a response, I say, "I want to speak directly with that part that would like to go to that child to help." I find that by creating a real life situation it is easy for the client to locate the helping part that can help the previously Vaded State.

Here is an example of the process. It comes after the previously Vaded State has elected to either remove, or allow to stay, any difficult **Introjects**.

> **Therapist:** Now, (client's name), I would like you to imagine seeing a, e.g., seven year old child who you care about crying and upset. This child would really love some help. What would you like to do?

> **Client:** I would like to go to her and help her feel better.

Therapist: What can I call this nurturing part of you that just spoke up and said he would like to help the seven-year-old child?

Client: "Helper."

Therapist: Thank you for talking with me, 'Helper' I want you to go to the seven-year-old Resource, now, that I have been talking with. You can help her, and do everything else you do all of the same time. The more you do the stronger you become. Just go to her now, put your arm around her, and let love flow from you into every cell and fibre of her being. This will feel good to you to, to receive love back from her. (Short pause) "Upset," how does that feel?

Client: It feels really good.

Therapist: You can give Helper a hug back if you like. It can be like two logs in the fire next to each other. They really glow by giving each other warmth. You can ask her if she will always be here for you, and she can be. (pause) How do you feel now?

Client: I feel really good.

Therapist: That's great! It seems like the name, 'Upset,' doesn't really fit you anymore. What would you like to be called now, a name that would better fit how you feel there with 'Helper'?

Client: I would like to be called, 'Loved'.

Therapist: That's a great name. From now on I will call you, 'Loved'. Loved, when you enjoy yourself, what do you like to do? (Remember, Vaded States were once Normal states before they became vaded. Now that the Resource is no longer vaded, it may again take up its original role. It would not have been able to participate in its original role while vaded, because it was carrying overwhelmingly negative emotions).

Client: I like to play.

Therapist: Maybe now that you're feeling better, when this adult gets a chance to play you could come to the surface and help her enjoy playing, really having a good time. At other times you can stay down where you are with, Helper, receiving and giving love to her. How does that sound to you?

Client: I can do that.

Therapist: That's great! And is it okay with you if at other times you let more mature adult parts handle the difficult things, while you can continue to enjoy where you are?

Client: Yes, that's OK.

Therapist: Thank you, "Loved." I'm glad that you are now getting the unconditional love that every child deserves.

At this point the Vaded State is resolved. It has released the overwhelmingly negative feelings that it held, and it is again able to take up its role as a Normal Resource. It will no longer come to the Conscious with the negative feelings that it once held.

If the client has experienced something difficult or tragic the memory of that will always be sad. If the client takes time to think back on what happened he or she may feel emotional and upset, but once the Vaded State is resolved it will not jump back into the Conscious interfering with the client's life. Resolving a Vaded State can be thought of as changing a painful seething sore to a scar. It is no longer a tender spot in the psyche, just a memory that may carry with it emotion.

(This is where the Find Resource Action may be used in the following way) Following the resolution of a Vaded State, it is good to find how the client would like to deal with a difficult situation like the presenting one. For example, if the client would previously become overwhelmingly upset if criticized at work, a statement and question can be something like, "Now, how would you like to respond externally, and how would you like to feel internally if your boss says something critical to you at work? I want to know how you would like to respond back to him, and how you would like to feel internally at the same time."

The client will not be bothered again by the state that was vaded, but it is preferable that she be able to respond in a way that she would really like. Therefore, it is good to help her find a resource that has this capability. When she answers the question about how she would like to respond, the next question is to ask her when had she been able to respond like that in her life, ever.

If she can think of the time that she has been able to respond like that previously, with anyone, a child, family member, in a work setting, with anyone at any place, then revivify that time and bring that Resource into the Conscious. The next step is to get a name for that state, to thank it for talking with you, and asked if it would be willing to help the client at work when she is being criticized. It will say yes, because Resources love time in the Conscious.

If the client cannot remember a time that she was able to respond externally and internally in the way she would like to, then ask her to describe someone who she knows that could respond like that. Have heard describe them in some detail, then stop her in the middle of her description and ask her to give a name to the Resource that is describing this other person. Then you can say to that state something like, "Strong," it seems like you really understand and have a good handle on what it is like to be able to respond appropriately. I know you may not have done this before, but it seems like you are the best part that (the client) has to respond to the boss at work. Would you be willing to help her out when the boss is critical by coming to the surface and responding in the way that you described?

The state will almost without exception agree to do this, because it has the ability. It understands what needs to be done. If you were to have asked a meek and fragile Resource if he would do that it would probably say no, because it does not have the ability and it knows this. Resources love being in the Conscious, and if they are asked to do something that they feel they can do, they will. Resources like being in the Conscious so much that they often conflict over which one has the Conscious. A rest state and a work state both want the Conscious at the same time. A state that wants to diet and a state that wants ice cream both want the Conscious at the same time. Resources love to be out.

The last important thing to do in the session is the Imagery Check Action, to revivify the time that the Vaded State would've normally come to the surface. In the present example, the client could be asked to imagine being at work, being behind her desk, and being criticized by her boss.

This does two things. If everything has worked well, it gets client confidence that she will be able to handle situations in the future, and it gives her some imagery practice in doing this. Very occasionally, the same overwhelmingly negative emotion is experienced. This means that the bridging has not gone to the right initial sensitizing event. If there is time in the therapy session, a second bridging can occur very quickly. The client is ready and has a high level of understanding about the process. Obviously, if there's not enough time in the session this would need to be done in the following session.

What most normally happens is, the client is pleasantly pleased with her ability to handle a situation that previously would have been overwhelming for her. It is not unusual for a client to say, "There is still some emotion there, but I can handle it. I have a choice. I did not have a choice before."

Action 8: Find Resource

Purpose: The purpose of this Action is to locate and gain access to the best Resource the client has to deal with a situation at hand. This is a very useful technique, and one that is often beneficial. For example, a State Vaded with Fear may have previously come to the Conscious each time a client has attempted to speak in public. That state is most normally a fragile part that, following resolution is not the best part to speak in public, therefore a part than enjoys communicating should be found and encouraged to take on the activity that the previously Vaded State had blocked. The Find Resource Action is used to find the best state to speak in public in the future.

Process: It is important that it is used in the proper sequence otherwise it will be ineffective. If a Vaded State is involved in the issue at hand that state will need to first gain resolution otherwise the client will not be able to gain access to the preferred resource. The angst of the Vaded State is often more powerful than the desire of the client to bring to the surface the correct state, even if that state (Resource) is known. For example, the person suffering with arachnophobia would not be able to merely bring a calm state to the surface when a large spider is nearby. The Vaded Resource holding the fear anxiety would first need to gain resolution otherwise it would force its way into the Conscious carrying with it the irrational fear that it holds.

The Find Resource Action is a 5 step process.

1. **Preference Question:** Following the resolution of the Vaded State the client should be intellectually reminded of the scene that was described during the **Vivify Specific Action**, along with the question, "In the future,

how do you want to react to this both externally and internally? How do you want to respond to the other person, and how do you want to feel internally?" These questions are for a thinking state, so no attempt to revivify should be made at this point in therapy. It is important for the therapist to get a clear definition of the preferred response, both the external response and the internal (feeling) response, before the next step.

2. **Locating Question:** When have you been able to respond like this (repeat the client's response) at any time in your past, with a friend, a child, a family member, or at work? [**Alternative step 2, 3 & 4**. Below if the client cannot think of any time that the wanted type of response was ever experienced, ask the client to describe in some detail what it would be like to respond like in the desired way. During this defining, when it is evident the client is in a Resource that can clearly describe what it would be like to respond in the desired way, stop the client and ask, "What can I call this part of you that is talking right now?" (Resource name is given) Then say, "It seems like this part really has a good idea of the best way to respond. (Name of state) since you have a real understanding of how to respond, would you be the part of (Client) that comes out at this time and helps. Even though you may not have done it before you seem to be the best part to really help at these times, and the more you practice at it the better you will get."]

3. The state that can describe an action clearly can do the action (i.e., a fragile state could not describe what it would be like to be really assertive), and states love to help when they feel they can. After finding this state and getting a name for it, and getting assurance that this state will be available to help in the future, move on to step 5 below.

4. **Vivify Specific** the time that the client has mentioned, making sure you get a name for the state. This state will be the resource that can be used in the future.

5. Calling this state by its name, ask it if it will be willing to help the client in the future, during times like the one described in Step 1 above.

An Anchor may be used, if it seems as though it would be helpful to assist the client to bring the wanted Resource to the surface. (For example, the client may be asked:

> "What animal do you associate with the feeling you are having right now, while experiencing this strong state? (Answer) Imagine being that animal right now with its strength and focus. (A short amount of time can be spent helping the client gain the feeling of the animal by mentioning attributes of the animal.) When you want to feel this way again, when you want to use this resource of yours, just picture this animal and how it feels to be this animal, and that will really get you into this great resource of yours."

This **Find Resource Action** is often the last Action before the **Imagery Check Action**. The **Imagery Check Action** will revivify the initial problem so the client will be able to gain practice using this Resource, so the client can gain confidence that the therapy has made a difference, and so the therapist can see if the correct intervention has been used to create change.

Action 9: Changing Chairs Introject Action

Purpose: The Changing Chairs Introject activity is a very powerful tool that can be used at different times during therapy. It is core to working with Resources Vaded with Confusion, and it can also be extremely useful working with other Resources in order to assist them to gain a higher level of understanding of Introjects.

For example, this activity is beneficial to allow a client who is having relationship concerns with a partner, neighbor, relative, friend, or acquaintance to have an interaction with the Introject of that person to gain a better understanding of the dynamics of the relationship, and to better understand what is likely possible, or impossible, within that relationship.

Another example when this Action is useful is with a Resource State Vaded with Confusion over the death of a loved one. When given the opportunity to interact directly with the Introject of that loved one, the client can gain a heightened level of understanding.

A client dealing with feelings of guilt or shame in relation to another person, or even a deity, can have an interaction in order to become resolved of those negative feelings. Action #14, The Separation Sieve, is a good technique to follow this type of release of guilt or shame so the client can gain clarity in relation to what it feels like to be free of the past.

Process: There are some important aspects that are necessary in order for the changing chairs Introject Activity to work properly, and to result in the most beneficial gain for the client.

These aspects are:

1. **Vivify Specific:** Make sure the pathological state is Conscious and named, e.g., 'Hurt'.

2. **Determine what needs to be said and/or asked:** Speak directly with the Resource, calling it by name, and find out what it would like to say to the Introject if it had a chance, and what questions it would like to ask.

3. **Create an understanding of the Introject in the other chair:** I.e., "Hurt, just imagine the presence of your brother sitting in the chair opposite you right now. Tell me when you have done this."

4. **Ensure complete expression and questions:** Tell the Resource that, since we know the Introject is really not in the other chair now this is a time that absolutely anything can be said completely and safely, and direct the Resource to express itself fully and **directly** to the Introject. If the client says something like, "I want him to know…" stop him or her and say, "Tell him directly. Say his name then continue with what you want him to know." The Resource can also ask any questions that it may choose or benefit from. The therapist should **encourage complete expression** and should take good notes of everything that is said, so when the Introject is speaking all appropriate cues can be made.

5. **Direct the client to move to the Introject's chair:** After the Resource has been encouraged to fully express and to fully question, the client should be asked to stand, move over to the other chair, and when the client is in the process of sitting down the name of the Introject should be called out clearly, e.g., "Anthony, thank you for being here."

6. When the client has finished sitting down **the Introject should be asked how it feels** about what was just said, e.g., "Anthony, she said a lot of things to you just now. How does that make you feel?" This helps the client settle into the skin of the Introject.

7. **Speak directly with the Introject:** Ask the Introject questions in relation to the needs of the Resource. Ask things that will enlighten the Resource about the abilities, feelings, and level of peace of the Introject. Look at the notes you have taken and make sure the Introject responds to all the comments and questions posed by the Resource.

8. **Direct the client back to the original chair:** Call the client by name (not the name of the Resource), and ask her to stand up and move over to the other chair, and as the client is sitting down, speak clearly the name of the Resource in order to re-engage with that personality part, e.g., "Hurt, what Anthony said was interesting. He said...."

9. **Debrief with the Resource:** Ask the Resource its feelings about what it has just heard, and see if it has anything else it wants to say to the Introject. Debrief.

Each of the steps above will be discussed in more detail below for added clarity: Because this Changing Chairs Introject Activity is often used while working with Vaded States, it is important that a good understanding of the Action is obtained. Following the more detailed step-by-step description below, some of the most common mistakes will be discussed.

1. **Vivify Specific:** It is very important that the pathological Resource is Conscious and that you have a name for it. Use the name often when you speak with it. Continuing to use the name in almost every sentence holds it in the Conscious and makes the therapeutic process clear.

2. **Determine what needs to be said and/or asked:** Before the conversation with the Introject begins, it is good to know the needs of the Resource. When the Resource is obviously in the Conscious and you're able to call it by name, ask things like, "If you could say anything that you wanted to to your brother, what would you like to say?" This is not the time the Resource

is actually speaking with the Introject, but it is the time that the therapist is able to gather information to make sure that when the Resource begins speaking with the Introject all information is covered. Also, ask the Resource if there is anything it would like to find out from the Introject. You can use these notes to make sure the Resource State, when speaking to the Introject, says and asks everything it needs to. When the Resource is speaking with the Introject you can remind the Resource about things that it has said, that it wants to say, or questions that it has shared that it wants to ask. Your notes on these statements and questions are important, because when the Resource later speaks as its Introject of the other person, you will be able to make sure that it responds to all the questions and statements.

3. **Create an understanding of the Introject in the other chair:** I will pull an empty chair in front of a client, and suggest the Resource that I'm speaking with, to just imagine, e.g., "The essence of your brother, Anthony, sitting in this chair" right now. Just tell me when you have done this." Having the Resource report when it is able to imagine the essence of the other person in the chair, ensures that the Resource is involved with the process and not just listening to the therapist.

4. **Ensure complete expression and questions:** By telling the Resource that we know the Introject is not really there, therefore you can say anything you like, we make it easier for the Resource to speak. Knowing that it has complete freedom to say absolutely anything, because really there is no one else in the chair, gives it the power to speak. I find it actually allows the Resource to connect more with the situation, rather than less, because a level of fear has been removed.

5. **Direct the client to move to the Introject's chair:** The next step is to have the client move over to the other chair and sat down. It is very important that this step is completed in the right manner. I never ask the client if he or she would like to move over to the other chair, I speak directly and instruct them clearly. Given clear instructions the client will respond to the therapist. Clients should not be given the extra stress of deciding

whether or not they want to participate in this useful Action. When told to clearly, the client will respond.

Therefore, the first thing I say is the name of the client, followed by the clear instructions to stand up, "John, stand up right now. That's right, just go ahead and stand up (and after he does), and go ahead and move over to the other chair (and after he does), and now sit down".
In the process of the client sitting down, while movement is still occurring, I will call out the name of the Introject that the client has been speaking to, and I will immediately ask how the Introject feels about what was just said. "Anthony. That was a lot that you just heard. How are you doing? What does that make you feel like, Anthony?" This helps the client begin speaking from the persona of the Introject.

6. The first question is simple. I am asking something personal about the **Introject's** feelings. I am not yet asking the Introject to answer any questions that have just been asked by the client, and I am not asking the Introject to speak directly back to the client at this time. I just want to make sure that I am drawing the Introject out so that there can be a feeling of authenticity when the client returns to his or her own chair.

Usually, the client will be able to speak immediately and directly as if he or she is the Introject.

Sometimes clients will have a question about what I want to happen, whether I wanted the Introject to speak out loud, or sometimes they will begin responding as the Introject but will respond in a way to make the Introject look stupid, rather than respond in a way that the Introject would actually speak. If either of these occur, I will say to the client, "Just be a great actor right now. Just forget about who you are, and let me hear directly from your 'brother', as if he were actually here speaking. Great actors can forget who they are and crawl into the skin of another person and speak. So when I ask Anthony a question, just be Anthony and answer the question, as Anthony."

When the client is able to feel an authenticity with the Introject, it is more likely that he or she will feel a level of clarification with reflection on what the Introject said.

7. **Speak directly with the Introject:** After the Introject has been called by name, and has been asked about how it feels about what has just been said, you will be able to use your notes from step two above to ensure that all statements and questions made by the Resource have been responded to by the Introject. When speaking with the Introject use the **Introject's** name a lot to ensure clarity in who you are speaking with. Speak empathetically with the Introject, showing understanding for the **Introject's** feelings, although not necessarily agreement. For example, if the Introject is a parent who says, "I am just too busy to pay attention to my child," it is okay to show an understanding about how frustrating that might be, "That must be very difficult for you to have all the things that put demands on you, and have a child at the same time." Think about speaking as you would speak to a person, and that is what you need to do to make this conversation feel authentic to the client.

8. **Direct the client back to the original chair:** After you make sure that the Introject has responded to all statements of the Resource, and answered all questions of the Resource you can call the client by name, and ask the client to move back to the other chair. As the client is in the process of sitting down, call the Resource by name and asked the Resource how it feels about what it just heard.

9. **Debrief with the Resource:** During debriefing it is good to reflect back to the Resource the different things that the Introject has said, and ask the Resource how it feels about those things. Often, the Introject will have explained feelings and, in my experience, if the Introject is of a deceased person, it will ensure the Resource that it is peaceful and that it loves the client.

Summary

This Changing Chairs Introject activity often leaves the client with a feeling of catharsis. The Resource makes statements and asks questions to its Introject of another person. Then, the client sits in the chair of the Introject and acts as the Introject, to respond in an authentic manner. Next, when the client returns to his or her chair there is a different level of understanding. At a guttural level the lack of completeness or the confusion is gone. This activity must be done properly, and when it is, it is very powerful.

Common mistakes that I find students make in attempting this activity include:

- Failing to ensure that either the Resource or the Introject directly speaks to the other.

- Failing to make sure that the Resource has expressed fully and has asked all questions of interest.

- Failing to ensure that the Introject has responded fully.

- Failing to debrief with the Resource and reiterate the responses that the Introject has made as part of the debriefing session.

This Changing Chairs Introject Action can be used to clarify issues with the current Introject of a living person, such as a roommate, a parent, or partner. It can be used to clarify issues with the Introject of a deceased person, such as a lost love one, with the Introject of a fetus, or even with the Introject of a pet (the client can still respond from the chair of the Introject). It can also be used to address the historical Introject of a person in the past. For example, an adult client may have a relationship with their living parent, but a childhood Vaded State may have a need to address the Introject of the parent of the time that the vading occurred.

Note: Changing chair work is not done when bridging is used. During Bridging the Client has eyes closed and can easily change from one Resource to the other, or from a resource to an Introject without changing chairs. When the eyes are closed the Introject Speak Action is used.

For a transcribed example of this the Changing Chairs Action see Leah discovered her sister had slept with her husband*, page 272.

Action 10: Retro State Negotiation

Purpose: Retro States, when Conscious, carry out behaviors that other states do not like. Retro State Negotiation is a process of talking with a Retro State in such a way that it becomes happy to take on behavior that is appreciated by other states. This is accomplished by it becoming aware that there is alternative behavior that can continue to fulfil its purpose, and that it will be appreciated by other states if it takes on this alternative behavior.

Note: The same negotiation process is used for Retro States regardless whether they are Retro Original (States that learned Retro behavior in childhood when this Resource was formed) or Retro Avoiding States (states that adopt a behavior to save the client from the negative emotions of a Vaded State).

For Retro Avoiding States the associated Vaded Avoided State must be resolved prior to this negotiation Action. Vaded Avoided States may be Vaded with Fear or Rejection. The Retro Avoiding State sees its role as imperative, to save the client from the negative feelings of the Vaded State. Even if the Retro Avoiding State agrees to cease its unwanted behavior, this behavior will most often return if the client re-experiences the angst of its associated unresolved Vaded State.

For example, let's consider a resource that was vaded with the experience of living through a family attack. A Retro Avoiding State may have learned to save the client from the re-emergence of these intensely fearful feelings, through an escape into OCD lock checking behavior. It is imperative that the Vaded Avoided State be resolved prior to using this negotiation Action, otherwise when those intensely fearful feelings return the Retro Avoiding State would again step in to save the client from those feelings.

As long as the Vaded Avoided State remains unresolved and continues to carry its negative feelings it must be avoided

- by the same Retro Avoiding State behavior,

- by that same Retro State adopting another avoiding behavior to avoid the negative feelings,

- by a different Resource taking on Retro Avoiding behavior,

- by changing the Vaded Avoided State to a Vaded Conscious State, where the negative feelings are externally experienced, or

- by suppressing the negative feelings.

While some of these five options are at times an improvement, none of them are appropriate. For example alcoholism might be changed to workaholism in certain individuals, but the person still experiences 'out of control behavior'. Therefore, the Vaded Avoided State should be resolved (see Chapters 5 and 6) prior to Retro State Negotiation.

Process: The negotiation process is rather simple, and when followed in the appropriate sequence, works very well. Resources like to be liked, therefore when the Retro Avoiding State discovers it can continue to have an important role and at the same time will actually be liked and appreciated by other states, it will change its behavior. It must first be presented with an alternative positive role, then another Resource must be questioned about how it would like the Retro Avoiding State if it were to take on this new role. This enables the Retro Avoiding State to experience the effect of being liked. It is then a very easy decision for it to agree to take on the new positive role.

Resources like to be liked, just like all people. Retro States have given up on the prospect of being liked, because they just believe they never will be, or because they feel they HAVE to continue with their important role, no matter what. The experience of being in the Conscious and speaking directly with a respectful, honoring therapist, followed by the experience of another Resource experiencing the Conscious and saying it will like the Retro State when it takes on the new positive behavior, allows the Retro State to return to the Conscious with the affective experience of feeling liked. It is a no-lose choice. It can do its job and it can be liked.

Here is the sequence of Retro State Negotiation steps:

1. **First resolve the Vaded State** if the Retro State has been coming into the Conscious to avoid the negative feelings of a Vaded State (see Chapters 5 and 6). If the Retro State is a Retro Original State just proceed to step 2.

2. **Use the Vivify Specific Action (# 2)** to bring the Retro State into the Conscious.

3. **Talk with this state to determine how it has helped** the client in the past, in order to become clear on its purpose. For example, a state exhibiting anti-social behavior may have protected the person from attack, or an

alcohol abusing state may have protected the client from the negative feelings of a Vaded State.

4. **Get a name for the Retro State** that is an indication of its purpose, not its role. For example, don't accept the name Smoker, rather acccpt a name like Relaxer, or Rebel. Don't accept the name Gambler, rather accept a name like Protector. You can suggest a name once the purpose is clear. Allow the Retro State to have input on its name.

5. **Show appreciation for how it has helped in the past**, even if the behavior has been negative. Praise the state for having been willing to be disliked by other states so that it could accomplish its important role.

6. **Line up an appropriate Resource**. If another Resource is needed to handle the situation that the Retro State has handled in the past use the Find Resource Action (#9). For example, if assertive behavior is needed rather than rage, anger or withdrawal, you will need to find a Resource that can be assertive by using the Find Resource Action. You can do this step even before the Retro State Negotiation starts, if you prefer. It is just important to have a state that can become conscious during some of the times when the Retro State had been in the past.

7. **Suggest an alternative or smaller role** that will allow it to continue to accomplish its purpose, a role that the other Resources can appreciate. At this time do not ask the Retro State if it will take on this new role. Say, "Let's just see what other states will think of you with this new (or modified) role." It is common for Retro States to at first believe they will never be liked, or to believe that what they have done in the past is all they can do. They will say things like, "They will never like me," or, "This is just what I do. I can't do anything else." It is amazing how quickly these attitudes change once they have experienced another state appreciating its new role. You can say things like, "I know it seems like they will never like you, but I bet they will if you take on this new way of helping. Let's just see."

8. **Speak directly with the Resource that has presented** the Retro behavior as an issue. Get a name for it. Suggest to it that it will like the Retro State if it changes, e.g., "You would like Protector, if Protector only comes out when the body is in real physical danger, and other times an Assertive part handles things. That would be really good to have a strong, Protector part,

if wild dogs were attacking, wouldn't it? Then at other times Assertive could handle things. That would be okay with you, wouldn't it?

9. **Speak again with the Retro State** to ensure it is now willing to take on new behavior or a reduced role, e.g., "Protector, did you hear that. Other states will like you with your new role. Are you willing to allow 'Assertive' to handle most things, while you are there in case the body is ever in real danger?"

There appears to be something almost magical about the change in attitude following the expression by the other Resource that it will appreciate the Retro State in its new role. The Retro State can still feel the experience of being accepted by the other state, having the body memory of that feeling still lingering. A Retro State that just a minute before may have stated that it would never be liked, or that it could never take on another role, becomes happy to take on the new role when it has felt the experience of being liked by other states. I like to drive this home by saying, "The other states will really appreciate you. They will pat you on the back."

Resources like to be liked and when they find they can be liked and still accomplish their purpose, they will be happy to change. When a Retro State takes on behavior that is appreciated by other states it is no longer Retro, it is Normal. The distinguishing characteristic of a Retro State is that it carries out behavior that other states do not like.

For an example of Retro State Negotiation see, Meagan could not stop buying clothes*, page 304.

Action 11: Conflicted State Negotiation

Purpose: Conflicted Resources are those that have a pathological level of disagreement. For example two states may disagree on having, or not having a dessert, but as long as a decision can be made without feeling a high level of anxiety the states are not considered to be conflicted. If one state wants to sleep and one state wants to think, and the conflict results in a high level of anxiety or a threat to good health then those states are Conflicted Resources and need Conflicted State Negotiation. It is often the case that work to resolve Resource conflict is necessary as part of work with Vaded States.

Conflicted State Negotiation is a process of assisting the **conflicted states** to learn to understand the value of each other, communicate directly, and learn to compromise. Following this, states that were conflicted will be able to compromise in the future as circumstances change.

Conflicted states are identified when the client makes statements like:

- I hate myself when I do that.

- I procrastinate.

- I don't know why I do that.

- I can't make myself do it.

- I try to sleep, but I just keep thinking.

- I embarrass myself.

- I can't control what I do.

The Table below outlines when it is appropriate to use this Action. Generally, the Conflicted State Negotiation Action is helpful to resolved emotional conflicts between two Resources, but when that emotional conflict is being fed by the pathology of a Vaded or Retro State, that pathology should first be resolved. If, after that resolution, there is still emotional conflict this Action should be used.

Table 22: When to use the Conflicted State Negotiation Action

Two states are in conflict and	Therapeutic Course re Conflicted State Negotiation Action
Neither is Retro or Vaded	Proceed directly with this Action.
One is Vaded	Resolve the Vaded State first then complete this Action.
One is Retro Avoiding	Resolve the Vaded State, then complete Retro State Negotiation. Normally no need to follow with this Action.
One is Retro Original	Complete the Retro State Negotiation. Normally no need to follow with this Action.
Following the completion of any intervention, if two states are still in Emotional Conflict	Proceed directly with this Action.

Process: There are nine steps to moving Conflicted States to Normality: Situate two facing chairs with the client in one, looking toward the other.

1. With the client in one of the chairs use the Vivify Specific Action to ensure one of the **Conflicted States** is in the Conscious, and then get a name for that state.

2. Call it by name and ask it what it feels about the other state that it has been conflicted with in the past. Take notes detailing what it says.

3. Show understanding for its feelings, but make a case to it how important and useful the other state can be.

4. Ask the client to stand and switch chairs then speak directly with the other Conflicted State, making sure you get a name from it for itself.

5. Call it by name and ask it what it feels about the other state that it has been conflicted with in the past. Take notes detailing what it says.

6. Show understanding for its feelings, but make a case to it how important and useful the other state can be.

7. Continue making a case until the Conflicted State begins to understand the utility of the other state, then ask it to speak directly with the other state, saying how it understands its importance and how it wants to work together with it in the future with a specified plan of compromise.

8. Again, have the client switch chairs and make sure the other state is able to respond in the same way, saying how it understands the other's importance and how it wants to work together with it in the future with a specified plan of compromise.

9. Show appreciation to both states for working together and suggest that in the future as circumstances change they will be able to continue to work together and compromise.

Example: For an example of Conflicted State Negotiation see, Stewart could not sleep*, page 325.

Action 12: Imagery Check

Purpose: At the beginning of therapy the Vivify Specific Action is used to identify the Vaded Resource that requires resolution. An Imagery Check is used to return to that initial image to see if this image still elicits a negative emotional reaction. If the Imagery Check reveals no negative emotional response then there is an indication that the therapeutic intervention has been successful. This indication also has a positive benefit to the client. It shows that a change has been made, and provides a practice for the future.

Process: The Imagery Check is an easy and straightforward process. As its usage is almost always at a time near the end of the session when the client is relaxed and focused, it is most often easy for the client to return to the image that had been stressful. The notes that were taken during the Vivify Specific Action should be returned to to revivify the time that had been initially presented as problematic.

For example, if the client, John, presented in therapy as wanting to change the way he reacted when criticized by a woman (see the example in the **Vivify Specific Action**), he would have been presenting with a resource vaded with either fear or rejection. This presentation would mean he suffered from a resource requiring bridging and resolution. As the first step in Bridging is to bring the Vaded Resource to the surface, a **Vivify Specific Action** would have been used to precisely vivify a time when he had experienced these feelings. The **Vivify Specific Action** would result in bringing the Vaded Resource to the surface for bridging and resolution. The notes taken during this **Vivify Specific Action** are required for the Imagery Check Action.

Example:

The following example continues from the example of John given in the **Vivify Specific Action** above. It comes near the end of the session to determine if Resource work was successful and to give the client confidence and practice. The **Find Resource Action** will often be used directly before the **Imagery Check Action** in order to make sure the client is connected with the best state for the purpose. Therefore, the **Vivify Specific Action** is used to bring the Vaded Resource to the surface so it can be resolved, resolution is achieved with the appropriate Actions, depending on the type of Vaded State, the **Find Resource Action** is used to line up the best Resource for the challenge, then the Imagery Check Action is used to determine if therapy has been successful. The **Imagery Check Action** should be carried out with the therapist speaking in the **present tense**.

> **Therapist:** Now, John, let's go back to the scene in the kitchen when you are sitting having cereal, it is almost 7 in the morning, and Nancy does not like the shirt you have on. She is standing above you, you have the blue shirt on that you bought in Bali, and she is commenting that it is not the best shirt to wear to work. Allow yourself to be aware of her mood, and tell me how you are feeling when she says this about your shirt.

> **John:** I don't like the way she is saying it, but I do feel different. It's like, maybe I should just change shirts. Yes, I feel like I have a choice how to react. Before I did not have a choice.

When the Find Resource Action has been used to assist the client in having the right Resource out during a time of previous concern, comments can be made during the **Imagery Check Action,** to ensure the client uses the best Resource. For example, had John determined that a **Wise** state would be the best one to use when being criticized by a woman the therapist could have said, "Nancy does not like the shirt that you have on. Your **Wise** state is able to hear what she is saying and is able to determine the best way to respond."

You can see how important it is to keep good notes from the **Vivify Specific Action.** It is important to be able to use the exact terms and the exact images that were presented in the Vivify Specific Action, so that the client can re-imagine the occurrence that had previously resulted in stress. When the client realizes that there has been a change, confidence is gained that therapy has been effective. The client has also been able to have practice in responding in a new way.

Complimentary Resource Actions

Action 13: Resistance Alliancing

Purpose: Resistance is caused by Protector Resources attempting to keep the therapist from bringing a Vaded State to the Conscious for resolution. These states do this in order to protect the client from the uncomfortable feelings of the Vaded State. Resistance Alliancing is used to form an alliance between the therapist and the protector state, so the protector state will allow the therapeutic process to continue.

Process: There are two methods to assist protector states to allow the therapeutic process to continue, 1) Acknowledgement, Appreciation and Suggestion, and 2) Engagement. The first method works with most Protector States, but often an Intellectual Protector State, if there, will maintain its resistance. Therefore, if an Intellectual Protector State is evident it is best to use the Engagement intervention method.

The Acknowledgement, Appreciation and Suggestion Method of Resistance Alliancing

This method consists of making a statement to the resistant Resource without starting a conversation with it. Protecting Resources see themselves as important. It is their job to keep the hurting state below the surface so the client will not have to experience feeling the feelings of the Vaded State. They work hard. Most of the time they will step aside, when their work is acknowledged as being important, and when it is suggested that now that the therapist is here a much deserved rest can be taken.

When resistance is noticed a statement such as this can be made:

"I can see there is a part there that is protecting a fragile part. I want to say thank you to that protecting part. I'm sure you have been protecting for a long time and that is very helpful. It must be very tiring to constantly be on guard. I am here to help too, and while I am here it might be a really good time for you to take a well-deserved rest. But, even though you are resting, keep an eye open just to make sure everything is alright."

This statement contains:

- **Acknowledgement** (I can see there is a part there that is protecting a fragile part.)

- **Appreciation** (I want to say thank you to that protecting part. I'm sure you have been protecting for a long time and that is very helpful. It must be very tiring to constantly be on guard.)   and

- **Suggestion** (I am here to help too, and while I am here it might be a really good time for you to take a well-deserved rest. But, even though you are resting, keep an eye open just to make sure everything is alright.)

Imagine being an angry parent visiting your child's school. If you are told to calm down or leave, you may feel a need to get even angrier. Compare the difference with being told (Acknowledgement), "I can see you are upset," (Appreciation), "A lot of parents don't even come here, and the fact that you are here and upset tells me that you care a lot about your child. That makes me want to help," and (Suggestion), "Come in and sit down so you can tell me all about it."

The upset parent is in a Resource that is out for a purpose. It will stay out as long as it feels it is needed. That angry Resource does not have to stay out when it feels acknowledged and appreciated. It is willing to listen to the suggestion that now is a safe time to take a rest and let another part talk. In the same way, the resistant part is out for a purpose, and when it can see that it is acknowledged and respected most often allows therapy to continue without resistance.

Following Acknowledgement, Appreciation and Suggestion, work may immediately continue and most of the time the resistant part is happy to allow that to happen. If the resistant part is still evident then the next method of direct engagement may be employed.

The Engagement Method of Resistance Alliancing

This method for allying with a resistant state may be used either for clients who seem to hide in intellectualizations, or for those who the first method proved unsuccessful. It is easy to understand. Like people, Resources are curious about what others think of them. If they say something or ask something, they are curious about how it was heard.

Therefore, the resistant state can be engaged with directly. For example, if a client continues to intellectualize during the Vivify Specific Action when you are attempting to bring out an emotional Vaded State you can say:

"This part I am speaking with right now seems like a good thinking part. Can I call this part of you 'Head'? (yes) 'Head', thank you for talking with me. I know you are aware of that fragile part that we have been talking about. What do you think of it? Do you like it, or do you just wish it would go away?"

Regardless of how the question is answered, the next step is to say:

"Alright, I just wonder what that state feels about what you just said. Fragile part, 'Head' just said '*whatever Head had said*'. How does that make you feel? I bet that makes you feel (either good or bad, depending on what the other state said), doesn't it?"

At this point two things happen. 1) 'Head' wants to know what the fragile part feels about what it said, so that part sits back and listens, without blocking, and 2) the Fragile part is given a direct opportunity to answer an easy question.

When the Fragile part answers the question, immediately thank it for talking with you, get a name for it, and continue to call it by that name, thus holding it in the Conscious.

Example: Trying to bring a Vaded State into the Conscious

A client presented because she would become extremely distressed each time she felt criticised by her boss at work. This is an example of a Vaded State coming to the surface with its unresolved feelings. There is a need to bring it to the surface in therapy so it can become resolved. During the Vivify Specific Action there is an attempt to bring the emotional Resource into the Conscious, so Bridging can follow.

Therapist: Right now, being at work, your boss is telling you he is disappointed with your work. What are you feeling?

Client: I know he is just a bastard.

Therapist: Yes, you know that, and how are you feeling. You mentioned before that you would get so upset you would have to leave work, and sometimes not return for two days. How are you feeling now that he has just said your work is no good?

Client: It is not surprising. He is like this all the time.

The client is avoiding responding to feelings, and is staying intellectual, therefore the Engagement Method of the Resistance Alliancing Action is used.

Therapist: This part I am speaking with right now seems like a good thinking part. Can I call this part of you 'Head'?

Client: Yes

Therapist: 'Head', thank you for talking with me. I know you are aware of that fragile part that we have been talking about. What do you think of it? Do you like it, or do you just wish it would go away?

Head: I just wish it would go away. It is always getting me in trouble. I just wish it would leave and never come back.

Therapist: Alright, I just wonder what that part feels about what you just said. Fragile part, 'Head' just said she wants you to go away and never come back. That must not feel very good to hear that. How does that make you feel? I bet that doesn't feel very good, does it?

Fragile Part: No it doesn't.

Therapist: I bet it doesn't. Thank you for talking with me. What can I call you, Fragile Part? What name or term fits you?

Little: You can call me 'Little'.

Therapist: Little. I understand you have not been feeling very well some time at work. That must feel bad when you hear the boss say bad things, doesn't it, Little?

Little: It feels awful.

At this point the Vaded State has assumed the Conscious and the resistant state has assumed the role of a listener.

Helpful Therapist Image

It may be helpful for the therapist to have the image of a protector resource as standing in front of a door restricting entry. If the therapist becomes aware of the type of protector and the reason it is protecting, more appropriate statements may be made. For example, it is common for some male clients to have a protector that exudes "I'm so strong you can't get past me." In this case a statement to the client like: "I'm not sure if you will be able to truly relax. Some people can do that and some are not able to. Only a few can do it really well." This can be heard as a challenge to a strong state so it makes sure a deep relaxation is experienced.

Another client may have a protector that protects because he or she feels a need to keep emotions from the surface. The client may hold a feeling that, there is too much difficulty in life to become emotional. Here a statement like, "I know you are a very important part that protects this person almost all the time. It is very important that you continue to do that. You can become even better at that by becoming aware of when it is truly safe to let some emotion be felt. That way all the states will really appreciate the work you do, and they won't feel held down, but they will be protected."

Action 14: The Separation Sieve

Purpose: The Separation Sieve Action is a very useful therapeutic mechanism that facilitates the client to use the metaphor of going through a sieve, in order to focus readiness and intent to accept change. This Action can be used to assist clients in letting go of guilt, letting go of connections to a past partner, or letting go of trauma.

When should it be used? This Action is most useful when the client is having difficulty letting go of guilt, shame, anger, trauma, or an unwanted connection to another person. It is important that the correct Resource be in the Conscious when this Action is used. For example, when this Action is employed to facilitate the client to release feelings of guilt, it is important that the Resource that has those feelings of guilt be in the Conscious.

Process: The Separation Sieve Action is not difficult, and is composed of 10 straight forward steps.

The steps will be listed below and then further explained.

1. Make sure the correct Resource is in the Conscious.
2. Check to see if the client is ready to let go.
3. Describe the sieve.
4. Describe coming through the sieve leaving everything negative behind.
5. Ask the Resource how it is feeling.
6. Ask the Resource to look back up in the sieve and described what that stuff looks like that was left behind.
7. Ask the Resource if it wants any of that stuff back.
8. Asked the Resource what color of light, or fluid, would sizzle that stuff completely away.
9. Provide the image of the stuff in the sieve sizzling away with the light or fluid.
10. Ask the Resource how it feels now.

Step 1: Make sure the correct Resource is in the Conscious.

The first step in the Separation Sieve Action is to ensure that the correct Resource is in the Conscious. Most often, when this Action is employed the therapist will be aware that the correct Resource is already in the Conscious, because that Resource will be expressing an unwanted emotional reaction relating to something such as guilt that the client would like to release. If the correct Resource is not already in the Conscious the Vivify Specific Action (see Action 2) can be used to make sure the correct Resource is out.

Step 2: Check to see if the client is ready to let go.

It is important to check on the readiness of the client to let go, e.g., of something like guilt, or the connection to a lost relationship. This may be obvious. It may be the reason the client has come to therapy, but sometimes the client may not be fully ready to let go. If this is the case the Sieve Action may be introduced as an exploration to help the client determine if he or she wants to let go. Therefore, it is not important if the client is sure about letting go. The Sieve Action can be used to help the client determine this.

Step 3: Describe the sieve.

Ensure that the client's eyes are closed, if they are not already. This can be done by saying, "Just allow your eyes to close right now." When the client's eyes are closed the image of the sieve can be constructed.

Example: "Just allow your eyes to close. There is a very powerful magic sieve. It is much more powerful than it needs to be. Nothing heavy, dark, sticky or negative can possibly come through the sieve, only lightness. You can come through the sieve but nothing heavy can possibly come through. No guilt, shame, anger, regret, or unwanted connections can possibly come through this sieve. Just as an experiment you will be able to come easily through the sieve down to where my voice is, then you will be able to decide if there is anything that was caught in the sieve that you want back."

Step 4: Describe coming through the sieve leaving everything heavy behind.

"This is just an experiment, so you can come through the sieve and then make your decision. So right now just allow the light you, the free you, the pure essence of you, to come directly through the sieve down to where my voice is, leaving anything heavy or sticky or negative behind. Come straight through now to where my voice is."

Step 5: Ask the Resource how it is feeling.

"How does that feel?"

Step 6: Ask the Resource to look back up at the sieve and described what the stuff that was left behind looks like.

"Look back up at the sieve and tell me what the stuff that is caught in it looks like."

Step 7: Ask the Resource if it wants any of that stuff back.

"Do you want any of that back?"

Step 8: Ask the Resource what color of light or fluid, would sizzle that stuff completely away.

"What color of light or fluid, would sizzle that stuff away, into complete nothingness?"

(If the Resource responds with only a color and does not say if it is a light or fluid, ask, "Is that a light or a fluid.")

Step 9: Provide the image of the stuff in the sieve sizzling away with the light or fluid.

(E.g., If the client answers, 'A blue light'.) "Okay, let's just allow that blue light, to be much more powerful than it needs to be, to go straight through the sieve sizzling all of that stuff completely away. Czzzzzzzzz, completely away, Czzzzzzzzzzzz."

Step 10: Ask the Resource how it feels now.

"How do you feel now?"

The client may now be told, "It is alright to just go ahead and allow your eyes to open so we can talk about this further.

After coming through the image of the sieve it is very unusual for a resource to say they want any of the stuff in the sieve back. Normally, when asked if they want any of that stuff back the response is definitely, "No, I don't want any of THAT back." If there is an exception to this a negotiation can be conducted to allow something that the client wants to keep to come through the sieve in a transformed, positive and beautiful form. What is unwanted, can be sizzled away. Following this process clients will often say they feel lighter.

Obviously, there is no three-dimensional sieve that separates clients from their unwanted emotional baggage. The imagery metaphor of the sieve allows the client to focus intent in a safe way. Clients understand that this is an experiment, and they will be able to have anything back the way it was, if they choose. This experiment allows to the client to experience what it feels like to let go of emotionally heavy feelings.

Action 15: Anchoring

Purpose: Anchoring is a useful technique that can assist the client to bring into the Conscious the preferred Resource State. For example, a person participating in a sport may want to bring into the Conscious the Resource that can best play that sport. A person taking an exam may want to bring into the Conscious the Resource State that studied. A person wanting to relax may want to bring into the Conscious a Resource that is good at relaxing.

Process: Clients are benefited in their ability to bring the preferred Resource State into the Conscious by a mnemonic memory technique. They are trained to associate a particular animal with the state they want to bring to the Conscious. By focusing on the experience of their chosen animal, they are better able to gain access to their preferred Resource State.

Clients will be able to bring their preferred Resource State into the Conscious as long as a Vaded State is not forcing its way into the Conscious, or as long as a Vaded State is not actively being avoided by a Retro Avoiding State. In other words, in order to be able to bring out the preferred Resource it is important that any related Vaded States first be resolved. It is easy to understand this by considering a person who has of phobia about spiders. It is impossible for this person to decide, "I just want to be relaxed now," before the Vaded State that underpins the fear is resolved. Until it is resolved it will overpower the ability of the client to bring out the preferred Resource State. Therefore, Anchoring is a technique that should only be taught following the resolution of Vaded States.

Here is an example of when it would be most appropriate to use Anchoring. A client presents due to the fear of public speaking. If the client describes a high level of anxiety when attempting to speak publicly, then a Vaded State is involved. RT Actions 2 to 8 can be used to resolve the negative feelings of the Vaded State. Next, a Resource State that enjoys communicating can be found using RT Action 9, Find Resource, and this Resource State can be given a name. The client will be wanting to bring this communicative Resource State out whenever any slight anxiety is felt while communicating in front of a group. The Anchoring technique will assist the client in being able to bring out the communicative Resource State.

The Anchoring technique can also be used to assist clients to bring out Resource States when Vaded States have not been involved. Examples of this include test taking (often a nervous Resource State assumes the Conscious when the client would prefer the Resource State that studied) and sport participation (a Resource State that is concerned about performance may hold the Conscious, rather than a Resource State that participates well). Even in these instances if the client reports experiencing exaggerated levels of affect, then a Vaded State will need to be resolved prior to using the Anchoring technique.

Anchoring Example

Matt wanted better sporting performance*

Therapist: Matt, I understand you have not been doing as well in tennis as you normally do.

Client: That's right. My game had been improving and I had been getting to, or near the finals in several tournaments. Recently I've been getting knocked out in the first round and it has been very frustrating to me. I know I can play better.

Therapist: That does sound frustrating. Tell me about your last match. Was that one that you felt you did not play as well as you should have?

Client: It sure was. I got knocked out in the first round. I was just not seeing the ball like I normally do, and my movement wasn't right.

RT Action 2, Vivify Specific

Therapist: Just allow your eyes to close so we can really focus in on that. Tell me the time of day, the temperature, and how you are feeling.

Matt: It's hot, but not too hot. I'm frustrated and I really want to do better, but it seems like the more I try the worse I play.

Therapist: The more you try the worse you play. That must be a frustrating feeling. You are on the court now, attempting to move, and it just seems like this isn't working for you. Is that right?

Matt: Yes, I just don't feel right.

Therapist: It sounds like right now, on the court, trying to do your best, you are being a bit critical of yourself. What would be a good term for you right now, as you are being critical of yourself?

Matt: 'Critic', I guess.

'Critic' did not show upset feelings. It did not show a level of affect that would be considered unusual, therefore it was not vaded. It was merely a Resource State that wanted improvement. It was not the right Resource State to be in the Conscious.

Therapist: I just want to continue talking with this same part of you. Critic, thank you for talking with me, and thank you for caring about how well Matt plays tennis. I know you want Matt to play really well, and I do too. You do want him to play well, don't you, 'Critic'?

Critic: Yes, I do.

Therapist: I think, Critic, you understand that you may not be the best tennis playing part that Matt has. You do understand, don't you, that sometimes Matt feels differently and plays much better?

Critic: Yes, I definitely do.

Therapist: Critic, I can see that you could be a good motivator, possibly before a match, but during the match it would be good if Matt had a part playing tennis that can enjoy playing, and play well. Critic, would you be willing to be a Resource for Matt before a match, and possibly after a match, so you can think about the match, and would you be willing to allow Matt's better playing part to actually play?

Critic: Definitely.

Therapist: Fantastic. Thank you, 'Critic'.

RT Action 8, Find Resource

Therapist: Matt, just allow your eyes to continue to stay closed, and tell me about a time when you really felt good playing tennis, about a time when you felt that you were playing well.

Matt: That's easy. At the first tournament of the year I won, 6-1, 6-0, against a player who could have beaten me.

Therapist: You are playing this match right now. It is in the second set. Describe what's happening and what your experiences are to me.

Matt: I'm actually surprised how well things are going. It just seems like I can't do anything wrong.

Therapist: Are you having fun?

Matt: I'm having a ball.

Therapist: Describe more about what you're feeling, and what's going on in your head.

Matt: I'm just feeling the groove. The only thing that's really going on in my head is occasionally I am surprised at how well I'm playing.

Therapist: What can I call this, Groove, enjoying, tennis playing part of you?

Matt: 'Groove'.

Therapist: 'Groove', thank you for talking with me. You really do enjoy playing tennis, don't you, 'Groove'?

Groove: I love it.

Therapist: And you don't really think that much, do you, 'Groove'?

Groove: I don't really think it all.

Therapist: It seems like you don't need to. 'Groove', would you be willing to be the part of Matt that is playing tennis more often, if other parts allow you to do that?

Groove: Sure, I love playing tennis.

Therapist: That's fantastic, Groove. Groove, there are a lot of different kinds of animals. What kind of animal do you associate with yourself? What kind of animal do you associate with being able to enjoy playing, and being totally focused on the moment, without other thoughts?

Groove: What kind of animal?

Therapist: Yes, Groove, what kind of animal do you associate with yourself?

Groove: It sounds funny, but the animal I thought of is a spider monkey. You know, the ones with long tails and long arms that swing and glide through the trees so easily.

Therapist: Yes, I know those. Groove, right now being a spider monkey able to swing, and glide through the trees easily, where do you picture yourself?

Groove: Swinging and gliding through tall trees.

Therapist: That sounds great, Groove. What does it feel like being a spider monkey, seeing those trees move by?

Groove: It feels great. Things are happening really fast around me, but I am totally in control.

Therapist: That does sound like a good feeling. Thank you for sharing that image with me. Matt, when you are playing a tennis match and want to make sure Groove is the part of you that is playing, just take a moment and feel yourself as the spider monkey. Feel yourself gliding through the trees, enjoying watching them go by. Feel yourself with the spider monkey's mindless ability to be focused. Let's try that right now. A tennis match is about to start, and you are going to receive a serve. You may have a little nervousness, so, pause, and feel the focus and movement of the spider monkey going through the trees. Feel 'Groove'. Now you're ready to play. How does that feel?

Matt: It feels great. I think I can do this.

Therapist: That's good. Remember that any time in the match, you can bring yourself back into 'Groove' by focusing on the spider monkey, by being the spider monkey gliding through the trees.

Matt: I really like it.

Therapist: I do too. It is a great image. You can go ahead and allow your eyes to open so we can debrief.

The Anchor of the spider monkey is used in this example to help Matt to connect with his best tennis performance state, 'Groove'. To anchor we first find the preferred state and make sure it is holding the Conscious, then ask that state what animal it identifies with. Then we make sure that the client gives a clear image of where the animal is pictured and a clear description of what it feels like to be that animal. It is the sensual experience of feeling like the animal feels that acts as an Anchor to the preferred Resource State. Then, when the client wants to bring that Resource State into the Conscious, revisiting the sensual experience of feeling like the animal (e.g., swinging through the trees) can help bring to the surface the preferred state (e.g., in this case, 'Groove').

GEMS: When working with Resource States

Basic concepts:

- All Resources should be spoken to with respect at all times.
- Each pathological state was in a Normal Condition prior to becoming Pathological.
- The purpose of treatment is to return states with pathology to a Normal Condition.

Naming the Resource State

It is imperative, when using this therapy, to get a name for each individual state that you are working with. Here are some of the benefits for getting a name for each Resource State that you are working with:

- As you speak with the state, you can continue to call it by its name. This helps ensure that it will stay in the Conscious.

- You can refer to a Resource State by name when talking with a different Resource State.

- You can return to a Resource State in the current session, or in a later session, by calling its name.

It is important for each Resource State to either name itself, or approve a name that was suggested by you. For example, a Work State might name a Resting State 'Lazy'. Obviously, the Resting State would not like to be named 'Lazy'. That Resting State might likewise name the Working State, 'Slave Driver'. When Resource States identify with, and approve their name, they respond to it better and respond to therapy better.

It is best to ask a Resource State directly, "What can I call you?", rather than, "What can I call this part of you?" Think about talking to one person in a room full of people. If you say to that person, "What can I call you," it is likely you will get a response directly from the person you are talking to. But, if you ask, "What can I call this person?" you may get a different person creating a name for them and giving it to you.

The name for a Resource can easily be changed. Therefore, I am happy to accept a name for a Resource that is indicative of a negative feeling, because after this Vaded State has been resolved, when asked, it will prefer to change its name to something more positive.

I am not happy to accept a name for a Resource State that indicates a negative behavior, because I have found that it takes longer to change that behavior if the Retro State is named for the behavior. I prefer to get a name for how that Resource helps the client, rather than for what it does. For example, I would not like to accept the name Smoker, but I would not mind accepting the name Relax, Rebel, or Socialize. If the Resource State has helped the client socialize by smoking, then it will be easier to find another way it can help the client socialize in the future when it identifies itself as the socializing part. Another example, I would not accept the name Abuser, but I would accept the name, Protector. That way the protecting part can find a better way to protect than by using abuse (See Action 10: Retro State Negotiation, page 123).

Therefore, it is fine to accept a name that designates a negative emotion, but it is not fine to accept a name that designates a negative behavior.

When I get a Name for a Resource State, I circle it in my notes so I can glance down and see the names of the Resources I am working with.

Sometimes a Resource State will have difficulty coming up with a name for itself. If that is the case, it is okay to suggest two or three names that sound like they would fit it. The Resource State may find one of them acceptable, or may then come up with a better name for itself.

The most important aspect of naming a Resource State is that it approves of the name that it has. That way it will easily respond to the name.

Work with, not against Vaded and Retro States

Speak to and about all Resource States with respect. Resources are like humans. They like to be respected. They are like humans for a very good reason. Every person you meet is in one of their Resources during the interaction. Our Resources are us, and like us, it feels good to them when they are respected. If you speak to or about a Resource with disrespect it will not like it, and will probably not be cooperative in therapy. When we feel someone likes us we are more cooperative.

Even when a Resource has conducted behavior that is not respectable it is important to speak with and about that Resource in a respectable way. For example, a Resource that has in the past been loud and overbearing may be complemented for its power and for its willingness to speak out to help the client.

This does not condone the negative behavior, and it prepares the Resource to be accepting of a new role, a role that can be appreciated by the other Resources within the personality. The therapist can say something like, "I can see you are a very powerful part of this person. That is really good. Everyone needs powerful parts. I think you know that there are some other parts of this person who do not appreciate the way you have been helping. It will be good when you have a role that is both powerful, helpful, and able to be respected by all other parts."

When a Resource is acknowledged and respected in this way it becomes more ready to be cooperative. That is why in all Resource work we should always talk both to, and about, Resources in a positive way. Resources should never be talked about in a way that would make them think you believe they are bad. They should never believe that you want them to go away. If they do they will not cooperate. We want Resources to feel respected and honored, and for them to discover a way that they can gain even more respect and usefulness within the personality.

Vaded States may not be involved in these presentations

Inner conflict: Two states both want the Conscious at the same time or two states may disagree on a future course of action (Conflicted States).

- A 'Work State' and a 'Rest State' may both want the Conscious at the same time. A 'Planning State' and a Resource that wants to sleep may both want the Conscious at the same time. A state that wants to study and a state that wants to play may both want to hold the Conscious at the same time.

- One Resource may want to continue with a relationship, and another may not. One state may want to go to university, and another state may prefer not to go.

(These inner conflicts may have nothing to do with a Vaded State, but sometimes a Vaded State is in conflict with another state, because another state may not like the emotion of the Conscious Vaded State.)

Emotional issues related to a situation where the level of emotion corresponds with what is happening (Dissonant States);

- An employer is difficult and the job is needed.
- A teenage son or daughter is causing stress to a level that might be expected.

- The client has found out he or she has a medical problem or terminal illness.
- Normal, non-complicated bereavement.

Organically based psychological issues;

- Schizophrenia, manic depression, and other psychological responses caused organically.

Retro Original Behavior;

- This is behavior that was first learned as a coping skill in childhood, but later becomes unwanted behavior. While Retro Avoiding Behavior is caused by the attempt to avoid the unwanted feelings of a Vaded State, Retro Original Behavior is not connected to a Vaded State.

Dissonant State;

- A Dissonant State does not like to be out, and wishes it did not have to be there. But it is not out of control, or fragile, although it is not be the best Resource in the Conscious at the time.

Vaded States (with Fear or Rejection) are normally involved in these presentations

Below are some specific presenting problems that are caused by Vaded States. This list represents a small fraction of the types of issues Vaded States cause.

- The client becomes extremely nervous when stepping into an elevator.
- The client experiences panic disorder or PTSD.
- The client has an unwanted emotional response during sexually intimate situations.
- The client becomes extremely upset when criticized by an authority figure.
- The client feels compelled to eat when there is no hunger.
- The client feels compelled to gamble.
- The client is blocked from professional accomplishment by fear.

- The client becomes extremely nervous when attempting to speak in front of a group.
- The client feels it is impossible to be assertive.
- The client fears spending or handling money.
- The client experiences OCD.
- The client feels compelled to purchase or to compete.

The common and recognizable feature of an issue that is caused by a Vaded State is the client has an emotional reaction that does not match the situation at hand. This is evident considering the list above.

Being extremely nervous to enter an elevator is an example of an emotion that does not match the safety of riding in an elevator. Obviously, experiences of panic disorder or PTSD are emotions that go beyond the current experience. Experiencing negative emotions during sexually intimate times with a trusted partner is another example. While it is normal to feel somewhat hurt when being criticized by an authority figure, having an extreme emotional reaction is not. The emotion of feeling compelled to eat when the body is not hungry is another example. When the client does not want to gamble, but feels compelled to gamble at certain times there is a feeling coming from somewhere other than what is currently happening. It is understandable that the desire to take on a new job can cause stress, but being completely blocked from being able to do so because of negative emotion is not normal. In the same way, it is normal to have some stress when talking in front of a group, but to be emotionally incapacitated means that a resource is coming to the surface with unresolved feelings. The person who has fear of speaking out, and being assertive has a fear that does not match the current situation. The same is true of the person who has a fear of spending or handling money. Feeling compelled to check the locks and taps over and over again, as some people with obsessive-compulsive disorder do, is obviously a feeling that does not match the situation at hand. After being carefully checked once, there should be emotional peace. Clients who feel out of control in their purchasing or in their need to be perfect have Vaded States that are emotional and interfere with their ability to make current decisions that are best for them.

After realizing that a Vaded State is at play, it is necessary to locate the specific state that is the core of the issue. When the Vaded State is the core of the problem it will either be, 1) holding the Conscious, causing the client to feel an emotion that does not fit the situation, and feel out-of-control, or 2) a 'Retro Avoiding State(helping state)' will be taking the 'out-of-control client' into another activity, often one that the client regrets.

If a Retro Avoiding State is involved there is some form of addiction, such as, drug addiction, gambling, OCD, eating disorders, some smoking activity, workaholism, self-harming behavior, and the list goes on. Unlike issues where the Vaded State is in the Conscious, the Resource that is actually doing the addictive behavior does not feel out of control. It is doing what it feels like its role is. Other Resources commonly may look at this activity and feel that the person is out-of-control, but during the activity the Resource that is actually conducting the activity feels it is doing the right thing.

Therefore, Vaded States can be the core of the problem when they are Conscious during the problem (Vaded Conscious States), or when they cause the client to escape (Vaded Avoided States) from their feelings of anxiety into some sort of addictive behavior (Retro Avoiding Behavior) .

Identifying Vaded Conscious States

Vaded Conscious States are the most easy to identify. The client will have presented his or her issues as being emotional, and will feel an inability to not be emotional. In other words, they present as having emotion that does not fit the current situation at hand, and feeling out of control.

There is normally a fight, internally, in an effort to keep a Vaded State out of the Conscious. Clients will describe trying to push these out of control feelings away, and they will often say that they just wish that that part of them would go away and leave them alone and never come back. While these actions and attitudes are understandable, they do not help resolve the hurt feelings of the Vaded State.

The client's description of the problem is often presented in a way that makes it easy to locate the associated Vaded State. It is merely necessary to ask the client to describe the recent time when this unwanted feeling occurred, and during this process ask the client to close his or her eyes and respond to a number of questions in order to revivify that time and bring the associated Vaded State into the Conscious. This is described in RT Action 2: Vivify Specific, page 88, and it is part of the Bridging process.

Identifying Vaded Avoided States and Retro Avoiding States

It is somewhat more difficult to identify Vaded States that have been forced out of the Conscious by some sort of addictive behavior. The key feature here is, the client feels out of control in participating in some kind of behavior (Retro Avoiding Behavior), such as addictive behavior, OCD, out-of-control eating, eating disorder behavior, self-harming, and others. The actual behavior that is being participated in is not the cause of the problem. Therefore, it is necessary to identify the causal Vaded State that is being avoided.

The best way to identify the causal avoided Vaded State is to identify the precise time that the client felt compelled to enter into the unwanted (retro) behavior. For example, if the client is lying in bed ready to go to sleep, then feels a compulsion to check the locks and taps; this is the time that the Vaded State is surfacing. You can ask the client to close his or her eyes, and just imagine lying in bed a bit longer without getting up to check the locks and taps. This 'Vivify Specific' imagery will bring the Vaded State further into the Conscious so that bridging and resolution may occur.

The key is to use imagery, preferably with the client's eyes closed, to identify the time just prior to the onset of the unwanted behavior, and within that imagery ask the client to continue what he or she is doing in the image without starting the unwanted behavior. The anxiety caused by this 'withholding of the unwanted behavior' is the causal Vaded State coming into the Conscious. When this occurs, you have identified the Vaded State that needs resolution and it is time to bridge to the initial sensitizing event. See the Vivify Specific Action.

It is important to first resolve the Vaded State, and second, work with the Retro Avoiding State to ensure if needed in the future, it will have a positive

role, see Chapter 10
Treatment of Retro Avoiding States page 301.

Chapter 5
Treatment of states Vaded with Fear

This chapter covers the types of presentations that are caused by states Vaded with Fear and their treatment.

There are two kinds of fear. There is external fear and internal fear. External fear is a good thing. If we get too close to the edge of the cliff external fear causes us to move away. External fear keeps us safe from what may cause harm in the present.

Internal fear is not needed. Internal fear is the fear of something from the past that can no longer hurt us. Internal fear is caused by Resources that have taken on fear from the past and have not been able to let it go. Resources Vaded with Fear are carrying internal fear into the therapy room, a place where it is safe. These Resources carry their internal fear everywhere they go and when they come to the surface they bring their fear to the surface with them.

A Resource Vaded with Fear is characterized by one of the following feelings, when that feeling does not fit the situation at hand.

1. General Anxiety.
2. Fear.
3. Panic.
4. Inability to be alone.
5. A feeling of being out of control.
6. Feeling Fragile.
7. Claustrophobia.
8. A feeling that the focus of anxiety is bigger than the client.

Related Pathologies

These states all have in common a resource that experienced a fearful event and was for one reason or another incapable of incorporating that event and understanding it. This Vaded Resource maintains within the personality an overwhelming feeling of fear and when it comes to the surface, to the Conscious, it brings with it that fearful feeling. It interrupts the ability of the client to respond to life's challenges from mature, adult Resources.

Below is a list issues that can be caused by Resources Vaded with Fear. Where further elucidation may be beneficial, items in the list will be described in more detail to explain the dynamic that is occurring within the personality.

Resources Vaded with Fear can cause these Pathologies

• Nightmares and sleep terror • Specific Phobia • Panic attack • PTSD • Agoraphobia • Self-harming behavior • Generalized Anxiety Disorder • Dissociative Identity Disorders	• Pathological Gambling • Addictions • Workaholism • OCD (or may be Vaded with Rejection) • Social Phobia (or may be Vaded with Rejection) • Business Phobia (or may be Vaded with Rejection)	• Compulsive Shopping (or more often is Vaded with Rejection) • Antisocial (or may be Retro or Vaded with Rejection) • Crisis reaction (benefitting from crisis intervention)

Vaded States carry the illusion that the past is present. They carry the illusion that an Introject from their past has power today. A Vaded Resource may imbue an Introject with so much power that the Resource can feel temporarily overwhelmed when internally facing what it has feared. Vaded States are stuck in the past. It is necessary for them to get from the present a resolution that allows them to feel safe, supported, and accepted.

Treatment Process

Three requirements for resolving States Vaded with Fear

- **Identify the State related to the issue:** The correct state must be identified by the therapist as the core cause of the presenting concern. (RT Action 1)

- **Bridge to the initial sensitizing event:** Bridging must take the Vaded State to the image of the original sensitizing event. (RT Actions 2 & 3)

- **Resolve the Vaded State Emotion:** The Vaded State must become empowered and/or reach understanding and be left with a feeling of safety, support, and care. (RT Actions 3-4, 6-7)

Following Resolution: Find the most appropriate Resource (RT Action 8) for future challenging situations using information gained earlier (described by the client during Vivify Specific, RT Action 2), and then check the client's ability to respond with RT Action 12.

Table 23: RT Actions used to bring States Vaded with Fear to Normality

---

Action 1: Diagnosis of Resource Pathology
Action 2: Vivify Specific   see page 88
Action 3: Bridging   see page 94
Action 4: Expression   see page 101
Action 5: Introject Speak
Action 6: Removal   see page 106
Action 7: Relief   see page 108
Action 8: Find Resource   see page 113
Action 9: Changing Chairs Introject Action
Action 10: Retro State Negotiation
Action 11: Conflicted State Negotiation
Action 12: Imagery Check   see page 131

The first step in helping the Vaded State is to bring it into the Conscious (RT Action 2) so that it can be talked with directly. It is not possible to bridge to the original sensitizing event unless the Vaded State is in the Conscious. Therefore, it is very important to make sure that the Vaded State is in the Conscious, and then Bridging can proceed.

Following the location of the Initial Sensitizing Event (Bridging), there are three steps in bringing a Resource in a Vaded condition back to a Normal condition. The first two steps are to empower, to make sure the Resource realizes it has more power than its **Introjects**, and the third step is to inoculate, to make sure that the Resource is left with safety, support, and care.

The three steps for resolution are:

- Expression: (see RT Action 4) Ensuring the Resource expresses its feelings fully. This is the first empowering step. When the Resource State is able to say absolutely everything it feels to the Introject, then it learns the Introject has no power.
- Removal: (see RT Action 6) Giving the Resource a choice to keep or remove from its image the **Introjects** that gave it negative feelings. This is not removing Introjects of the same person from other Resource States, only from the Vaded State.
- Relief: (see RT Action 7) Bringing a nurturing, caring Resource of the client to the fragile state to ensure that it gets immediate and ongoing support and care.

Case Example with Transcript

Peggy could not enjoy sex with her partner*

Peggy was a 26-year-old client who reported being in a relationship with a partner that she loved very much. She had previously been married and divorced. Her presenting concern was an inability to enjoy any kind of intimate sexual activity.

Peggy reported that she had been able to deal with the sexual relationship she had with her husband because there was little or no foreplay and he was quick.

She said she could get through that, although she never enjoyed it. But, with her new partner, a much more sensitive man, her dislike of any sexual activity had become a real problem for her.

She said that she did not even like it if he told her she looked nice. She said, "I just HATE it when he says that." She was not blaming him. She saw that there was something that needed attention in the way she was reacting.

During the first session, when Peggy was presenting her issue, she said, "There is something I probably should mention. I don't think it has anything to do with my problem, but I was raped by two older cousins when I was 10 years old. I don't really think it bothered me that much, and I don't actually remember feeling anything about it."

Obviously, this could have been associated with her dislike of any sexual activity, especially since she could not remember feeling anything about the rape. It would have been more normal, and emotionally healthy for her to have experienced feelings, and to talk to someone about them. But, in working with Resources we do not have to guess about which initial sensitizing event is related to the current sensitive Resource. Bringing out the appropriate Vaded State and Bridging directly to where its feelings started is much more accurate than guessing.

I find that often when clients come to therapy they think they know why they react the way they do, and I find they are often wrong. Bridging demonstrates this, and when they experience the direct emotional connection that Bridging facilitates it becomes clear to them and to myself what the initial sensitizing event really was. If clients, who have lived their life and have their own memories often do not ascribe the right initial sensitizing event to a Vaded State, then how can the therapist play Sherlock Holmes and hope to get the right reason for the feelings clients are experiencing.

It can be detrimental to the emotional health the client to spend time working in the wrong area of their past. Too many therapists, upon learning that a client has been sexually abused, automatically ascribe their sexual abuse as the reason for their presenting concern. Often, the clients, themselves, do this. It serves no benefit to dredge up bad memories when they are not connected to what the client wants to change.

Therefore, I did not want to automatically assume that Peggy's rape was directly related to her inability to enjoy sexual experiences. In this case, it was.

Peggy said that her new partner was a sensitive man, who wanted to say nice things to her about her body, and who wanted to spend time with her in extended foreplay, as well as extended time in sexual intercourse. She said she was totally incapable of doing this with him. She said that she knew her friends would love to have a partner like him, and she said that she knew there was something wrong with her for something to be keeping her from being able to enjoy such a wonderful man. She said she did not want to lose him, and that she would like to be able to have positive sexual experiences like the ones her friends talked about.

In our second session Peggy was talking about how she felt when her partner said she looked nice. She said, "Even when he says he likes what I'm wearing, I JUST HATE IT."

It was obvious by the way she expressed her last four words that they came from a Vaded State. They were spoken with strong and deep emotion. It was clear to me that an underlying Vaded State had just risen to the Conscious and expressed its feelings, "I JUST HATE IT." So I said the following.

RT Action 3, Bridging

Therapist: Peggy, close your eyes and, say, I just hate it, again, just like you did, then tell me exactly how you are feeling.

Because the Vaded State was already there, I did not have to work to bring it out, I did not have to revivify a situation. She made it easy for me, as a therapist.

Peggy: I JUST HATE IT, I don't know if this is what you mean, but it just feels like I can't move. I feel like I'm being held down. I feel like I don't know if I should be angry or what I should feel. I just want to get away. I JUST HATE IT. I don't know if that helps any.

Therapist: I think it may help a lot. Just, allow your eyes to stay closed for a moment and listen to what you just told me when I repeat to you, and tell me what image comes up for you. I JUST HATE IT, I feel like I'm being held down. I don't know if I should be angry, or not. I just want to get away. I JUST HATE IT.

This was a different kind of Bridging. Since Peggy had already told me about her cousin's raping her, and because the feelings expressed by the Vaded State were so clear, I just restated what she had said and let the image come to her. This is where understanding the concepts of Vaded States is so useful in therapy. There is no cookbook that should always be followed. There are some really good techniques that can help clients to reconnect with their initial sensitizing event that has vaded a normal Resource, but the better the therapist understands what a Vaded State is, the more skilled the therapist will become in working with Vaded States in elegant and creative ways. During the learning stages of working with Vaded States, it is okay to follow the steps presented in this book, but the more you work with them the more elegant your work will become.

Peggy immediately started to cry.

Peggy: How could they do that to me?

This was not the Vaded State that spoke. This was a state that realized what had happened, and how upset she had become. I did not want to lose communication with the Vaded State.

Therapist: Right now, wanting to move and not being able to, being pinned down, what can I call you, the part that is so upset? What name or term fits you, right there, right now with your cousins?

Peggy: I don't know, 'Pinned'?

RT Action 4, Expression

Therapist: Pinned, thank you for talking with me (Calling a Vaded State by name, and speaking with it directly most often pulls it into the Conscious and keeps it involved in the conversation.) Pinned, I want you to know that this is not really happening right now so you can say exactly what you want to your cousins. They are not really here right now so you can look at them and tell them exactly what you want to. They are just illusions so you can say anything you want. Go ahead and tell them, out loud so I can hear you, exactly what you want to say.

This was said, both to make it safer her to speak, and to make it safe for her to stay in the image of the initial sensitizing event.

Pinned: Why are you doing this? I thought you liked me. Why are you doing this?

Therapist: Pinned, this is our seen and we can have it anyway we want. Let's have your cousins on the other side of the room, totally powerless, and you can tell them if you think they are wrong in what they were doing.

Pinned: You are wrong. You should not have done that. That was a really bad thing to do.

RT Action 6, Removal

Therapist: That was really good, Pinned. This is your space and they have absolutely no power in it. Right now, do you want them to stay in this inner space of yours or do you want them out of it. Do you want them to leave this inner space of yours?

Pinned: I want them to leave. I want them out of here.

Therapist: Just tell them to go.

Pinned, Get out!

RT Action 7, Relief

Therapist: Pinned, that was amazing. You really told them how you feel, and now you're space is your own. I want to bring in an older part to make sure that you always feel really safe there. I will want to talk with you again, but right now I want to speak with an older part. Peggy, if you saw a 10-year-old girl who you know and care about, who had been really upset and frightened, who really needed a hug, what would you want to do?

Peggy: I would want to go over and give her a big hug.

Therapist: What can I call this part of you, the part of you that just said that? What name or term fits this part of you?

Peggy: 'Strong'.

Therapist: Strong, I know you have been hearing what Pinned has said, so go to Pinned right now right where she is, put your arm around her, and let her know you will always be there for her on the inside. You can do this, Strong, and everything else you do all at the same time. The more you do the more powerful you become. So, just go to Pinned right now, put your arms around her, and let love, safety, and your strength flow into every cell and fibre of her being. She has done a great job, already. (pause) 'Pinned', can you feel Strong there with you? How do you feel now?

Pinned: Yes, she is here. I feel much better.

Therapist: That's great. It sounds like you feel better now, and safe with Strong there with you. What would be a better name for you now, a name that describes how you really feel now?

Peggy: 'Contented'.

Therapist: That is a great name. From now on when I refer to you I will call you 'Contented'. Contented, now that you are safe and supported and feel much better, is it okay with you to stay with Strong and let one of Peggy's more mature parts enjoy sexually intimate times?

Contented: Yes, that's Ok.

RT Action 8, Find Resource

Therapist: I want to talk to a part of Peggy that will like to enjoy intimate times with her partner. This is probably a part that enjoys feeling the body, feeling sensual, like being in a hot bath, or feeling ocean waves.

> This is probably a part that doesn't think that much, but really enjoys body sensations. Just say, I'm here, when you're ready to speak.

Peggy: I'm here.

Therapist: Part, thank you for talking with me. What can I call you? What name or term fits you?

Peggy: You can call me, 'Body'.

Therapist: 'Body', it sounds like you had not had much time in the past to be out to enjoy sensitive times, sexually. Is that right?

Body: That's right.

Therapist: That's too bad. But, now that the part that used to feel pinned is Contented, Peggy needs you to help her enjoy sensual times with their partner. Would you be willing to help Peggy by being the part that is out during the times she wants to enjoy sensuality? You are a very important part of Peggy, and you could help her a lot.

Resources love to have jobs. They love to be able to do what they can do. Previously, Peggy's Body Resource was not able to assume the Conscious during sensual times because it was overpowered by a Vaded State. It would now be able to assume the Conscious during those times because no other state would be fighting for that time.

Body: "Okay. I'll try."

RT Action 12, Imagery Check

Therapist: Right now, Body, just imagine Peggy's partner touching your hand and stroking it in a nice way. How are you feeling, now, as that is happening?

Body: It feels really nice. I feel nice.

Therapist: That's fantastic, Body. Thank you for being available to help Peggy in this way. I think you will really enjoy it, and that will make Peggy really appreciate you being there. Thank you for talking with me. (Pause) Peggy, go ahead and allow your eyes to open. (Pause) How are you feeling right now?

Peggy: I actually feel really good. I feel such relief.

I told Peggy that it might be nice to think of herself as a teenager, exploring intimate activities for the first time. I asked her if she thought her partner would allow her to set the speed of any intimate activities for the first few weeks. She said that she knew that he would be happy to do that.

Six weeks later Peggy dropped in at the clinic when I was working at my desk. She knocked on the door, and told me she just wanted to come by and say, "I love sex." She said that she could not imagine missing out on the intimate times that she and her partner now enjoyed. I thanked her for the feedback.

Peggy had had a Resource Vaded with Fear. It had experienced a frightening event, one that she had not talked about. That Resource had not received any resolution and therefore had become vaded. The Resource, she had named, 'Pinned', had come into the Conscious any time any kind of sexual activity was attempted. It even came into the Conscious if a male would complement her on how nice she looked.

It is normal for sexual activity to be enjoyed, so her negative feelings around sex indicated that she had a Vaded State. She had emotions that did not fit the situation. When this Vaded State became empowered, and received the help and safety that it needed it no longer carried feelings that would jump out and interrupt her ability to enjoy life the way she wanted.

Variations to treatment for Classification Categories

DSM categories may be caused by different types of Vaded States. For example, addictions are most commonly caused by Resources Vaded with Fear, but they are sometimes caused by Resources Vaded with Rejection. In either case there is a subconscious mechanism where a Retro Avoiding State relieves the client of the pain of the Vaded State with the use of the addictive behavior. As long as the Resource remains vaded there will be an inner compulsion, a perceived inner duty, to get the pain filled state out of the Conscious with what has proven to work in the past.

A business phobia, an inability to proceed professionally, can be caused by Resources Vaded by Fear or Rejection. Here, when the client considers taking on a new or challenging role the Resource Vaded with Fear or Rejection comes to the Conscious and makes it difficult or impossible for the client to continue. If the state has been Vaded with Fear the client will be literally afraid to continue, while if the state has been Vaded with Rejection the client will feel not good enough and incapable of continuing.

Nightmares and sleep terror

Nightmares and sleep terrors do not happen randomly. Anxiety is often manifested in sleep, resulting in nightmares, and night terrors. The Vaded Resource that has caused a nightmare is not difficult to access, especially when the client has a clear memory of the dream. Just like using a past event to bring a Vaded State into the Conscious, a dream can be used to bring a Vaded State into the Conscious so that it may be Bridged to and resolved. The client should be asked to retell the dream in detail, the therapist should have the client do this with eyes closed while eliciting as much sensory information from the dream as possible. Information can be asked about where the lighting was, what the room was like, what the temperature was, what was being worn, etc. in order to revivify the dream, and to assist in bringing the Vaded State into the Conscious. When emotion is exhibited by the client, indicating that the Vaded State is in the Conscious, normal Bridging techniques can assist the client to return to the initial sensitizing event so the resolution can be completed. Once the Vaded State that caused the nightmare is returned to a Normal Resource condition, the client will no longer have nightmares initiated from that State.

Working with sleep terror is not as straightforward, as the connection made between sleep terror and the causal Vaded State has to be made indirectly, due to the fact that there is no dream memory associated with a sleep terror. Even so, this association can still be made, and most usually the correct initial sensitizing event can be found with the first Bridging.

The client should be asked to describe his or her night sleep. During this description questions should be asked like, "Tell me as much detail as you can about your experience of your sleep terror. As you do this, please allow your eyes to close to improve your memory."

The client should be watched for any expression of emotion during this time, either in the voice or the body language. When an expression of emotion is noticed the client should be asked to describe exactly where in the body they are experiencing this feeling, right now. Then the bridging techniques (See Action 3, Chapter 4) can be used to bridge to the original sensitizing event.

The client who is concentrating on an issue will normally display emotions that are connected to that issue, and when those emotions are further brought into the Conscious, the Vaded State associated with the presenting issue comes into the Conscious. This is the precise state that needs to gain resolution, to ensure it is empowered, safe, and that it feels supported.

Specific Phobia

Phobias are the direct result of a Vaded State coming into and holding the Conscious. This state is called a Vaded Conscious State. No Retro Avoiding States are involved in assisting the client away from the Vaded State, so the client has complete exposure to the overwhelming feelings of that state. Sometimes phobias are a result of the states becoming vaded with a near identical initial sensitizing event to what onsets the phobia. For example, a person may gain a phobia of driving (the onset) after having a car crash (the initial sensitizing event).

Other times, the initial sensitizing event may have only an indirect connection to what onsets the phobia. For example, a person with arachnophobia, the fear of spiders, may bridge to an initial sensitizing event where he or she was being pinched and bothered by older children, and at that time felt overwhelmed and powerless to get them to stop.

As therapists, we do not have to do detective work to determine what the initial sensitizing event was. We merely revivify a time when the client felt the phobic fear, make sure that the Vaded Resource is in the Conscious in the therapy room by observing an emotional reaction, then Bridge to whatever initial sensitizing event becomes evident, and work to empower, bring safety, and care to that state.

Panic attack

The dynamics of panic attacks are very close to the dynamics of phobias. This makes sense, because phobias bring on panic attacks. The experience of a panic attack is the experience of the Vaded State, with its unresolved feelings of panic, taking over the Conscious. The state that is Conscious and out is a Vaded State that held panic, was overwhelmed by it during an initial sensitizing event, and gained no resolution thereafter.

In order to locate the Vaded State that is holding onto the experience of trauma, the therapist should revivify a time when the client experienced trauma, then Bridging and Resolution should follow.

In order to do this kind of work it is necessary for the therapist to feel comfortable in dealing with the emotional reactions of the client. It is the negative emotions that Vaded States hold that must be addressed. The most direct way of helping these states is to access them directly, speak with them, and make sure they get their needs met. Necessarily, this process means the therapist will be exposed to the emotional reactions that the state's exhibit prior to their resolution.

PTSD

A symptom of PTSD can be panic attacks, which was the case in the earlier case study here, where the client, when a 10-year-old girl, thought she was going to drown. Because PTSD relates to life threatening incidents the unresolved anxiety can be severe, when the Vaded State that holds it comes to the Conscious.

PTSD results when the client has a Vaded Resource that maintains an illusion that a feared Introject still has internal power. It is not unusual for the life-threatening Introject to be an inanimate, as was the case in the near drowning incident. Floods, fires, tornadoes, hurricanes, blizzards, near drowning incidents, car crashes, and many other inanimates can cause a person to fear for his or her life. It is also common for a person to fear another individual may kill them, such as in war, robberies, disturbances, and other instances.

The most important thing is that whatever form the Introject has within the personality (a person or an inanimate); the Vaded Resource needs to become aware that it is not physically in the therapy room, so there is only an illusion that it has power. The illusion that the Introject still has power is broken when the Vaded State is encouraged to, and is able to express fully to the Introject. Being able to say absolutely anything the state feels and thinks, and by seeing that it has complete power to do this, is a demonstration of the internal powerlessness of the Introject.

The Vaded State realizes even more power when at the end of the process of expression it is given the choice as to whether the Introject can stay within the Resource's inner space, "Do you want it to stay in your immediate space, or do you want it to leave, so your space will be clear of it? It is totally up to you." Knowing it has the power to make this decision is empowering to the Resource.

These two steps, 1) full expression, and 2) the choice whether, or not, the Introject can stay in the inner space of the Resource, proves to the Vaded State that the Introject has no power. That is a major realization to a Resource State that may have lived in fear for many years.

Agoraphobia

Agoraphobia is a specific type of phobia where the client fears things like wide-open spaces, or leaving the home environment to venture out. When exposed to places that feel non-safe a panic attack can ensue.

The dynamic here is not complex. A resource Vaded with Fear is brought to the surface when the client feels threatened by being in a non-safe place.

This is an example of a Vaded Conscious State. The Normal Resource is forced out of the Conscious by the Vaded State and the client experiences the unresolved feelings of the Vaded State. Unlike a Vaded Avoided State, where the overwhelming feelings only come out temporarily and then are replaced by some type of addictive behavior, the Vaded Conscious State comes out and holds the Conscious, resulting in the client feeling out of control for the entire period of time that the state is out. These unresolved feelings of the state are overwhelming to the client.

A common cognitive behavioral intervention for Agoraphobia is systematic desensitization, where the client is trained, over a period of time, to take small steps in moving out, until he or she is able to overcome the fear feelings and begin geographically re-engaging.

This intervention gives the client a coping skill that is useful, by training a Resource to be able to maintain the Conscious without allowing the Vaded State out. While beneficial to the client, this intervention leaves the Vaded State vaded. It may reappear later, especially at times when the environment seems scary, and it may be felt internally by the client where an inner peace appears illusionary.

A better resolution to Agoraphobia is to empower the Vaded State and leave it with a feeling of safety, support, and care. This resolution allows the client to feel able to make reasoned decisions about safe behavior, and it does not leave the client with a lingering internal sense of something unfinished.

The Actions described in Chapter 4 will bring the Vaded State to the Conscious, facilitate bridging to the initial sensitizing event, and will resolve the state using the Expression, Removal, and Relief technique

Self-harming behavior

Self-harming behavior is an example of a Vaded Avoided State. The overwhelming anxiety felt directly prior to the onset of self-harming behavior is a Vaded State coming to the Conscious, then being forced from the Conscious by the self-harming behavior. The self-harming behavior is a coping skill that brings more peace to the personality than having the experience of the Vaded State in the Conscious.

The Resource that does self-harming behavior is a Retro Avoiding State, a helping state, and it should be spoken with respectfully. It believes that it is important, and it will want to continue the self-harming behavior as long as a Vaded State remains vaded and attempts to come to the Conscious.

The resolution of the Vaded State will allow the 'helping state' to cease the self-harming behavior. It will no longer feel compelled to harm in order to protect the Consciousness from angst.

The resolution techniques described in Chapter 4 can resolve this type of Vaded State, although it is imperative that the right state be brought into the Conscious for this resolution to be effective. The Retro Avoiding State is not the Vaded State. The Vaded State is the anxiety experienced directly before the self-harming behavior.

The best way to ensure that the appropriate state is brought into the Conscious is to revivify a time that the client felt compelled to harm. Then, while inside this image of feeling compelled to harm, ask the client to imagine waiting a bit longer. This, waiting, is quite anxiety producing for the client, and it is the anxiety that is displayed that is the Vaded State. When it is obvious that the client is uncomfortable within the image of needing to self-harm the Bridging procedure described in Chapter 4 can begin.

Following the resolution of the Vaded State, the coping, 'Helping State' will not have a role. I like to praise this state, appreciate it for helping in the past, and find a role for it where it can be a positive addition to the family of states in the future. This, 'Helping State', is a Retro Avoiding State, a resource that had a role that is not wanted. It can take up a new role that fits its level of skill and ability. It can be spoken with directly, given a name, and negotiated with to find a role that is positive.

A 'helping state' that has previously self-harmed has skills of dissociating and getting a hard job done. This can be a great skill to finish menial tasks. When the client has jobs such as, washing windows, polishing, or other time-consuming, menial tasks Resources that have self-harmed previously can be very useful. A good name for these states can be, 'Focused Worker', but the name should be negotiated with the Retro Avoiding State. When this state takes up a positive role and no longer maintains a role that is unwanted it becomes a Normal functioning Resource, no longer Retro functioning.

Generalized Anxiety Disorder

This disorder can be caused by a resource Vaded with Fear and it can also be caused by Conflicted Resources. For example, difficulty in going to sleep, being easily fatigued, difficulty concentrating, and being restless can occur when Resources are in conflict, when work Resources deny a Rest State its ability to have time to recharge the body. Difficulty in sleeping, specifically, can be caused when a Resource that has a need to plan comes in conflict with the Resource that wants to sleep. Often the Resource that wants to plan can keep thoughts generated and can prevent the body from sleeping. When this disorder is caused by **Conflicted States** a Negotiation Intervention is preferred (Emmerson, 2013).

A Resource Vaded with Fear may also make it difficult or impossible for the client to rest. In this case, whenever the client attempts to shut down, to allow the body to rest, to sleep, or the proverbial, "Put the feet in a stream on a sunny day," the Resource Vaded with Fear may surface. This may be better understood when considering the difficulties that some people have in clearing their mind for meditation. A person with the Vaded State will have anxiety surface during quietness, and this will prevent the ability to have a clear quiet, mind.

Individuals suffering from generalized anxiety disorder have almost no ability to have a clear, quiet mind. When they attempt to rest, to be at peace, or to be relaxed, anxiety surfaces. This, surfacing anxiety, is a Vaded Resource coming into the Conscious. This Vaded State needs resolution.

When the Vaded Resource is the causal factor in generalized anxiety disorder it may be accessed by having the client close his or her eyes and imagine relaxing at home. Assist the client to imagine sitting quietly at home, doing nothing, and ask the client to describe this experience. Especially, if you introduce ideas about things that they tend to think about that disturbs their rest the client will begin to experience anxiety as the Vaded Resource comes into the Conscious. The more you are able to build the image so that the person is able to experience anxiety of their Vaded Resource, the easier it will be to Bridge when you follow the steps in Chapter 4.

By Bridging to the Resource that experiences anxiety when the client attempts to sleep, rest, or carry out the normal daily functions, and by bringing resolution to this Resource where it can feel comfortable, safe, and supported, the Normal mature Resources will better be able to carry out daily activities without the experience of a Vaded State bringing anxiety into the Conscious.

Dissociative Identity Disorder

There are a number of Dissociative Identity Disorders. The one I refer to here is more popularly known as Multiple Personality Disorder.

Severe and chronic abuse in early childhood can result in DID. The Resource State or States that experience abuse almost daily obviously find this abuse horrifying. Other Resource States that handled daily jobs, school, or routines, do not want to revisit the experiences of this abuse while it is not occurring. A subconscious coping mechanism allows the states to get better and better at not thinking about the abuse. This chronic attempt to shut off communication between the abused states and the non-abused states results in the atrophying of the synaptic connections between Resource States. This coping skill allows the chronically abused child an opportunity to experience the next day without the constant mental images of the abuse. This is quite a good coping mechanism, although it results in the dissociation of Resource States.

There are other examples of communication links between Resource States atrophying. The experiences of most of our childhood Resource States are not revisited often in adulthood. Therefore, the links between these states atrophy to such a point that it can be difficult to remember many childhood experiences.

Even non-DID individuals have some Resource States with poor communication links. It is not unusual for a person to discover after driving for a few minutes that there is no recall of the last 10 or 15 minutes. These two Resource States, the one that was driving first, and the one that was driving second, both obviously know how to drive and are both spending driving time in the Conscious. This is not an indication of DID, but of two Normal States that have a low level of synaptic connection.

Sandy had Dissociative Identity Disorder

An ex-student of mine rang me to inquire about working with a DID client. My student said that she had been working with her client for a few weeks, her client had been diagnosed as DID and had told her about some of her different personalities, but only one had been evident in therapy. My ex-student wanted to know if she could bring her client to my office to observe my bringing out different alters so she could continue to work with this client. I was happy for her to do that.

They drove about an hour to get to my office, the client riding with my ex-student, her therapist. Introductions were made, my ex-student sat on a couch at the side of the room, and I begin working with the client. After speaking with her (Sandy) for a couple of minutes I brought to the Conscious another alter (Rachel), and began a conversation. Rachel stopped the conversation and asked me who that woman was sitting over on the couch. I told her that it was her therapist, and that Sandy had been seeing her. I told her that Sandy had ridden down with her and I introduced Rachel to her therapist.

After a few more minutes a third personality, Liz, was brought into the Conscious. I asked Liz if she knew who the lady was that was sitting on the couch. She did not, so I introduced them.

Sandy, Rachel, and Liz only knew of each other from what other people had told them. They each felt somewhat resentful of the others. They each thought it was their body, and their life, and the others were stealing some of it.

Just like when working with Resource States, it is important to speak to and about alters in a positive way. This helps the different parts of the personality feel more peace.

One of the first steps in working with DID is to help each alter gain a positive impression of the other alters, and a second step is to facilitate the communication that may result in their integration. That is, the growth of synaptic connections between each alter so that a memory can occur when moving from one alter to the next.

Sandy was a quiet, reflective alter and Liz was rather loud and assertive. When speaking with Sandy about Liz I said how lucky she was to have a strong part that could help when a strong part is needed. I told Sandy that it was great that she was a sensitive, quiet part and that it was also good that if she needed her, Liz was there to back her up and protect her.

Sandy said this was the first time she had thought about Liz in that way. I placed an empty chair in front of Sandy, facing her. I asked her if she would like to take a moment to thank Liz for being there to protect her, and to be assertive when she was needed.

Sandy spoke to Liz in the empty chair, and I wrote down her words **verbatim**. Then, I asked Sandy to stand up, move over to the other chair, turn and sit down. As she was in the movement of sitting down, I called out the name loudly, LIZ, and begin saying, "Liz, you are a very strong part. I really appreciate your strength. Thank you for talking to me again." This is a good way to move the conversation from one alter to another.

There is an opportunity during movement, like in the process of sitting down, to call out the name of another alter to get its attention. Then after getting its attention it is important to say things that it relates with, quickly and clearly, in order to help it come into and hold the Conscious. This same technique works to help call out any Resource State.

I asked Liz if she could recall anything that Sandy had just said. Liz remarked, "Sandy was here?" I said, yes she was and she was speaking directly to you in this chair that you're sitting in now. She was speaking to you and she said (reading verbatim only), "Liz, I want to thank you for being strong and for helping me when I need you. I am glad that you are there."

Liz said, "Sandy said that?"

I confirmed that she had and spoke to Liz in a way that helped her understand the importance that Sandy adds to the personality. Then I had Liz say some nice things to Sandy, speaking to the empty chair across from her.

We moved back and forth two or three more times, each time having a positive interchange, and each time my repeating the words in a verbatim fashion. There was no time that any alter indicated a memory of what had been said by another alter. If this procedure is continued over weeks, and months, alters will begin to remember what was said.

I find the best way to begin work with alters is to gain their trust, to help them gain a positive impression of the other alters, and to begin rebuilding synaptic connections in the way that I just described. It takes time. Rebuilding those synaptic connections is a little like rebuilding the synaptic connections after a stroke to regain muscle control. It takes repetitive work over, and over again.

Sandy commented to her therapist on the drive back that she could not remember a time when she felt as good about herself. This may have been the first time some of her alters began to think positively about each other.

Beyond the work to help the states feel more inner peace and experience more integration there are normally, 1) alters that fear you will try to make them go away, 2) alters that are very protective of fragile states, and 3) alters that can have negative behavior. The best way to effect change in all cases is to find positive things you can say about states and find ways they can incorporate into the personality with a positive role that is appreciated by all other states. This can be done using the same RT Actions that are used with any Resource States.

While DID clients will have had severe and chronic abuse, often surface alters have no awareness of this abuse. It is inappropriate to ever suggest that abuse has occurred to a client. False memories can be generated when therapists suggest things have happened. It is sufficient to notice the errant emotions of Vaded States, Bridge to the initial sensitizing events, and utilize appropriate RT Actions.

A good thing about Resource Therapy is that we do not have to be Sherlock Holmes, and we do not have to make suggestions. The information is all there as long as we facilitate the correct states to come to the surface and lead us. The correct state can be found using RT Actions 1 and 2.

Pathological Gambling

Pathological gambling is described in some detail in other parts of this book, and a therapeutic example is given, see Michelle had a gambling Addiction*, page 212. Pathological gambling is distinguished by the client being out of control when gambling. Many individuals are able to gamble as a recreation, stop when they choose, and see the amount of money that is lost as the cost of the recreation.

Pathological gamblers are not able to do this. They cannot stop when they choose, and they lose the ability to completely cease gambling. They have a Vaded Avoided State that is driven from the Conscious by a Retro Avoiding State that uses gambling for this purpose.

As with all Vaded Avoided States, it is not the 'helping state' that gambles that should be the focus of therapy. It is the anxiety filled Vaded State that drives the individual to gamble that must be the focus, if pathological gambling is to be resolved. Following the resolution of the Vaded State (see chapter 4) it is best to find a new role for the Retro Avoiding State, as described in the section on self-harming behavior.

Addictions

There are two causes for addictive behavior. These are, 1) psychological causes, and there are 2) physiological causes. There are addictive behaviors that are caused by a combination of both.

Here, we are interested in the psychological causes of addictions, as well as their interplay with the physiological causes. Often, an addiction will begin due to psychological causes, a physical addiction may develop, and the effort to stop the addiction is complicated by both the physical and psychological causes.

Physical addictions are easy to understand. One can be addicted to drinking coffee, eating sugar, or any other number of drugs. The body becomes accustomed to having a substance and when that substance is withheld the body demands the return of that substance. These addictions can be very difficult to overcome. If I do not have a cup of coffee by two o'clock in the afternoon I get a headache and flulike symptoms. This is the result of a physiological addiction. I have found, if I want to stop drinking coffee, the best way to do that is to cut my coffee consumption by one third over a period of several days. Without doing this, my body severely demands coffee.

Therefore, if the body's demand for coffee is difficult to overcome, the body's demand for harder drugs can be extremely challenging. Even, those who have been taking antidepressants can attest to the fact that it can be very challenging, physically, to cease taking them.

Psychological addictions are caused by Vaded States. Addictions are actually clever coping mechanisms to avoid the experience of a Vaded State. This is the case, whether it is a drug addiction, gambling addiction, or even workaholism.

A resource can be vaded with an experience so overwhelming that escaping from that feeling into addictive behavior is easily the lesser of evils. Normally this escape is a subconscious process where a 'helping' Resource has found a way to relieve the psyche from the experience of the Vaded State. For example, the zoning out experience of going into a casino, risking losing money, seeing colorful and flashing lights, can create and a relieving diversion from a Vaded State that holds overwhelmingly unpleasant feelings.

Drugs can block states from coming into the Conscious. If an individual has experienced the angst of the Vaded State, then finds a drug that blocks that state from coming into the Conscious, it is very appealing for that individual to return to that drug over and over again to receive the peace that it gives. It takes the Vaded State out of the Conscious. When an individual finds a drug that helps them in this way, this is called their "Drug of choice."

Some people experiment with drugs without ever becoming addicted. It is likely that these individuals do not have states vaded to a level that creates a need for them to escape. It is even possible for these people to become physically addicted to a drug if they return to it over and over again, purely for recreational purposes.

It is very difficult for the individual who is both physically and psychologically addicted to a drug to stop their habit. They have to, at once, deal with the physical addiction and the return of the Vaded State when they stop using the drug. Because of this, it is beneficial for their Vaded States to gain resolution so that all they have to deal with is the physical addiction.

This is tricky, because while the person is under the effects of the drug, the Vaded State that needs resolution is blocked. This means that it is also blocked from a therapeutic resolution, because the therapist has no access to the Vaded State while it is being chemically blocked. In order for the therapist to gain access to this Vaded State that has been blocked by the drug it is necessary for the individual to stop taking the drug long enough for it to reappear.

I instruct my clients who want to cease the use of a drug to stop using that drug for a period of time long enough before their session so they will be yearning for that drug during the session. The number of times they are unable to do this is disheartening, but when they can, they come to the session with the Vaded State associated with their addiction easily accessible.

The only way to remove the psychological need for the drug is to resolve the Vaded State that the drug has blocked. Once the Vaded State is resolved, then the individual will only have to deal with the physiological addiction, if there is one. That can be a difficult task in its own right.

These understandings help us see that drug dependency can be very difficult to break. Clients respond better to therapy when they realize their therapist understands this. They also respond best when the 'helping Resource' that has used a drug to give him relief feels respected. This, drug taking Resource, is most often abused and misunderstood both by other people and by other Resources of the client. It feels that it is important and that unless it does its job, helping the person cope, there will be a lot of pain in the personality. The best way to get this personality part on side is to thank it for the help that it has given in the past, and let it know that it is important that it will be available in the future to help client and other ways.

It is always good to have all Resources cooperating with the therapist. If a resource believes that it is not respected, or that the therapist is against it, it will likely not cooperate. The important part of helping a client with an addiction is resolving the Vaded State. When that Resource that had previously felt overwhelmingly uncomfortable when coming to the Conscious, finds peace, support and care, there is no longer a need to escape from that state into addictive behavior.

This is the case no matter what kind of an addiction the client presents. It is not unusual for individuals to find an addictive behavior that they can live with that helps them block the experience of a Vaded State. These may include things that on the surface may not appear problematic, like gardening, cooking, cleaning, or workaholism. It is not good when an individual feels compelled to do something. They feel out of control.

Some individuals will become so used to having an addiction that they do not want it to end. I suspect many of the most famous people in history were addicted to their work, that is, they could not stop working without their Vaded State returning. Some people like this become proud of their accomplishments and find it difficult to imagine themselves not feeling compelled to work. While excellent work can be accomplished by individuals who are not addicted, it is true that workaholism can result in exceedingly large amounts of hours spent working. The sad part is that these people feel out of control.

People who are addicted to work often find it difficult, or impossible, to take time out, put their feet in the stream, and experienced a relaxed moment for any period of time. Quiet moments allow Vaded States to rise to the surface. When Vaded States are resolved our moments are our own, to work, to relax, to choose to spend time alone, or with our family or our friends.

What is important for therapist to remember when working with addictions, is that the way to bring resolution to psychological addictions is to bring resolution to the Vaded State that fuels the addiction. To gain access to this state there must be a withdrawal of the addictive behavior so the Vaded State will come to the surface. This means there must be a withdrawal of the drug, if the addiction is a drug addiction, and if the addiction is not a drug addiction there must be a withdrawal of the activity, that prevents the Vaded State from coming into the Conscious. If the addiction is not a drug addiction, this can be done very easily with imagery.

Have the client imagine a time immediately prior to beginning the addictive behavior, then have him or her to imagine continuing without starting the addictive behavior. For example, have the client imagine exactly where they are when they feel compelled to go into a casino. Revivify that seen in detail, and have him or her to imagine continuing to state where they are, without going into the casino. This will bring the Vaded State into the Conscious and Bridging can proceed.

It is important for the therapist to remember that the Retro Avoiding States that have been taking on addictive behavior have been doing this for the benefit of the client, to relieve the client of the overwhelmingly bad feelings of the Vaded State. Therefore, this 'Helping State' needs to be praised, understood, and eventually a new role needs to be found for it so that it can feel it is able to benefit the client without continuing with the addiction. It will be able to do this only when the Vaded State is resolved, and not before.

Workaholism

Workaholism is an addiction. It is an addiction that some people are reluctant to give up.

Workaholism, like all addictions, is caused by a Vaded Avoided State. The 'helping state' that helps the client avoid the Vaded State uses work as an escape. The workaholic is generally unable to stop working without feeling the anxiety of the Vaded State. Often, people who suffer from workaholism will also suffer from out-of-control shopping and other escape techniques to avoid their Vaded State from coming to the Conscious.

It is interesting that workaholism and out-of-control shopping often are experienced by the same individuals. One reason might be that those who suffer from workaholism have the funds to shop.

While the workaholic is out of control, this person may appreciate the benefits of the work that is done. This person may appreciate the income, the notoriety, and the pride that is sometimes felt from high levels of productivity.

The negative aspects of workaholism include the inability to enjoy extended quiet moments in life. There's often a difficulty in being able to quietly reflect, enjoy time off, and enjoy rest. The holidays of workaholics are often crammed with activities that require energy and work.

It is, of course, the decision of the client as to whether they continue with their addiction to work or seek a life where they do not feel compelled to action. Obviously, those who seek therapy for workaholism are seeking a change from feeling out of control.

The same therapeutic techniques used for other addictions should be used for workaholism. The problematic Vaded State that feels uncomfortable when the client is not working should be the focus of therapy. Have the client imagine taking time off and not working. This will cause a level of discomfort to rise in the client. This discomfort is the Vaded State coming into the Conscious. It is because of this Vaded State that the 'helping state' drives a person to work.

The techniques in Chapter 4 can be used to bring a resolution to this Vaded Avoided State after it is brought into the Conscious by using the imagery of non-work behavior. It is helpful to build a picture for the client of working for enjoyment and productivity, otherwise these clients will often fear that they will do nothing. It is important for them to understand that they have Resources that actually want to work, that they have Resources that want to be productive, and that they can, and will, work even when they do not feel compelled to work.

It is possible to use empty chairs to isolate Resources that like to work, and those that like to rest, so all Resources can learn to respect each other and respect that each has time to do what is important. It is important that Resources that like to rest have time to do that, and it is important that Resources that like to work have time to do that, also.

OCD (or may be Vaded with Rejection)

Obsessive Compulsive Disorder is an addiction. It is the escape from a Vaded State into a 'zoned out' compulsive behavior that is much more palatable to the psyche than the experience of the Vaded State.

Certain drugs have the ability to block specific Resources. Antidepressants may block Vaded States, if the correct antidepressant is found. This is why antidepressant medication is sometimes effective with obsessive-compulsive disorder. It is not unusual for a number of antidepressant medications to be trialed, in an attempt to give relief to the symptoms of obsessive-compulsive disorder. Here, what is happening is a search for the right chemical compound that can block from the Conscious the Vaded State, thereby negating the necessity for a Retro Avoiding State to engage in compulsive behavior. Obviously, it is better to resolve the Vaded State than to attempt to block that state with medication.

My work with clients suffering from obsessive-compulsive disorder was frustratingly ineffective until I discovered the dynamic at play. I had attempted to work with the state that carried out the obsessive behavior, rather than the Vaded State that it was assisting the personality to escape from. I would speak directly with these 'helping states' and I would get assurance from them that they would cease the obsessive compulsive behavior, only to have the clients return and report that their unwanted obsessive behavior continued. Both the client and I were frustrated by this.

There is a reason for everything. If the car will not start, there is a reason. It may be a bad battery, bad fuel, or one of many other reasons, the good mechanic can often find the reason and fix it. When the client exhibits obsessive-compulsive behavior, behavior that the client does not want to continue, yet continues with that behavior, there is a reason for it. The reason is, that behavior provides a subconscious relief for the client. If the client does not need relief, i.e., if the client does not experience the Vaded State, then there is no need for the obsessive compulsive behavior.

In order to stop the need for obsessive-compulsive behavior it is necessary to find, and bring to the Conscious, the Vaded State that fuels that behavior. Just as with gambling addiction, the best way to do this is to locate the time when the client first feels compelled to carry out obsessive behavior, revivify that time, and then through imagery, have the client to withhold his or her obsessive behavior. This will bring the Vaded State further into the Conscious, as it begins to feel higher levels of anxiety. Then, bridging can be used to locate the ISE and bring resolution to the Vaded State.

Social Phobia (or may be Vaded with Rejection)

Social phobia is a situationally based psychological disturbance. Therefore, it has a psychological root. There is a reason that the client experiences this anxiety, there is something that this anxiety is connected to, and this is a Vaded State.

Social phobia may be caused by Resources Vaded with Fear or Rejection. Because this phobia is most often caused by Resources Vaded with Rejection, refer to the Social Phobia section on page193. When social phobia is caused by Resources Vaded with Fear, the client will demonstrate fearful anxiety, rather than anxiety indicating, "I am not good enough." When this is the case follow the steps in Chapter 4 to help resolve the Vaded State and bring it to a state of normality.

Business Phobia (or may be Vaded with Rejection)

Business phobia has the same causes as social phobia, with the only difference being the situational cues that bring the Vaded Resource to the Conscious. The Vaded State intervention is the same for business phobia as it is for social phobia. It is most often caused by Resources Vaded with Rejection, but can also be caused by Resources Vaded with Fear. If the client describes the experience during their reaction in such a way that indicates that they feel small, and that something larger may hurt them, then this phobia may be caused by fear. As with social phobia, if their presentation is one that indicates that they do not feel good enough, then the phobia will be rooted in a Vaded State suffering from Rejection.

Two client examples in this book can help illustrate this distinction. Luke, illustrated in the example on page35had been screamed at by his father for not being a good worker. This caused Luke to feel afraid and upset. His overwhelming feeling was one of fear, rather than not being good enough. The screaming father frightened Luke, therefore he was left with a Resource Vaded with Fear and he could not speak in front of a group. When Luke's Vaded Resource came into the Conscious he would feel incapacitated and useless.

Anthony, see page 239, had felt rejected by his mother who went out when he was 10 without telling him where she was going, leaving him on his own. Anthony had felt that he was not good enough. He was not afraid of his mother, but he did feel rejected by her. It was more important for Anthony to experience the feelings of his mother's Introject so that he could understand that the issue was in her inability to share love, rather than his inability to be lovable.

The interventions for Resources Vaded with Fear and Resources Vaded with Rejection are very similar, with only the exception that Resources Vaded with Rejection almost always benefit from the experience of speaking from the Introject of the person who rejected, so that an understanding can be internalized, that the issue is with the rejecting person, and not with a child.

Compulsive Shopping (more often is Vaded with Rejection)

Because compulsive shopping is a symptom that is more often related to Resources Vaded with Rejection, it will be discussed further in the section about Resources Vaded with Rejection, below (see page 231). For a case example see, Meagan could not stop buying clothes*, page 304.

Antisocial behavior (or is Vaded with Rejection)

Antisocial behavior is the behavior of a Retro Resource. This behavior is not necessarily related to the Vaded State, but often it is. Retro States carry out activities that had a purpose in the past but do not continue to be beneficial to the client.

For example, if the child cannot get the needed attention with positive behavior, that child may take on antisocial behavior that can result in attention. Later in life, the individual may continue to resort to antisocial behavior to satisfy the need for attention. A Vaded State is not part of the dynamic in this example. A Retro Original State is.

Crisis reaction (benefitting from crisis intervention)

Resources can be vaded in adulthood. A Resource is vaded when it has a negative experience that it cannot incorporate. This most often happens in childhood, as children have not had enough life experiences to be able to understand and incorporate what happens to them, and as they are not good at talking to others about what has happened. They can feel embarrassed, they can feel that they would be in trouble, and they may just not even consider attempting to have a difficult conversation.

As individuals become more mature and get a larger context on the types of incidents that occur they become better at understanding and incorporating events, and they get better at talking about events to friends, family, or therapists. Still, major events can occur in the lives of adults that are difficult to incorporate, and maybe difficult to talk about. An obvious example is an incident in war, where the soldier experiences something completely out of the ordinary, and where talking about it may be avoided.

Other obvious examples include being the victim of a mugging or robbery, experiencing a flood, fire, storm, or other natural disaster, a car crash, a sudden or unexpected death, or having any other type of experience that is difficult to incorporate and may not be fully discussed.

When incidents such as these occur, the Resource that has been in the Conscious during that incident may become vaded. If so, this Vaded Resource, with its unresolved emotions, can continue to cause the client to feel emotional and out-of-control in relation to what has happened.

There is one major difference in treating a client with crisis reaction compared to other clients who present with Vaded States. No Bridging has to occur. The client presenting with crisis reaction already is acutely aware of the major incident that occurred. It is easy to revivify this incident to a level where the Vaded Resource assumes the Conscious, exhibiting emotion.

The Expression, Removal, Relief, Actions described in Chapter 4 for resolving Vaded States is an excellent intervention for individuals experiencing crisis reaction. As soon as the image of the experience is revivified and the

Vaded State is noticed to be in the Conscious the Expression, Removal, Relief Actions can be initiated.

Sexual abuse

Clients who have experienced the same symptoms will often have different causes for the symptoms. Clients who have experienced similar histories will have different reactions to those histories.

Clients who have experienced sexual abuse may have a Resource State Vaded with Fear, Vaded with Rejection, or Vaded with Confusion, especially guilt related. RT Action 1, diagnosis, will help the therapist determine what type of pathological state, if any, the client has. I will talk a little bit more about that later in this section, but I want to say some general things about working with clients who have experienced sexual abuse.

Often, if the client has experienced sexual abuse he or she will automatically ascribe that as the cause for practically any presenting concern. Some therapists are almost as quick to do this. It is obviously true that the experience of sexual abuse can result in psychological issues. But, it is also true that people who have not been sexually abused have psychological issues. Too often, sexual abuse is blamed for pathologies when the cause of those pathologies may have nothing to do with that abuse. Revisiting sexual abuse when it has nothing to do with the issue that the client presented not only wastes time in therapy, but requires the client to reconnect with a painful part of life for no reason.

A good aspect of Resource Therapy is that Bridging allows the therapist to determine the initial sensitizing event for unwanted emotions, therefore time does not need to be spent reprocessing something else.

If Bridging takes the client to the time of sexual abuse, then the Expression, Removal, Relief Actions can be used to empower the client in regard to the Introjects relating to the abuse. There is no need for the client to go into any kind of detail in terms of any abuse. The only thing that is needed is for the client to become empowered, for the client to come to the understanding that the Introjects from the past have no power, so the States that were abused can have a clear, safe space, made even safer by bringing in more mature nurturing

Resource States. The perpetrators from the past can be internally shrunk, and sent out of the inner space of the abused State, and strong, nurturing, Resource States can replace them.

If sexual abuse has become a focus of therapeutic intervention it is appropriate for the therapist to check and ensure that clients feel no guilt associated with their abuse. Guilt is a common symptom of clients who have experienced sexual abuse.

I find a good technique to help resolve guilt is to place an empty chair in front of the Resource State that feels guilty. (It is imperative that the state that feels guilt is holding the Conscious, for this, or any technique, to be beneficial in relieving the guilt.) I ask the Resource State that feels guilty if he or she believes in any kind of loving, all-powerful being, such as a God, or any other manifestation which they identify in this way. One client who did not believe in God, believed in Mother Nature, so we invited Mother Nature into the other chair.

The next step is to invite this loving, benevolent manifestation into the empty chair. Then, I say to the Resource State that feels guilt, calling it by its name, to express itself to the being in the other chair, e.g., "Regretful, now that God is sitting in the other chair, and knowing the power there, now is your opportunity to say to God exactly how you feel. Tell God exactly how you feel about what happened. Just tell God how you feel about your feeling of guilt."

It may seem hard to understand that a survivor of sexual abuse can feel guilt, but it is a very common reaction. Because it is so common, it is a good thing to check out when working with clients who have experienced sexual abuse. Those who feel guilty afterward normally feel guilty about something they interpret as inappropriate behavior on their part. Of course, all blame belongs with the perpetrator, but when survivors carry guilt, it should be attended to.

After the Resource State (in this example, Regretful) has expressed fully, and has said exactly how badly it feels about any role it had, I have the client to rise and move over and sit down in the other chair. As the client is in the process of sitting down I call out clearly the name of whatever manifestation has been agreed to to be in the chair, e.g., "God, thank you for joining us. I know you are everywhere but I especially want to thank you for being here now. I know you heard what Regretful just said. God, how does that make you feel?"

The response from the Introject in the other chair is invariably loving and forgiving. I ask the Introject how it would like Regretful to feel, and then I ask it to go ahead and give Regretful whatever it would like Regretful to have. I say, "I know you have a lot of power, and can do whatever you want, so in whatever way you do this, just go ahead and give Regretful exactly what you want her to have."

Most often, when the client returns to the other chair and I call out the name of the Resource State that had felt guilt, the guilt is gone or greatly diminished. At that point I asked the state if it still wants to be called the name that it had (e.g., in this case, Regretful) or if it would like a different name that better fits how it feels now. It almost always chooses a different name.

It is important to see, and speak with a client who has experienced sexual abuse not as a, "sexually abused person," but as a, "person who has experienced sexual abuse." There is a big difference.

It is also important to allow our empathetic voice to match the tone that we get from the client at all times, especially when sexual abuse has been involved. Too many therapists show more shock and disdain in their empathetic voice then they hear from the client. We should never make an issue appear bigger to the client than it is. We should also not make it smaller. Our voices should reflect what we hear from the client, whether it is about sexual abuse, loss of a pet, loss of a loved one, aging, the discovery of a disease, or anything else. We should accurately reflect what we hear and allow the Bridging techniques to guide us.

Case Illustrations of Resources Vaded with Fear

Mia could not drive without stopping (OCD)

This example using a Resource with OCD reveals the process of separating the behavior from the cause (the angst of a Vaded Resource), bringing the Vaded State into the Conscious, bridging to the initial sensitizing event, resolving the Vaded State, and then finding a positive Resource to assist the client in the future.

I had a client, Mia, who had great difficulty driving anywhere because each time she saw even a small object on the road she would begin obsessing that someone would hit that object, have a car crash, and die. Mia would attempt to drive on, her obsession with what might happen would become so strong that she would have to turn around, drive back, park, and remove the object from the road. She intellectually understood that this behavior was probably more dangerous than leaving the object on the road, but she could not cease her obsessive behavior. She hated herself for doing this, and it greatly interfered with her ability to travel.

This is an example of one Resource disliking another Resource, and this is extremely common for OCD clients. One, or more, other states really hates the state that continues to carry out the obsessive behavior, but the Retro Avoiding State that carries out this behavior is actually attempting to bring peace to the personality. It feels its role is necessary, and important. It is willing to sacrifice its popularity, both within the personality and outside, in order to do the job it feels is important.

Her Vaded Resource was the one that would feel anxiety when she saw an object on the road, it was not the one that would turn around, park, and remove the object from the road. Therefore, I asked her to close her eyes and imagine driving along the road that she often travels. I had her to describe how she felt driving, what time of day it was, what she was wearing, and what she saw as she looked out the windscreen of the car.

Then, I said, "I'm not sure if you have noticed it yet, but up in front there's a small object on the road. As we approach it tell me what it looks like." Here, after revivifying her driving experience I brought the conversation into the present tense so she could imagine being there, as if it were happening currently. This is an important aspect of bringing the Vaded State into the Conscious.

Mia described to me what the object looked like, and I asked her to tell me her feelings as she drove around the object, and drove on. She said she really wanted to go back and remove it from the road.

I told her I understood that, and asked her to, "Describe exactly what you are feeling right now, as you continue to drive further away from the object." She began to show a heightened level of emotional distress, which indicated that the Vaded Resource was assuming the Conscious. At this point I was able to use Bridging techniques described in Chapter 4 to locate and help bring resolution to her Vaded Resource. It is imperative that the Vaded State is in the Conscious, showing emotion, otherwise Bridging techniques will be ineffective in locating the initial sensitizing event associated to the Vaded State.

Following Bridging, and the Expression, Removal, Relief Actions to help resolve the Vaded State, I had the client to return to the image of driving. Again, I revivified the scene of her driving, and I introduced the vision of an object lying in the road. I asked her how she felt.

Mia said she felt different. She said she was still somewhat nervous, but felt that she could drive around it and continue without having to stop.

I asked her just to continue with the image of driving and describe to me, 'What is happening'. She said that she was able to continue, and the further away from the object she got the less she thought about it.

I asked her to tell me how she would most like to feel when she sees a small object on the road in the future. She said that she would like to just notice that it was there, and if it seemed too small to cause problems she did not really want to think about it at all.

I asked her to tell me about a time in her life that she noticed anything small, and then did not think about it afterward. I had to clarify my question a time or two so that she understood what I was asking.

She reported that it did not bother her at all to see a small paper on the ground, so I revivified a scene where she had seen a small paper on the ground and had her to report exactly how she was feeling at that time. This was done to bring into the Conscious a Resource that could be helpful for her when she noticed small objects on the road.

With questioning, she was able to give me a name for this Resource that was able to notice small papers and easily dismiss them. I called the state by name, and asked it if it would be willing to help Mia while she was driving, when she noticed small objects on the road. I told this part that it was very good at noticing inconsequential things and appropriately dismissing them, and that Mia could use its help in noticing inconsequential things on the road to appropriately dismiss them. It said that it would be willing to help.

Then, I again revivified the scene of her driving and noticing a small object on the road, I mentioned by name the Resource that she possessed, and I asked her to describe how she was feeling within this image. She reported feeling very confident.

This was a process of finding a Resource that could help her with her needs. This process would not have worked prior to the resolution of her Vaded State, because the Vaded State would have overpowered any other Resource that tried to come to the Conscious. But, after her Vaded State had returned to a Normal Resource condition, she was able to use one of her Resources (the Resource that could see things as inconsequential) to satisfy her needs (being able to drive without constantly stopping).

I told her that she could go ahead and allow her eyes to open so we could discuss the session further.

At the end of the session, during the debriefing, Mia asked, "Will this really work?" I replied, "I don't know. Sometimes it's just nice to be surprised." This is an honest response, because we never really know how well an intervention will work, but it is also a response that prevents some clients from wanting to prove the therapist wrong. See Chapter 4 – Starting and Ending Sessions.

Mia later reported that she was somewhat nervous in driving, but that she found she would forget to notice objects on the road. At the end of a trip, she could think back and remember that there had been small objects, but that she had not really thought about them. She found it hard to identify with, and even remember, the anxiety that she had once felt.

Adam was robbed at gunpoint

Here is an example of a service station attendant who was robbed at gunpoint. It was first appropriate to talk about the difference between an internal fear and an external fear. I told the young man that it is appropriate to hear things that may hurt us on the outside, like getting too close to the cliff, or a pack of wild dogs. I told him that the fear that we experience at these times helps protect us. I also told him that when we carry fear from the past, from something that happened previously, it does us no good. Fear from the past only keeps us from feeling peaceful on the inside.

He indicated that he understood this concept. I told him that the fear that he had had during the robbery was probably a good thing at the time. It may have made him careful, may have given him extra adrenaline, and it may have helped him do the right thing to protect himself. I said that it did not really matter if he had done the right thing or not, but what was important now was that that fear that may have been useful in the past is not useful now. I told him that the robber was not in the room at the present, therefore having a fear of the robber was not protecting him inside the therapy room. He, again, indicated that he understood this concept.

I told him that we would use an imagery to help him become empowered in relation to his internal feelings. I asked him to close his eyes and tell me in some detail about his experience of the robbery. In this case, I did not have to work to revivify the scene by asking for a lot of detail. When he started telling me about the robbery he immediately exhibited fear, and negative emotion.

I told him to keep his eyes closed, and that we can now do anything we want with this robbery scene because it is not happening right now, because the robber is actually not in this room right now. Then I said, "Let's just have your image of the robber, keeping your eyes closed, standing across the room next to the door. We know he is not really there, so right now you can say absolutely anything you want to him in complete safety. Go ahead and speak out loud and tell him exactly what you feel and think about him."

Telling the Client that the negative Introject is not present in the room actually allows the client to more easily imagine the Introject being there. The fear level is lowered so the imagery can become clearer. There was a pause, and I could see that the client was having difficulty feeling confident to speak.

I said, "Let's just shrink the robber down to 1 inch tall. He's not really here. He is just an image, so we can do anything we want. He is now shrunk to 1 inch tall, and he has a squeaky little voice. Please don't step on him, because I want you to be able to tell him exactly what you want to say. Would you like me to say something to him first?"

The client indicated that he would like me to speak first.

I said, "You stupid idiot. I can't believe how stupid and uncaring you must be to take that stupid little gun that you have just to take a little bit of money. Look at that crazy expression on your face. I feel sorry for someone with an expression like that. That's just sad." Then I said to the client, "Now, you tell him. Tell him exactly how he made you feel, and how you feel about him right now."

The client told the Introject of the robber how frightened he had made him feel, and he continued to tell him that he was a bad man, and that they should lock him away forever. I continued to encourage the client to say absolutely anything, and everything, he could think about to tell the robber. This, Expression phase, was important to allow the Vaded Resource to understand that there was nothing to fear from this Introject, and that he could not be hurt by this Introject no matter what he, the client, said to him.

After he had fully expressed to the Introject of the robber, I told the client to allow his eyes to stay closed a little bit longer, and I told him that he could now decide whether he wanted this image of the robber to be in his inner space or if he wanted his inner space completely clear of this man.

I knew what the answer would be. The client said he did not want him in his space, so I said, "Just tell him to get out then." He did. This was the Removal phase of resolving the Vaded State. He would not have been able to ask him to leave prior to his becoming empowered by saying everything he wanted to the Introject of the robber, because he first needed to prove that he could do so safely.

He told the robber to get out of his space.

I then went on to the Relief phase of the process. I asked the client, "If you saw someone who you cared about and who was upset after being robbed, and it was safe but they were still upset, what would you want to do?" He told me that he would just like to go and talk with him, so I asked him what I could call this part of him that would like to help the person who had been upset. I got a name for the helping Resource, and I asked to speak with it directly. "Helper, I can see you are a very good part. I know you've heard what has been going on. Would you be willing to go to the part that experienced the robbery? That part that experienced the robbery is been very brave and told the robber exactly what he wanted to. Would you be willing to help this part feel safe and supported now and in the future?" That nurturing Resource said it would be willing to do that.

I told it that he could do that, and continue to do everything else that it does, and that the more it does, the stronger it gets, and that it can do many things all at once. I thanked it for its help and asked it to go directly to the positive experience of the robbery, and do whatever is best to help it feel safe and totally supported. Then, I asked the client how he was feeling, and he indicated that he was feeling much better. I told him he could go ahead and allow his eyes to open.

His Resource that had been Vaded with Fear had been able to safely express itself fully. The Resource Vaded with Fear had been able to better understand its experience at an emotional level, and had gained the inner support and safety offered by a stronger, helping state. After this time, he would have still felt negative emotions surrounding the robbery, but it would not be something that would interfere with his day on a daily basis, and it would not be something that would cause him to feel any kind of panic attack or PTSD symptoms.

In summary, the Expression, Removal, Relief Actions are excellent for crisis intervention, and no Bridging needs to occur. It is easy to bring the Vaded State into the Conscious by revivifying the crisis situation. After the Vaded State has been resolved the client will feel much more empowered in relation to what has happened. Any grieving will be able to occur more naturally.

Chapter 6
Treatment of States Vaded with Rejection

This chapter covers the types of presentations that are caused by states Vaded with Rejection and their treatment.

Resources Vaded with Rejection feel unlovable. This can cause many psychological issues. The Resource of a young girl who felt unable to win the love of her alcoholic father may be left with an unfulfilled yearning for that love and may seek out relationships with alcoholic partners in an attempt to gain it. Because adult relationships do not heal childhood Vaded States, even if she is able to gain the love of an alcoholic partner her Vaded State will continue to hold its unfulfilled yearning. Therefore, she may seek out a relationship with a second alcoholic in another attempt to gain emotional closure. This process will never be fulfilling. Her underlying Vaded State needs to get the understanding that it is lovable.

Resource Vaded with Rejection is characterized by:

---

1. Feeling not good enough.
2. Feels positive when the client has pleased another person, but feels terrible when the client has disappointed another person.
3. Feelings of worth are based on the impressions of others.
4. Feels like a fake, and feels that if others saw the real person they would be disappointed.
5. Is unsure if it is loved.

A client who has a Resource Vaded with Rejection may have a need to be perfect. The underlying feeling is, "I have to do everything right to be accepted," but in truth there is never a feeling of being good enough because the Vaded State has not found resolution. These clients may have difficulty ever feeling like they have found the love they need.

Resources Vaded with Rejection are the root cause for the eating disorders of anorexia nervosa and bulimia.

Related Pathologies

These states all have in common a Resource that experienced an event that caused that part to feel unlovable, and was unable to incorporate that event and gain an understanding of it. This Vaded Resource maintains within the personality an overwhelming feeling of Rejection and when it comes to the surface, to the Conscious, it brings with it that feeling of being unlovable.

Below is a list of issues that can be caused by Resources Vaded with Rejection. Where further elucidation may be beneficial, items in the list will be described in more detail to explain the dynamic that is occurring within the personality.

Resources Vaded with Rejection can cause these Pathologies

- Social Phobia (or may be Vaded with Fear)
- Business Phobia (or may be Vaded with Fear)
- Narcissism
- Anorexia Nervosa
- Bulimia Nervosa
- Antisocial (or may be Vaded with Fear)
- Feeling Unlovable
- Business Phobia (or may be Vaded with Fear)
- Compulsive Shopping (or may be Vaded with Fear)
- Over competiveness

Contentment is something that eludes clients who have Resources Vaded with Rejection. Nothing they do leaves them with a consistent feeling of being 'good enough'. They may feel temporary elation following a success, but that feeling quickly reverts back to a sense of incapacity.

Resources Vaded with Rejection carry the illusion that they are unlovable. These States need to gain the understanding that all children deserve unconditional love, and that it is not them that is unlovable, it is the person whose love they desired that had difficulty loving, or expressing their love. This Resource needs to gain a clear shift in perception from, "I am unlovable," to, "The other person had difficulty loving or expressing their love."

As with all work with Resources, this understanding cannot be merely an intellectual understanding of a mature Resource. It has to be an emotional understanding of the Vaded State. When this Vaded Resource is able to gain the understanding that it is loved, it again returns to a Normal Resource condition. In order for the Vaded Resource to gain this understanding at an emotional level, part of the process of resolution is to have the client speak as the parent. When the client speaks as the introject of the parent, being a great actor, the client can get a better understanding that the problem was that the parent was not at that time able to show unconditional love (real perception of the client). Understanding at an emotional level that it was not the child that was unlovable, but the parent that was not showing the love the child needed is a central part of resolving a Resource State Vaded with Rejection.

Treatment Process

It is important for the reader to gain an understanding that Resources are physiological neural pathways that have been created by the repetitive actions of a coping mechanism that has worked for the individual. Resources cannot be removed, as they are a structural part of the personality.

Vaded States feel overwhelmed by their impressions of certain Introjects. Introjects are powerless impressions held by Resources, of other persons, animals, or inanimates. These impressions can be changed, and this is important because it is the impression the Vaded State holds of Introjects that has prevented it from returning to normality.

Table 24: RT Actions used to bring States Vaded with Rejection to Normality

---

Action 1: Diagnosis of Resource Pathology
Action 2: Vivify Specific   see page 88
Action 3: Bridging   see page 94
Action 4: Expression   see page 101
Action 5: Introject Speak   see page 104
Action 6: Removal   see page 106
Action 7: Relief   see page 108
Action 8: Find Resource   see page 113
Action 9: Changing Chairs Introject Action
Action 10: Retro State Negotiation
Action 11: Conflicted State Negotiation
Action 12: Imagery Check   see page 131

- The correct state must be identified by the therapist as the core cause of the presenting concern.

- Bridging must take the Vaded State to the image of the original sensitizing event.

- Ensure that the Vaded State is truly in the Conscious to the needed level.

- Get the age of the Vaded State at the time of the initial sensitizing event.

- Funnel the focus of the client into the initial sensitizing event.

- The Vaded State must become empowered and/or reach understanding and be left with a feeling of safety, support, and care.

- Expression: Ensuring the Resource expresses its feelings fully.

- Introject Speak: All the Vaded State to speak as the rejecting Introject so it can better understand the inability for the Introject to share love.

- Removal: Giving the Resource a choice to keep or remove the **Introjects** that gave it negative feelings.

- Relief: Bringing a nurturing, caring Resource of the client to the fragile state to ensure that it gets support and care.

Note: When it is clear that an Introject was not able to show unconditional love, that does not mean that the actual person who that Introject represents was actually that way. It merely means that is the way that person was internalized by the Vaded State. We, as therapists, have no real way to know what reality was, but it is our purpose in therapy to work with the reality of the client to help that client gain resolution.

Case Example with Transcript

Michelle had a gambling Addiction*

Michelle could not stay away from poker machines. The family budget was non-existent because of her problem. Many times, she had convinced herself that she would never go into another place that had poker machines. Then, it would happen again, and again.

She said that she had never been into a casino, and had no desire to go into one before her husband talked her into it. Her habit had started slowly, at first. Then, she found she could not control it.

This is not unusual with an addiction. Because addictions are coping skills to stay away from the feelings of a Vaded State, sometimes it takes practice to learn what can keep a Vaded State from taking over the Conscious. This learning is a sub-conscious process. When a 'Helping Resource' finds a coping skill that can relieve the person of the overwhelmingly negative feelings of a Vaded State, this Helping Resource feels compelled to help the person by returning over and over again to the addictive behavior.

Michelle's 'Helping Resource' had discovered that when she was in front of a poker machine, having the excitement of possibly winning or losing, seeing the lights and hearing the noises provided her with a 'zoned out' experience which kept her safe from the anxiety of her Vaded State.

In order to help Michelle break her gambling addiction it would be necessary to resolve the negative feelings of her Vaded State. It is extremely difficult to break an addiction by working with the 'Helping Resource', as this state feels it is important that it do its job. It does not like to see another state in pain, and it is totally willing to sacrifice its own popularity to keep the Vaded State from experiencing its pain.

Sometimes, with great effort, a person can break an addiction without attending to their Vaded State, but this is very difficult and it leaves their Vaded State with its negative feelings. Often, another addiction ensues, sometimes one that the person can better accept.

RT Action 2, Vivify Specific

I wanted to bring into the Conscious the Vaded State that drove Michelle's addiction so I ask her to allow her eyes to close and to explain in detail the time when she entered the pub where Pokey machines were. She said she would be driving home from work with no anticipation of going into the pub, then, about the time she passed a certain bridge she would feel compelled to pull into the pub parking lot and go inside. She said once this process started she no longer felt bad about going into the pub and staying for a period of time. It would be later, when she left the pub that guilt feelings would overtake her and she would be very angry at herself for what she had done.

This description indicated a normal addictive process. She was driving home from work in a Normal Resource, then as an anxiety filled Vaded State started to take over the Conscious, a Retro Avoiding State would direct her into the pub and keep her there for a period of time. When she would leave the pub this helping state would relinquish the Conscious to a Normal Resource. Once back in a Normal Resource, she would realize what she had done, and she would be flooded with guilt feelings and remorse.

It would be my role to locate the Vaded State, bring it into the Conscious, Bridge to the initial sensitizing event, and resolve the feelings of the Vaded State so that it could again become a Normal Resource.

I asked Michele to tell me more precisely about the exact time when she would begin to feel compelled to go into the pub. She said it was just before she got to a certain bridge on the way home from work. I worked to revivify the scene of her driving her car, asking her what she was wearing, what time of day it was, to tell me exactly how she was feeling, what she saw when she looked through the windscreen, and the very first feelings about turning into the pub parking lot.

The length of time it takes to revivify when a Vaded State was in the Conscious will vary, but it is necessary to continue with the process until you can see that the client is uncomfortable. This means the Vaded State is assuming the Conscious. I asked her if there was a moment of indecision, a time when she first felt the pulling for her to turn in the pub, and I asked her what that felt like.

She said it was a very uncomfortable feeling, then she started to open her eyes. I told her to just go ahead and allow her eyes to remain closed for a while, and I asked what I could call this part of her that was having this uncomfortable feeling, and she said, "Stressed." I spoke directly to 'Stressed'.

Therapist: 'Stressed', I know you're driving the car now and feeling uncomfortable, and I want you to continue driving further without turning into the pub and tell me how you feel.

Withholding coping from a Vaded Avoided State brings the state further into the Conscious, causing the person to feel even more compelled to enter into the coping, addictive behavior. Therefore, withholding coping is a good way to bring a Vaded Avoided State into the Conscious so Bridging can ensue. I could see by observing her body language and voice tone that she was becoming even more uncomfortable. Tears were coming down her cheeks and she was uncomfortably shuffling in her seat.

RT Action 3, Bridging

Therapist: Right now, where in your body are you experiencing this discomfort the most? Survey your body and tell me where you are feeling this the most.

Stressed: It is around here.

She pointed to her upper chest or lower throat, and that she was having difficulty speaking.

Therapist: As you try to speak, does it feel like your voice is adult or younger?

Stressed: Someone younger.

Therapist: About how old does this voice feel right now?

Stressed: I don't know. About 8, maybe.

Therapist: Stressed, feeling upset like you do and being about eight, having difficulty speaking, does it feel more like you're inside a building or outside a building?

Stressed: Outside a building.

Therapist: Does it feel more like you are alone, or with someone else?

Stressed: There are other people.

Therapist: Tell me where you are right now and describe what is happening.

Stressed: I'm in the street. There are a bunch of kids around. They're making fun of me.

Therapist: That's terrible. What is happening? How are they making fun of you?

Stressed: They are friends of my brother. I just wanted to play with them, and now they're making fun of me. I don't know why they won't let me play, and I don't know why they're making fun of me.

This was the initial sensitizing event. As a little girl of about eight years old, Michelle had wanted the play with her brother's friends. She looked up to them and she cared about what they thought of her. Not only did they not allow her play, but they made fun of her. This caused her to feel devastated, and this is something she never received resolution for afterward. Michelle said that her brother was making fun of her too.

Therapist: Look at one person who is making fun of you and tell me if it is a male or female.

Stressed: It is my brother.

RT Action 4, Expression

Therapist: My voice is right there with you right now, and we know that none of those kids are actually here so you can say anything you want to them. Look at your brother, right now, and out loud so I can hear exactly what you say, tell him how you are feeling. You can do this now, because he is not really here. Just say anything you want to him, right now.

This is the 'Expression' step in resolution.

Stressed: Why won't you let me play with you? I just want to play. Stop making fun of me.

She was crying when she said this, and quite distressed. Her eyes were still closed tightly.

Therapist: Tell me what expression he has on his face, right now after you told him what you have.

If he had had a mean or angry expression on his face I would have asked her if it was okay if I say something to him, then I would have told him that he was a silly person, that he wasn't even here, that he thought he was really something with that stupid look on his face and it was just making him look dumb, so he should just get serious and listen to what was happening.

She reported that her brother had a surprised look on his face. That indicated to me that her Introject of her brother was not belligerent, so I thought it would be good for her to experience his feelings so she could better understand what was happening.

RT Action 5, Introject Speak

Therapist: Stressed, you have done a really good job telling your brother how you feel. Right now, I want to speak with him directly. I want you to be like a great actress going right into his skin so I can talk to him and see how he feels. A great actress forgets herself and just becomes the other person, so when I talk to him you can answer as your brother. What is your brother's name? (She said it was, Mark).

With her remaining in the same chair with her eyes closed, I said loudly and clearly, "Mark, thank you for talking with me. Mark, your little sister is quite upset. She really wants to play with you and your friends. What does that make you feel like, Mark?"

Michelle as Mark: She is too little. My friends are all bigger than she is and they don't want a little girl messing up what we are doing.

Therapist: I understand that Mark. She is your little sister. I just want to know what it makes you feel like to see her so upset.

Michelle as Mark: I don't feel good about it. If it was just me I would let her play. I don't like to see her upset.

Therapist: I think I understand better now, Mark. You would like her to be able to play, but you are a bit embarrassed about your friends. What would you like your little sister to know, Mark? What would you like to say to her that might make her feel better? You can say anything you want and your friends will not be able to hear it, because they are not really even here right now. Just go ahead and tell her, right now, exactly what you would like her to know. Speak to her out loud directly, so I can hear you.

Michelle as Mark: Michelle, I'm sorry you can't play. I would like to play with you, but right now my friends are here and I want to play with them for a while. I will play with you later.

Therapist: Thank you for talking with me, Mark. I appreciate your honesty. (Slight pause)

Therapist: 'Stressed', I was just talking to your brother, Mark, and I can understand why you have been upset. I know he is bigger, but he was not acting very big. He was afraid of his friends. He wanted to play with you, but he was afraid of his friends so he rejected you at the time. That was not fair. I would be upset if that happened to me, too. He does seem like a nice boy, though. He said he wants to play with you when his friends are not here. How does that make you feel, Stressed?

Stressed: I feel a bit better, now that I know he really does want to play with me, but I still want to play with his friends.

Therapist: I can understand that stressed. It seems like the problem is that you are smaller than they are. Since this is not really happening right now we can do anything we want. So let's just let you to be as big as they are, or maybe just a little bit bigger. You may even be a little bit bigger than your brother. We can do this right now, because this is your scene so we can change it anyway we want. So, right now you can be a little bit bigger than Mark's friends, and a little bit bigger than Mark, and everyone wants to play with you. How does that feel?

A big smile appeared on Michelle's face. The negative emotions disappeared completely. (Because clients are telling about something that happened in the past, something that is not happening currently, any scene can be changed. This, of course, does not change history, and clients will continue to remember the actual events, but it does change the emotions from the event.)

Stressed: They all want to play with me.

RT Action 6, Removal

Therapist: Yes, they do. Is it okay with you if your brother plays too?

Stressed: He can play.

Therapist: That is very nice of you. You are a very nice person. You know, it seems to me that the term Stressed does not fit you anymore. What would be a better term that fits how you are feeling now?

Michelle: I think I would like to be called, Leader.

RT Action 7, Relief

Therapist: That is a wonderful name. From now on I will call you, Leader. Leader, I can see you are doing much better, but I still want to get another part that can stay with you to make sure that you are always feeling good. I will want to talk to you more in a minute, but right now, Michelle, I want to talk to a part of you that would like to make sure the little girl always has a friend. Michelle, if you were to see a little girl who looked lonely, possibly a daughter or a family member, what would you like to do?

Michelle: I would like to go and talk with her and make sure she was okay.

Therapist: What can I call you, the part that just said that? What name or term fits you, as you would like to help a young person feel okay?

Michelle: 'Mature'.

Therapist: 'Mature', thank you for talking with me. Mature, you are a great part of Michelle, and I am glad you are here. Right now, I want you to go to where Leader is, let her know that you will always be there supporting her without getting in the way, and that she will always have a friend there with her because you will always be there. You can put your arm around her right there on the inside where she is right now and let her know that you will always be there with her. You can do this and everything else you do. The more things you do the more powerful you become, Mature. (Pause) Leader, how does that feel?

Leader: That feels really good.

Therapist: Is there anything else you need?

Leader: No, I'm feeling good now.

Therapist: That is really good, Leader. You have done very well. You are now bigger than your brother, and you are able to play with him and his friends. It was very nice of you to allow your brother to play also. That tells me you are a very nice person, Leader. You also have Mature there with you, and she will always be with you, forever. I'm glad you're feeling much better now. Is it okay with you, Leader, if Michelle's more mature parts make decisions about gambling, and you can stay down there with Mature and enjoy playing with Mark and his friends?

Leader: Yes, that is okay.

Therapist: Is there anything else you need? How are you feeling, right now?

Leader: I'm feeling really good.

Therapist: That's great, Leader. Is it okay with you, if you stay down there with Mature, Mark, and his friends and let other adult Resources take care of things on the surface? When Michelle wants to play, you might even come to the surface and help her enjoy playing, and the rest of the time you could stay down there and enjoy the inside. What do you think about that?

Leader: I can do that.

RT Action 8, Find Resource

Therapist: That's great. Michelle, now, when you are driving home from work and you come up to the bridge that in the past has been a problem area for you, how do you want to feel, and how do you want to act?

Here, I wanted to start the process of finding a resource that Michelle would like to have out during the time that had been problematic for her in the past. The Vaded State that had caused her helping state to flee to the poker machines in order to escape was no longer vaded. Therefore, I wanted to make sure that Michelle had other Resources that would be able to fill the time that had previously been filled by the Vaded State and her Retro Avoiding States. This process would have been worthless unless the Vaded State had achieved a normal Resource condition, because the anxiety that is felt by a Vaded State can be overpowering.

Michelle: I just don't want to think anything about it. I just want to be able to drive on past the bridge and go home.

Therapist: That sounds reasonable. You just want to continue driving as you normally drive. Tell me, Michelle, how you normally feel while you are driving?

Michelle: I don't know. A bit mindless I guess. I'm just thinking about whatever pops into my head.

Therapist: Just imagine driving now, feeling a bit mindless, just letting your mind go wherever it goes. You are sitting behind the steering wheel seeing the road go by. What can I call you, as you are experiencing this, right now?

Michelle: 'Driver', I guess.

Therapist: 'Driver', thank you for talking with me. Driver, I know you have been hearing what has been going on. Michelle needs you now to be in control while she is driving home, all the way home including past the bridge, so she can get home safely, just the way she wants to. Would you be willing to help Michelle do this, all the way home?"

Driver: Sure.

RT Action 12, Imagery Check

Therapist: Thank you, Driver. Driver, now just imagine driving the car down the hill toward the bridge, and imagine just driving the car on past the bridge on the way home. How did that feel?

Driver: Good. No problems.

Therapist: Thank you, Driver. Thank you for being helpful and for being available. Now, Michelle, go ahead and allow your eyes to open and tell me how you feel.

Michelle: I feel really good. That was a bit strange. Will I really be able to drive past the pub?

Therapist: How did you feel when you imagined doing it, just now?

Michelle: It was easy. I just drove straight on by. But, will I really be able to do it on the way home from work?

Therapist: We never really truly know the future. Sometimes it's just nice to be surprised. You did really well in the session.

Michelle did not gamble for two years following the session. Two years later she came back to see me because she was afraid that she might start gambling again. She had felt so confident in her ability to not gamble that she had started accompanying her husband to casinos. After doing this for a while, she felt so confident, that she had put some money into a slot machine. It scared her and she made another appointment to see me. There was an RT Action (10) I now attend to that I had not previously done with Michelle.

The Retro Avoiding State that had helped her avoid the negative feelings of the Vaded State was still there, and it could in the future offer another state with upset feelings an escape into gambling. This Retro Avoiding State needed to learn a new behavior so if it was needed again it could help without gambling (see RT Action 10). Now when I work with clients for addictive behavior, I always attend to the Retro Avoiding State after resolving the Vaded State to make sure it is able to offer a behavior that will be appreciated by other States. See Meagan's father was not good at showing love, page 310, for an example of Retro Avoiding State Negotiation.

Variations to treatment for Classifications

Social Phobia (or may be Vaded with Fear)

Social phobia may be caused by Resources Vaded with Fear or by Resources Vaded with Rejection, although Social Phobias are most often caused by Resources Vaded with Rejection, it is not difficult to determine which is the case.

During the client presentation, if the client describes the anxiety that is experienced in social situations in a way that indicates that the client does not feel good enough, or feels they may be judged, then the Resource that is the root of the symptom is Vaded with Rejection. If, on the other hand, the client presents feelings in social situations of a general fear and body anxiety, where the client feels a sense of being overpowered by fear, the phobia is caused by a Resource Vaded with Fear.

As with all phobias, the sense of being out of control and the anxiety experienced is the direct reflection of the Vaded State coming into the Conscious. The client, at this time, is experiencing the unresolved feelings of the Vaded State.

In order to assist the client suffering from social phobia, a revivification (Vivify Specific, Action 2) of a time when these out of control feelings were experienced will facilitate the Vaded State to enter into the Conscious so therapeutic intervention can continue. This is best done by asking the client to close his or eyes as soon as a specific time and location when the social phobia was experienced. Immediately, the therapist should begin using present tense language while vivifying the precise scene with the client, i.e. "With him looking at you right now, what are you noticing in your body?"

After bringing the Resource that is Vaded into the Conscious, using a revivification of a time when the client has experienced these out of control feelings, the steps in Chapter 4 can be followed to help move the Resource Vaded with Rejection to a Normal Resource condition.

Narcissism

Narcissism is one of a number of possible reactions to a Resource Vaded with Rejection. The Vaded Resource feels unlovable so other Retro Avoiding States overcompensate with behavior that often appears arrogant. These helping Resources may actually learn to believe the superiority they pretend, but they are fuelled by the deep feelings of, "I am not really good enough."

When the related Vaded Resource is able to experientially understand that it is lovable, the Resources that have exhibited arrogant behavior no longer will have to overcompensate. They may have a habit of this type of behavior that will continue for a period of time, but when they no longer need to protect a fragile Resource Vaded with Rejection their behavior will be moderated.

Narcissistic behavior is behavior that is beyond the control of the client. Just as addictive gambling behavior provides an opportunity for the individual to avoid the anxiety of a Vaded State, narcissistic behavior allows the individual to avoid the anxiety of not feeling good enough. In this way, narcissistic behavior is similar to addictive behavior.

The metaphor, the tougher the shell the softer the core, applies to narcissistic behavior. Individuals who exhibit narcissistic behavior have a very fragile Resource that needs protection. The example below will elucidate this further, see Julie: Narcissistic Behavior, on page 233.

Anorexia Nervosa

Anorexia Nervosa appears to be almost exclusively associated with Vaded States that have had initial sensitizing events of rejection. The child has felt unable to have an unconditionally accepting relationship with a parental figure. This does not mean that such a relationship was not offered. It does mean it was not interpreted as unconditionally loving by the child.

The child becomes extremely needy for clear emotional connection, and is finally able to achieve that connection through the demonstration of real concern that is exhibited when the child stops eating. This subconscious dynamic is very difficult to break, as the need for a loving connection is being fulfilled by the parent's attempts to keep the child safe and healthy. The child who has experienced, over time, an unconditional acceptance, becomes more resilient to incidents that could be interpreted as rejection.

When the client suffering from Anorexia Nervosa, during therapy, assumes the Introject of their strongest parental figure, they reveal a difficulty to share unconditional love. For example, if Annette is the client who suffers from Anorexia Nervosa, and she is asked to sit in the opposite chair and assume the identity of her mother, when, as her mother, she speaks back to Annette she will have difficulty showing unconditional love.

The parental Introject is the child's internalized impression of the parent, and does not necessarily reflect the real parent. It is the Introject that is directly connected to the feelings of the client. The parental Introject of the client suffering Anorexia Nervosa, at these times, will say things like, the following.

Therapist: (After hearing from the Introject that she loves her daughter) Just tell her that you love her now. Tell her out loud so I can hear you.

Parent: She knows I love her.

Therapist: Just tell her now.

Parent: Well, she knows that.

Therapist: I want to hear you say it. Just tell her that you love her.

Parent speaking in an insincere and matter-of-fact fashion: "Well, of course I love you."

This statement, spoken like this, does not come across as sincere and is not heard as unconditional love. The experience of clients suffering from Anorexia Nervosa is that, no matter what they do, it is not good enough. They have attempted, sometimes for years, to receive, and feel unconditional love. Then, they discover that by controlling the amount they eat they can get real concern from the parent whose love they have felt deprived of. They discover that, by controlling what they eat, they can see concern and loving emotion for possibly the first time in their life.

While they have a Resource that is Vaded with Rejection, a 'Helping Resource' (Retro Avoiding State) learns on the subconscious level that the expression of love that has been needed can be received by losing weight. The more weight they lose the greater the expression of concern they receive. This coping mechanism to receive sincere emotion is not understood by the client. The client merely feels out of control, and has a powerful driving force to be thin.

Clients can become creative in ways they achieve thinness. They can use many different techniques for this, or combinations of techniques, that include under eating, over exercise, laxatives, and Bulimia.

As long as the client has a Resource Vaded with Rejection that client can maintain issues with food, even in older adulthood. The Vaded Resource needs to be brought to the Conscious, needs to understand through the experience of taking on the persona of the introjected parent, that the problem is the parent's inability to express love, not that the child is unlovable.

This Resource needs to understand that, as does every child, it deserves unconditional love no matter what it does. It needs to experience this unconditional love in the 'Relief' phase of resolution (see chapter 4). Many clients with anorexia nervosa have difficulty finding an unconditionally nurturing part of themselves to offer love to the Vaded State. This can slow therapy, as this part often needs practice becoming more nurturing (see Find Resource, for how to find a Resource that can learn new behavior).

When the Vaded State can gain this understanding, that it is lovable, and when it can gain an experience of being loved, it will feel comfortable remaining as an underlying state, continuing to gain love and acceptance from a nurturing part of the personality. This resolution of the Vaded State with Rejection, bringing it into a Normal Resource Condition, allows the mature Resources of the client to make decisions that are healthy and empowered.

Bulimia Nervosa

While a client that has Anorexia Nervosa may use Bulimia to achieve weight loss, often individuals may become Bulimic completely independent of Anorexia Nervosa. Bulimia can be a way that clients with Resources Vaded with Rejection can compete with others in their desire to gain love.

Because individuals who have Resources Vaded with Rejection have a tendency to compare themselves with others, they often have concerns about their body image. Their concern about not being lovable enough can translate to high anxiety if they feel other people have an advantage over them. They can be driven to be 'just as good' or 'better' than others. When they see others with bodies they feel compete better than theirs they can become highly motivated to lose weight.

It is not unusual for a person who has never been Bulimic to learn bulimic behavior from others and take up the practice. Of course, bulimic behavior is very hard on the body. It can be injurious to organs, the stomach acid can destroy the teeth; it can shorten life, and even kill.

When the Bulimic individual gets a resolution to the Vaded State with Rejection that person will no longer be driven by high anxiety to compete. He or she will still be able to make reasoned decisions on eating and lifestyle, but those decisions will be within the control of the individual.

Clients who suffer from Bulimia that is not associated with Anorexia will often respond quickly to the therapeutic intervention for States Vaded with Rejection. When Bridging leads to the correct ISE and the associated Vaded State is resolved, a positive outcome can be expected.

The difference between having a Vaded State and having a Normal State is the ability to be empowered and have control in life. Often, the person who feels like they have low control is actually very controlling. They constantly attempt to control things because they have a Resource that feels out of control. That Resource will remain out-of-control until it receives resolution, then the individual will be able to actually be in control, and feel in control of their own life. That person will no longer have to fight control. He or she will be able to use reason and assertive Resources to make decisions and carry them through.

Feeling Unlovable

Feeling unlovable is the general feeling of the person with a Resource Vaded with Rejection. This feeling can cause the person to end relationships, because 'I am not good enough for the other person'. It can also cause the individual to seek and gain a relationship to prove worthiness to be loved, yet when the relationship is won, because the Vaded State still is not resolved, this person may feel that the relationship is not enough because they are not fulfilled.

When an individual has a Resource Vaded with Rejection it is having an unquenchable thirst to be loved. Nothing that the adult can do will satisfy this thirst. No relationship, no achievement, no gratification satisfies this thirst, because the underlying Resource Vaded with Rejection still feels unloved by the Introject of the past that rejected it. It can only gain resolution by revisiting the initial sensitizing event so that the actual Resource that is vaded can finally get the love that it has always wanted.

Business Phobia (or may be Vaded with Fear)

I have had a number of clients who have presented with business phobia. They have been trained and they believe that they are ready to begin their new business, but something keeps them from continuing. They just can't make themselves take the first necessary steps. When they are asked about the feelings they have when they attempt to make these first steps it is obvious that a Vaded State is involved. They will report feelings of anxiety that tend to be expressed as feelings of fear, or feelings of unworthiness.

I find that business phobia is most often related to feelings of unworthiness, and these feelings come from Resources that have been Vaded with Rejection. Because the person has a resource that feels 'not good enough' it tends to come into the Conscious when they consider doing something that might result in failure.

Compulsive Shopping (or may be Vaded with Fear)

Compulsive shopping is a form of addiction. Two pathological states are normally associated with compulsive shopping, as with all psychological addictions. These two states are States Vaded with Fear or Rejection, associated with a Retro Avoiding State.

I find that compulsive shopping is most normally associated with States Vaded with Rejection, although this will become evident during diagnosis (RT Action 1) and Bridging (RT Action 3).

When an individual suffers from compulsive shopping it does not matter if that person needs to buy something or not. Shopping is done as an escape. The individual will experience much more positive feelings while shopping, than the otherwise negative feelings that would have been experienced had the Vaded State assumed the Conscious.

Attempting to work directly with the Retro Avoiding State that is doing the shopping is almost always wasted therapy time. As long as the individual feels anxiety that can be relieved by shopping it will be very difficult for that person to avoid shopping. Therefore, it is necessary to first focus therapy on the anxiety that is felt immediately prior to going shopping.

Time should be spent talking with the client about his or her emotional experience immediately prior to making the decision to go shopping. The Vivify Specific (RT Action 2) technique can be used to bring to the surface the Vaded State that is the driving force for the compulsive shopping. In order to do this it is important to ensure that the client speak very specifically about how he or she felt immediately prior to making the decision to go shopping. After vivifying this point in time it is powerful if the therapist asks questions about what the client would feel like if shopping is put off. This will help increase the level of affect and ensure that the Vaded State is in the Conscious.

In order to gain a better understanding of this technique it would be good to study the case example, Meagan could not stop buying clothes*, page 304.

Over Competiveness

Competition can be good. There is nothing wrong with being competitive. It is good to compete, to compete hard, and enjoy winning. But, if the person does not win it is healthy to still have enjoyed the contest. It is healthy to appreciate that someone always has to win, and this time was not my turn. Many people are able to complete this way. While they enjoy competing, they do not feel compelled to compete, and they do not feel emotionally depleted if they do not win.

Some individuals with Resources Vaded with Rejection feel compelled to compete. They emotionally feel as if they have to win, or they will not be good enough as a person. Competition for them is not an enjoyment, it is something they are driven to do.

They tend to compare themselves to others in a hierarchical way. They place themselves above some people and below others. When they see someone who has something they do not, or does something better than they are able to do, or has achieved something they have not, it feels like something has been taken away from them.

They are able to enjoy others' achievements if they can win some value for it, such as: They are from my school, it is my child, or they are from my club. They can be rather annoying because they are always comparing achievements, incomes, jobs, children, cars, etc.

It is not their fault. They have a Resource Vaded with Rejection. They feel compelled to compete and compare as a means of keeping score to see if they are good enough. There may be times when they feel a level of elation because they have won, but this elation is short-lived because their Vaded Resource will chronically cause them to compare.

When the steps are used in Chapter 4 to assist them to resolve their Vaded State and return it to a Normal Resource condition, then they can internally relax and stop constantly comparing.

In order for the steps to work it will be necessary for the right Resource to be in the Conscious prior to Bridging. This is the Vaded Resource that compels them to compete and compare.

It is possible to have this client to explain a time when he or she felt upset over a loss in competition. This will bring the Vaded State further into the Conscious so Bridging can take place.

Prior to Bridging, it is important that they exhibit a real need to compete or compare. They will be feeling a real anxiety, or a frustration. This is an indication that the Resource Vaded with Rejection is in the Conscious, therefore bridging can begin.

Case Illustrations of Resources Vaded with Rejection

Julie: Narcissistic Behavior

Julie's friends enjoyed her company. She had a quick wit, and provided her friends with information about the latest fashions, and trends. She came to therapy because she felt that she was falling behind her friends in the things that seemed important to her in life. While she did well professionally, and while, outwardly, she had a positive self-image, she was not partnered and had no children.

There was a part of Julie that really wanted marriage and children, but she continually found herself living a life focused on individual achievements rather than forming a partnership. She felt driven to succeed, and she was talented in demonstrating how successful she was, without being too blatant about it.

Julie presented in therapy with the issue of not being able to maintain a relationship that could lead to marriage and children. She was an attractive woman in her late 30s who dressed well and was successful in her vocation. Listening to her presentation sounded like she had the perfect life. She described how important her job was, how nice her house was, how new her car was, and how many friends she had.

It was difficult to get her to focus on what she wanted to change because she kept telling about the successful aspects of her life. It was as though there was an underlying understanding that there was something that was keeping her from being able to attain a long-term relationship, but the Conscious Resources were unwilling to entertain that there was anything wrong.

I repeatedly asked her to say what she wanted to achieve in therapy. There would be a moment of reflection and an indication that she would like a partnered relationship and had never been able to achieve one, then she would return to talking about the successes in her life.

This is an indication of the narcissistic client. Those who make it to therapy will often have a resource motivated to change, but it is very difficult for other Resources that are accustomed to covering up any frailty to allow the client to disclose any weakness. Because of this, narcissistic clients are often frustrating to their therapists.

It is difficult to get a feeling of authenticity when working with the narcissistic client, because when they are open and authentic their Resource Vaded with Rejection might surface. Being aware that more fragile states exist, and speaking directly to them, helps these Resources come to the Conscious and respond.

Therefore, it is especially important when working with a narcissistic client to avoid the trap of allowing helping Resources to continue to talk about peripheral topics. A narcissistic client can waste a session by making the time fly by, talking about peripheral topics.

Even though I am aware of this, it often takes me several minutes into the session to recognize what is happening when I am confronted with a narcissistic client. I tend to allow myself to be drawn away from the central topic until I become frustrated that nothing is happening. With Julie, it was probably the third time I asked her to re-state what it was she wanted to change in therapy before I noticed this dynamic.

Therapist: Julie, I am a little bit unclear about what exactly it is you are ready to change. What is it in your life that you want different? What do you want to be different when you are finished with therapy?

Julie: I see my friends having children and moving on. I really want that to happen in my life. I have a lot of success in my life. I make almost twice as much income as any of my friends do, and I get to travel all the time.

It was helpful to ignore the ego building sentences of her response, and speak only to the Resource that wanted change.

Therapist: Okay, I think I'm hearing more clearly what you really want. You feel there may be something that is interfering in your personality with your getting what you want in life, and you want to make sure you have the opportunity to get what you want.

Julie: Yes. I don't want to be held back. I know I'm good at things. I see my friends who are not as good as me at many things, and they have husbands and children. I'm not sure why I don't.

Therapist: That must be very frustrating to understand that you want something, and that it seems to always elude you. What pattern have you noticed in your relationships? When your friends might have continued with relationships, what has occurred in yours?

Julie: I have had live-in relationships, but when I think back on them they rarely last more than three months. It seems like I have difficulty

> sharing my space. I don't want to go to my partners place and I don't want him to have too much of my space.

Narcissism shares with many personality disorders the common feature of negative or annoying behavior that works as a coping skill with the client. This behavior can be negative or annoying both for others and for the client, and it can work so well that the dynamic may be very hard to break.

Julie was a good example of a narcissistic client. The part of her that wanted children and a long-term relationship was probably a healthy, Normal Resource. It wanted things that it valued, and it felt frustrated at having experienced many years of not being able to attain what it wanted. It had become unable to attain what it wanted because of Julie's 'helping Resources' that were protecting her Resource Vaded with Rejection.

This particular dynamic is especially difficult to break, because when the protecting states become aware that the fragile, Vaded State is becoming exposed, which it must do for resolution, they work harder to protect it. This, of course, is at a subconscious level to the client. It is probable that most narcissistic individuals never come to therapy, because of this dynamic.

Julie wanted some magic fix that would allow her to move forward in her life without having to show vulnerability. This was not possible. Although it appeared that at the end of the session Julie had become clearer about what she wanted, and about how fragile feelings might be associated in keeping her from getting what she has wanted, our work had just begun.

A couple of days before our next session, Julie rang and cancelled. She thanked me for seeing her and said that her timetable was going to be busy for a few weeks so she would ring me after it cleared up a bit. She never rang back.

It can be difficult not to feel like we have failed a client. Possibly, if I had said things in another way, or moved at a different pace Julie would've been able to continue with therapy and gain a resolution to her issues.

I mention this case here as an example because outcomes such as this tend to be more common than a straightforward resolution for narcissistic behavior.

In order for resolutions to occur a time needs to be revivified when the helping Resources would normally make positive statements in an attempt to protect the State Vaded with Rejection. This is to get the Vaded State into the Conscious so Bridging can begin. Because the narcissistic client tends to use these helping Resources almost all the time, this can often be done within the therapeutic setting without the requirement of remembering a time in the past.

For example, the therapist can ask the narcissistic client to continue talking without saying anything positive about themselves, about what they own, or about anything that is inflating to them. This can be very hard for the client to do. It is good to begin this procedure near the beginning of the session. The procedure will be frustrating to the client before Bridging can occur, therefore, there needs to be enough time in the session in order to Bridge and achieve a resolution, using the Expression, Introject Speak, Removal, Relief Actions.

When the therapist asks the narcissistic client to continue talking without making any positive remarks about themselves, the client is almost always unable to do this. Therefore, each time a positive remark begins, the therapist needs to indicate to the client, "Stop, you started to say one there."

As the conversation proceeds, especially if the conversation is focused on something that the client may not do well, the more anxiety the client will experience. This anxiety belongs to the Vaded State. This is the activity that I would have used with Julie had she come back for the second session.

It would have been of no value to focus on the state that wanted change. It wanted to have children and that was not happening. There was nothing wrong with that state.

There would have been no value to focus on the Retro Avoiding States that were protecting the Vaded State. They were just Julie's coping skills to get through life. They were helping her.

It would have been valuable to withhold her from using these helping states, so that the state that they were protecting would feel exposed. When the Vaded State comes to the Conscious then the Bridging steps in chapter 4 can be used to gain resolution. The trick with narcissistic clients is to get them into therapy, and to keep them there when it becomes obvious that the Vaded State may come to the surface.

There is an interesting corollary to this in posture and dress. A client who slumps down in the chair, and does not straighten up and look the world straight in the eye is often hiding from the world. If this client is asked to straighten up for a moment and explain the feelings that are experienced at this time, the feelings that are explained are normally feelings of being exposed. The feelings that are being explained, the feelings of being exposed, belong to a Vaded Resource. If that Resource is brought in to the Conscious, by continuing to have the client stay straight in the chair and feel exposed, then Bridging steps can take the client back to the original sensitizing event where a resolution can result. After the resolution, the client will be able to sit straight up in the chair without feeling a need to slump.

Occasionally a client may have hair combed almost over the whole face, hiding the face. While there is nothing wrong with various hairstyles, if it appears that the client is hiding behind his or her hair, with the client's approval, he or she can be asked to pull their hair back and hold it back to reveal the face. This can be hard for the client. It can cause a feeling of exposure. Here again, by highlighting this feeling of exposure the related Vaded Resource can be brought into the Conscious so that Bridging can occur, taking the Vaded State back to the initial sensitizing event, followed by the Expression, Removal, and Relief phase of the process.

Resources that cause a client to want to hide with bad posture or with the way the hair is combed can be Vaded with Fear or with Rejection. Either way, the techniques to bring these Resources to the surface are identical, as are the Bridging techniques. The only real difference in resolution is in assisting the Resource Vaded with Rejection to understand that the initial sensitizing event was due to the **Introjects** inability to feel or show love, while this is not a component of working with Resources Vaded with Fear. Resources Vaded with Fear merely need to become empowered over their Introject, and continue to feel support and internal safety from another nurturing Resource. These different treatment regimens are defined with more specificity in Chapter 4 Resource Therapy (RT) Actions, page 73.

Anthony: BUSINESS PHOBIA, Psychology Practice

Anthony had completed his degree in psychology along with all the training and supervision he needed for registration. He had been able to do all paperwork and jump through all the necessary hoops to attain registration as a psychologist, but then he found that he could not take the next steps to actually see clients.

When he would consider seeing clients he would experience a high level of anxiety and he would fear that he would let the client down and be a failure himself. His fear included a high level of anxiety about what the client would think of him. He was afraid that the clients he saw would think he was incompetent.

I asked Anthony to imagine that he already had an office and that his first client was in the waiting room. I had him to describe to me his office, what he had on, what the client chair looked like, and how his body felt sitting in his own chair. I had him to imagine the minute hand on the clock being at the top of the hour, the time that the client would be entering his room.

With this image, Anthony became very anxious. I asked him to describe exactly what he was feeling, "Right now."

He said that he was afraid that he would let the client down. I told him to tell me more about that feeling, and as he did, I asked him where in his body he was experiencing it.

He said that he was experiencing it in his stomach. From that point forward I followed the steps that are presented in Vaded with Rejection, page 82of this book, to continue bringing the Resource further into the Conscious, to Bridge, and to use the Expression, Introject Speak, Removal, and Relief Actions, to make sure that his Vaded State was able to return to a Normal Resource condition.

Anthony's initial sensitizing event had occurred when his mother used to leave him home for rather long periods when she went out. It was not clear to him where she was going or for what reason, but he felt abandoned at the times that she was gone. During the Bridging he went back to a time when he was crying, and asking her not to leave. She had said to him, "What kind of boy are you? I did not think I was raising a girl here." She then slammed the door and left. He felt devastated, not good enough, and like he was letting her down while at the same time he was longing for her.

In the resolution, during the Introject Speak Action after Anthony was encouraged to say everything he wanted to say to his mother, he was asked to speak as his mother, and as he was speaking from her Introject, she said she did not think she had a life, felt burdened by having a child, and could not get enough time for herself.

When Anthony was again speaking as the Vaded State, I said to him, "I can really understand why you feel the way you do. Your mother is not really ready to have kids right now. I hope later on in life she gets to a better place, but right now I don't think you're going to be able to get from her the love and support that every child deserves. I want to make sure you get that because every child deserves to get unconditional love and support."

Next, I asked to speak with a mature loving part of Anthony that would like to help a 10-year-old child feel loved and supported. I brought these two Resources together and the Resource that had been Vaded was able to feel loved and supported. It was left in a different state than it was found.

Following this procedure Anthony was able to begin his psychological practice. He had been a good student, and he would be a good psychologist. He had just been blocked by a business phobia from being able to begin his new profession.

Chapter 7
Treatment for states Vaded with Disappointment

This chapter covers the types of presentations that are caused by states Vaded with Disappointment and their treatment.

Psychological depression is caused by a resource becoming vaded by the perceived difference between expectation and reality. That is, a Resource takes on an overwhelming feeling of disappointment because of the gulf between what was desired or expected in life and perceived reality. It is not the magnitude of what has happened that vades a resource, it is the interpretation of what has happened that vades the state. Two people may experience the same reality, and one may acquire a Resource Vaded with Disappointment, while the other may not.

A Resource Vaded with Disappointment is characterized by:

---

1. Very low energy
2. Difficulty relating to a time when things were good
3. A reluctance to re-engage
4. A lack of permission for other Resources to take up positive engagement.

One person may view the loss of a pet cat as a minor occurrence in their life, while another person may view the loss of a pet cat as the loss of their best friend. One person may view the loss of their job as an opportunity to move forward, while a co-worker may view the loss of their job as the loss of a security that they thought they would always have.

I held a position in one university for 18 years. Because of government cutbacks in education, packages were offered to long-term employees so they could be replaced with new employees at a reduced rate of pay. At the same time, also because of government cutbacks in education, working responsibilities were increased. The employees who had been at the University for a number of years were generally unhappy with the new work requirements, while new employees who had not held positions in a university appeared to be very pleased to get jobs with those same work responsibilities. One group was upset at the work requirements, because they held different expectations, while the other group were more pleased with the work requirements because compared to the jobs they had had previously, they seemed preferable. The difference in the level of their angst was a difference in the gulf between their expectations and their perceived reality.

When a resource is overwhelmingly disappointed by its perceived reality it can be like a semi-trailer turned crossways on the freeway. It can keep all other Resources from having positive energy.

There is a resource corollary to this in relationships. When a husband, wife, or partner, discovers their intimate mate is having an affair one Resource can become so upset that it will block all other Resources from enjoying the relationship. It will not allow the Resource that enjoyed physical activity to continue to do that, it will not allow the Resource that enjoyed conversations to continue to do that, and it will not allow the Resource that enjoyed travel with their partner to continue to do that. Because it is so upset with the sexual affair it shuts down all positive activities with the offending person.

In the same way, when a resource becomes overwhelmingly disappointed, becomes Vaded with Disappointment, it can shut down all other Resources from enjoying life. It will not allow any other Resource to have positive energy. This is depression.

Related Pathologies

Resources Vaded with Disappointment all have in common a resource that experienced an event that caused an overwhelming feeling of disappointment, and was unable to incorporate that event and understand it. This Vaded Resource maintains within the personality an overwhelming feeling of disappointment, often refusing to allow other Resources to enjoy living because of the disappointment it feels.

Below is a list of issues that can be caused by Resources Vaded with Disappointment.

Resources Vaded with Disappointment cause these Pathologies

- Depression
- Relationship blame
- Prolonged and intense feelings of loss

Depression can be caused by non-psychological, organic imbalances, but psychological depression is caused by a resource Vaded with Disappointment. This can happen at any time during life.

It appears that the psyche becomes comfortable with expectation, and when expectation is not met there can be a level of discomfort. If the person creates a comfortable reality that their spouse will be with them for many years, then an overwhelming disappointment can be brought about by something that makes that impossible. Even if they have warning, for example, if they find out their spouse is dying of cancer; their disappointment can still be overwhelming when the death actually occurs.

Therapeutically, it is not important what the issue is that brought about the disappointment. If the disappointment is perceived to be overwhelming, the Resource that is disappointed is Vaded, so the focus of therapy is on the Vaded State. It will be important for that state to be able to return to a functional state of normality. Often it is able to do this with a different or lesser role, while understanding life will not be as it was expected, or hoped, to be.

It is beneficial to show an empathetic understanding for the loss the Vaded State feels, regardless of what has vaded it. For example, the person who has a state Vaded with Disappointment over the loss of a pet should be shown the same empathy as the person who has lost a partner. One of the worst therapeutic statements is, "It's not that bad." This is a statement that proves to clients that you do not understand their feelings. For them, it is that bad, or they would not be sitting in front of you.

Treatment Process

Table 25: RT Actions used to bring states Vaded with Disappointment to Normality

Action 1: Diagnosis of Resource Pathology
Action 2: Vivify Specific
Action 3: Bridging
Action 4: Expression
Action 5: Introject Speak
Action 6: Removal
Action 7: Relief
Action 8: Find Resource (x 2)   see page 113
Action 9: Changing Chairs Introject Action
Action 10: Retro State Negotiation   see page 123
Action 11: Conflicted State Negotiation
Action 12: Imagery Check

- There must be a determination that the Vaded State suffers from disappointment, as characterized by an exhibition of malaise; the shutting down of energy, and an inability to engage in life activities with enjoyment or excitement. (Action 2 – Identify Pathology)

- Two Resources should be located that have previously experienced enjoyment or excitement in an activity which would still be possible for the client to engage in.

- A time when one of these activities was enjoyed should be revivified until it is obvious that the client is experiencing a level of joy or excitement within the imagery. (Action 8 – Find Resource)

- A name for that Resource should be negotiated and that Resource should be asked if it would be willing to again engage positively in the activity that it had in the past, if internal permission can be gained.

- Step three and four should also be completed for the second Resource in step two.

- The Resource that is Vaded with Disappointment should be brought to the Conscious and permission should be gained from that state for the two Resources to reengage in the activities they have enjoyed in the past.

- Work should proceed with the Resource Vaded with Disappointment to determine its purpose and find adjusted or new roles where it can continue to fulfil that purpose.

Case Illustrations of Resources Vaded with Rejection

Case Example with Transcript

Ken suffered DEPRESSION after losing his job*

Ken was a conservatively dressed man in his mid-40s. He was married, had three children, and had benefited from a secure job at a major bank. He was relatively financially secure, and his wife was a mother/housewife who supplemented the family income with a part-time job by teaching one afternoon a week at the local high school. She taught an elective religious class, although she was not a registered teacher.

Ken was conservative politically, and he mentioned a few times during our sessions that he did not like individuals who took advantage of the government. He said that he did not want his tax dollars paying for someone to sit at home and watch TV.

Life seemed to be going well for Ken until his manager called him in for a talk about his future. Ken said that he knew the 'future planning discussion' was a euphemism for letting people go, but he said everyone was invited to one of these discussions and he did not dream that he might lose his job. He said he had always worked hard, had always been there on time, and had anticipated that he would retire at the bank.

Ken said that he thought that even if he had been selected to leave that he would be able to negotiate a way that he could stay. He said that he would have taken a pay cut or would have put in more hours for no extra pay. Ken was told that the discussion was about what opportunities he would have outside of the bank, and he was given no opportunity to negotiate. The decision had been made.

Ken was given a monetary package that meant that he would not have to find a job immediately. He said they told him that this is a great opportunity for him to walk away with a lump sum of money and enter directly into another job. Ken did not see it this way.

He was embarrassed, humiliated, and reported feeling emasculated. Ken did not tell his wife for two weeks. He was still working at the bank during this time. He said he thought they might come in and tell him that there had been a mistake, but that he really knew they would not. He said he knew he should be checking out other job opportunities, but for some reason he did not. He only told his wife when she demanded to know what was wrong. He was not sleeping well, not eating well, and reported just going through the motions of living. His energy was very low.

When he came to see me Ken had finished his job at the bank a few weeks previously, but had not been to a job interview. He felt guilty about this, but he just could not bring himself to do it. He only came to see me because his wife insisted.

In this case example it was obvious what the initial sensitizing event was. It was when Ken lost his job. He had a Resource State that felt secure in that job, and that anticipated the job would continue. This was important to him so when his reality negatively stopped matching his anticipation he became depressed.

Ken's Resource that worked hard and thought it would always be rewarded for that work no longer had a job. It experienced feelings of rejection and failure. It blocked Ken's other Resources from being able to enjoy the things that they had in the past. It even blocked Ken's ability to look for other work.

Ken was not interested in going out, he was not interested in sexual activity with his wife, and he had no energy to enjoy playing with his kids.

It was my role to show empathetic understanding to the Resource that was vaded, to show that it had a right to feel the way that it did, and to begin to get it on side and cooperative. If I had indicated that I did not feel that it should feel the way that it did, it would not have wanted to engage. It would have just felt misunderstood and separate.

Following that, and along with showing an empathetic understanding with the Vaded State, it was my role to find two Resources that could begin to reengage in positive activities. Then, it would be my role to get permission from the Vaded State for these states to reengage. Finally, it would be my role to negotiate with the Vaded State to find its purpose and a new role that could fit the purpose.

Show Empathy and Respect to the State Vaded with Disappointment

Therapist: Ken, I can't imagine how bad it must feel to have been told that your services were no longer needed at the bank. It makes sense to me that you are upset. I think it would be really surprising not to be upset. I also think you probably will be for a while, but even now I would like to talk with you about a couple of the things you used to like to do before you lost your job. Is that okay with you, Ken?

This statement is highly paraphrased. These kinds of comments were made in conversation over half of the session. It takes time to gain the confidence of a Resource Vaded with Disappointment. It feels a bit like a person standing on an island with no one else around. If you say things to it that it can relate with it will engage, but if you say things that discount the feelings that it has, it just feels like, 'There's someone else who doesn't understand me'.

Ken: What do you mean?

RT Action 8, Find Resource

Therapist: I want you to tell me about a couple of things you enjoy doing. I understand you have not been enjoying much lately. I want you to think back and remember something you used to enjoy doing, before you lost your job. Just remember back, and tell me something you enjoyed doing in the past.

Ken: I don't know. I can't really think of anything right now.

When clients are depressed it is very difficult for them to even remember a time when they had fun. They actually can't connect with the fun, but they will be able to connect with an intellectual memory of a time they had fun.

Therapist: I know it is hard to think right now about that. But, even if you don't really connect with it, tell me just one thing that you did with your time, before you lost your job, that you enjoyed doing?

Ken: I guess I liked playing with the kids. Sometimes I try to do that now, but I really just don't feel like it. I feel guilty because I don't play with them much.

Therapist: I can understand that. How, and where, did you play with them, back when you enjoyed it?

Ken: Jimmy and I used to play with his train set. We both enjoyed that.

Therapist: "Tell me about that. What room is his train set in, and what time of day did you play with him?"

Ken: The train set is in his room, and we would play while Maggie was fixing dinner. Sometimes, she would have to call us two or three times.

Therapist: Ken, just allow your eyes to close and picture playing with Jimmy right now in his room. Is the train making a noise?

Taking a client back to a time when a resource was out enjoying itself brings that state into the Conscious. As it comes into the Conscious, it brings its affect with it. The client will begin to exhibit more positive feelings, and this is an indication that the Resource is Conscious.

Ken: No, it doesn't really have a motor. It just has lots of track that you can build and it can go up and down along the track. When you let it go at the high point it will roll down on its own."

Therapist: How do you feel as you and Jimmy watch the train rolled down the track?

A slight smile came on Ken's face.

Ken: Pretty good, really. Both of us actually like to play with the train.

Therapist: I can see that this part I'm talking with right now is enjoying playing with the train, and is enjoying playing with Jimmy. What can I call you, as you enjoy playing with Jimmy? What name or term fits you here?

Ken: I guess, 'Playful'.

Therapist: That's a great name. When I want to talk to this part I will call it, Playful. I'm talking with it right now and I want to continue talking with it for a while. Playful, you really do enjoy playing with the train with Jimmy, don't you?

Playful: (Smiling) Yes I do.

Therapist: I can see that, Playful. Playful, you are a great part of Ken. You help him bond with his children, and you help him enjoy life. I think you know, Playful, that Ken has not been very happy lately. If I can get permission from the part that is upset for you to enjoy playing with your kids, Playful, would you be willing to play with your kids a little while each day, so you and your kids can enjoy it?

Playful: If I can, I will.

Therapist: That's all I wanted to know. Thank you, Playful. I will want to talk with you some more later. (Pause) Ken, that was very good. Just leave your eyes closed for a while, as we talk. I will tell you when it is a good time to open them. Playful seems like a great part of you. I would like you to tell me one more thing that you enjoyed doing, other than playing with your kids, in the past. It can be anything. Just remember back, and tell me something else that you enjoyed doing.

RT Action 8, Find Resource

Ken: I really used to enjoy having breakfast with Maggie. We used to talk about things, and it was a really good part of the day. I haven't been going down for breakfast. Just really don't want to face her.

Therapist: I can understand that. Your life hasn't been very easy lately. Just think back now to a time when you are sitting with Maggie, having breakfast and really enjoying the conversation. Are you at a table?

Ken: Yes, we have a table in the kitchen.

Therapist: Are you eating, right now, as you talk with Maggie?

Ken: No, I'm sitting at the table, and Maggie is fixing the meal.

Therapist: Is she able to talk as she does that?

Ken: Yes, we both enjoy talking in the morning.

Therapist: Are you drinking anything?

Ken: Yes, we both have a cup of coffee. I made it before I sat down.

Therapist: (I notice that Ken's mood has lightened, so I ask) How does it feel, sitting there drinking your coffee, talking to Maggie?

It is important to continue working to revivify a time when the client was having a good time, until you see a mood change. When you can see a lighter mood, it is an indication that a Resource that can have a good time is in the Conscious.

Ken: It feels really good. I like talking to Maggie. (This was said with positive energy.)

Therapist: I can see that. What can I call you, as you like talking to Maggie? What would be a good name or term for you?

Ken: I don't know. 'Talker', I guess.

Therapist: I like that name. Thank you for talking with me, Talker. You really do like talking to Maggie in the morning, don't you?

Talker: Yes, I do.

Therapist: Talker, I'm going to ask you the same question I asked another part earlier. If I get permission for you to come out and enjoy talking with Maggie, would you be willing to come out and help Ken enjoy talking with Maggie again in the mornings. It seems like that would be good both for you and for Maggie. Would you be willing to do that, Talker?

Talker: Yes, if I can.

Therapist: Thank you, Talker. I appreciate that. (slight pause) Ken, I know you have not been feeling very well lately. I have just been talking with two very nice parts that you have, Playful and Talker. I liked both of them. Ken, tell me, leaving your eyes closed, more about how you have been feeling during the last few days.

Here, I am wanting to bring out the Resource that is vaded. This is not difficult to do, as in a depressed client the Vaded Resource is dominant. In order to bring out the Vaded State all I have to do is have Ken describe how he has been feeling lately. It will be the Vaded Resource that gives that description, because it will be describing its own feelings.

Ken: Really, nothing has had much meaning to me. I know it should, but I just can't make myself do anything.

Therapist: I can hear the frustration. What would be a good name for me to call you? Would 'Low' or 'Down' be a good name, or would there be a different name that is better?

Ken: You can call me, Low.

Therapist: Low, thank you for talking with me. I know it was horrible, about you losing your job. I can understand that must feel awful. Low,

I want to spend some time with you to make sure you find something really worthwhile to do, but in the meantime I have a favour to ask you. Low, I know you don't feel good, and you have every right not to feel good, and I want to work with you to help you feel better, but I have just been talking with two really nice parts, Playful and Talker. They are both able to enjoy some things in life, playing with the kids, and talking with Maggie. Low, I wonder if you would be kind enough to allow Playful and Talker to enjoy some time when they can come out. It is understandable that you still won't feel very good most of the time. Would it be okay with you, Low, if these two parts were allowed some time where they could enjoy playing with the kids and talking with Maggie?

Low: Yes, they can do that. I still feel awful.

Therapist: I know you do, Low, and I want to help you feel better, but right now I just want to say thank you for letting those other two parts have some time out for the good of everybody. Thank you, Low.

Low: That's okay.

Therapist: Playful, did you hear what Low said? He said it would be okay for you to have some time to come out and enjoy playing with the kids. That would be a really good thing for you to do. The kids would enjoy it, and you would enjoy it, and you have permission from Low to do that. Playful, are you still willing to have some time where you play with the kids?

Playful: Yes, I would like to do that.

Therapist: Just imagine, right now, coming home and spending some time playing with the kids. How does that feel?

Playful: Really good, actually.

Therapist: Good. Thank you again. Now, Talker, are you still willing to spend some time in the morning at breakfast talking with Maggie?

Talker: Yes, I would enjoy doing that.

Therapist: That's great, Talker. Just imagine doing that, right now, tomorrow morning and tell me how that feels. (Pause.)

Talker: Really good.

Therapist: I'm glad, Talker. Now, you and Playful both have permission to do what you do best, enjoy communicating with your kids and your wife. The two of you can start doing this immediately, thanks to Low's willingness to give permission. (Pause) Ken, you can go ahead and allow your eyes to open now, so we can talk about the session.

This is a good place to finish the therapy session. It is a good place for multiple reasons. One reason is time. This is about as much as can be accomplished within the session, therefore it would not be appropriate to start working with 'Low' on issues that would take some time to deal with. Plus, it is good to end the session right after talking with the two positive Resources so the client is able to leave holding these states fresh in memory.

At this point the Resource that is depressed, Low, has been heard and respected and has given permission to two other Resources for them to begin engaging in life in a positive way. It is actually easier to begin working with the Depressed Resource after the client has already begun engaging in some life activities in a positive way. When you begin working directly with the depressed state you will be using a form of Retro State Negotiation, in order to find a new and positive role for the Depressed State. The Depressed State has actually become a Retro State, in that its role of shutting down all states is not one that other states appreciate, so it needs to be negotiated with in a highly respectful way to find a new role where it can contribute in a manner that will be appreciated by other states.

This technique of speaking directly with Resources that can engage positively, and getting permission from the Resource that has been shutting down the personality, makes it much easier for the client to take on positive activities. Just encouraging the client to take on positive activities is often not enough to get them to do this. The client can find this too difficult. But, most often I find clients who return after the procedures above report that there was very little effort involved in them engaging in a positive way.

If nothing else is done other than the above procedures the depressed client will improve, but there is more work to be done. The depressed Resource needs to find a more limited, or a different role, so it can engage in a positive way, even though life's circumstances have changed. In order to do this it is necessary to find the purpose of the Depressed Resource and find a way it can fulfill that purpose, given the current life circumstances.

There are two real problems in accomplishing this:

11. The first is that many clients who present with depression are already on antidepressants. It is very difficult to work with Vaded States when the client is on antidepressants, because the antidepressants work by blocking the emotions of Vaded States. It is very difficult to work with emotions when those emotions are being blocked chemically. Antidepressants do not always block the Vaded State. Sometimes I find that clients on antidepressants can have access to emotional, Vaded States, although this tends to be the exception rather than the rule. When the client is on antidepressants the work goes more slowly, more weeks are added to therapy, and often the resolution is not complete until they return after finishing with the antidepressant medication. Still, much improvement can be made even while the client is on antidepressants.

12. The second, more minor, problem in helping the Depressed Resource is that the level of energy of the client is generally very low. This is one reason I prefer to work with the depressed Resource after a couple of other Resources have already begun engaging in life in a positive way, as this tends to raise the Depressed Resource level of energy.

The Resource Vaded with Disappointment tends to see all life as being disappointing, and tends to have difficulty envisaging a life where it will have a positive role. While working with the Depressed Resource it is important to continue to appreciate the fact that it has a right to feel the way it does. This helps it see the therapist as being understanding, and on its side. When a Resource sees the therapist is being understanding, and as on its side, it becomes more cooperative.

Simply put, the role of the therapist in the second stage of working with Depression is to determine the purpose of the Resource Vaded with Disappointment, and to find a way that it can fulfill that purpose within the current life situation. The abbreviated illustration below, while spanning a number of sessions, will help illustrate this.

Therapist: Ken, how has the past week been for you?

Ken: You know, it has been a bit better. Although, I still don't feel like going to work.

Therapist: Have you been able to play with you children before dinnertime, and talk with Maggie during breakfast?

Ken: Yes, I have done those things. That is a change.

Therapist: That's really good, Ken. I'm glad that can continue. I guess I am also hearing that you have been experiencing the part of you that we named, Low. It sounds like Low is still feeling pretty bad.

RT Action 10, Retro State Negotiation

Ken: Yes, I would say that is true.

Therapist: Ken, I would like to talk to 'Low' directly right now, so just allow your eyes to close and go into that feeling that you have been experiencing through much of the week, that low feeling. (Pause) Low, tell me what you are feeling right now, sitting in the chair that you are sitting in.

Low: About the same. I don't really think I'm good for much.

Therapist: That must not feel very good, feeling like you're not good for much. Just survey your body, and tell me where you feel this feeling the most.

Low: It goes all over my whole chest and my head. It covers the whole area.

Therapist: That must feel like not much is left, like you are in a real fog. Low, think back to when you were still working at the bank, before you found out that you're going to lose your job. Low, what was your role then? How do you normally help Ken? What do you normally do for Ken, Low?

Here, I first made sure that I was speaking with the Resource that was Vaded with Disappointment prior to asking what its purpose was. I wanted to make sure that it was out and in the Conscious, so I could engage with it directly. I did this by asking how it was feeling, by locating where that feeling was in the body, and by speaking directly with it, using its name.

Low: I'm the solid type. I work hard and I expect to be rewarded for my work. I expect things to be fair.

Therapist: It sounds like you have a very important purpose. Everyone needs a part that works hard. So, your purpose is to work hard, and expect that you will be rewarded for that purpose?

Low: Yes, I think that's right.

Therapist: It seems like you did your job. You worked hard, but then you were disappointed when you were not justly rewarded the work you did. You did not deserve to be asked to leave.

Low: You've got that right.

Therapist: Low, I think Ken still needs you. He really needs a part right now that can work hard. He needs a part that can look for a job. That is hard work. He needs a part that, when he finds a job, can work hard at it. It seems like there is no guarantee that a person can keep a job. It sounds to me like, Low, you may not be the best part to deal with rejection. It does also sound to me like you are a very good part to get work done. Would that be right?

Low: Sounds right to me.

Therapist: Low, I wonder if you would be willing to help Ken by doing hard work again if I find another part that can deal with rejection. Since there is never any guarantee about a job it seems like it would be good for there to be a part there that can handle bad news if it comes. The truth is, Low, Ken really needs you. He needs you to work for him. It is not fair that you have to do two things all at once, to work and to deal with rejection. Is it okay with you if I find another part that can deal with rejection, if it comes, and then all you would need to do is what you do really well, and that is work?

Low: I certainly don't like rejection. It makes me feel that all the work I do is not appreciated.

Therapist: I can understand that, Low. You should be appreciated for the hard work you do. I want to leave you for a moment, and find two other parts, one that will appreciate the work you do and one that can be good at dealing with rejection. Thank you for talking with me, Low. [Pause] Ken, what do you feel about people who you know who work hard?

Ken: I have a lot of respect for them. I think people should work hard.

Therapist: I thought you might say that. What can I call this part of you that said that, this part that respects people who work hard?

Low: I guess you can call this part, 'Honor'.

Therapist: Honor, thank you for talking with me. Honor, I understand you appreciate hard work. You respect those people who work hard. You heard me talking with Low earlier. What do you think of Low, Honor?

Honor: I like the fact that he works hard, but I think he's a little weak.

Therapist: I can understand why you said that, Honor. But, he does work hard and he really would like respect for the work that he does. Honor, since you are a part that really respects work would you be willing to go to Low right there where he is and let him know how much you respect the work that he does? You can do this as well as everything else you do, Honor. The more you do the more powerful you become. Would you be willing to share your appreciation of work with Low for the work that he does? That would make him feel much better.

Honor: Yes, I can do that.

Therapist: That's great. Just go to Low right now there on the inside. Let him know how much you appreciate the hard work he has done, and the hard work he will do. Let him know how much you value that. This will help him feel much better. Thank you, Honor. (Pause) Now, I want to talk to a part that is very intellectual. I want to talk to the part that can do math problems or work on the taxes. This part pretty much just thinks. It does not feel much, because it is too busy thinking. It is very much a head part that just thinks. Just say 'I'm here' when you are ready to speak.

Ken: I'm here.

Therapist: Thank you for talking with me, part. What do you do for Ken?

Ken: Like you said, I do his math problems. I do his taxes. I help Ken figure things out.

Therapist: It sounds like you are an important part. Can I call you, 'Head', or what would you like to be called?

Ken: You can call me, 'Thinker'.

Therapist: Okay. Thinker, I think you have heard what's been going on here. Ken really needs a part that can intellectually consider criticism or rejection and make a decision on whether it is justified. Ken needs a part that can understand other people's decisions, and can determine whether they are making good decisions are not. It seems to me like you are a much better part to consider criticism or rejection than one of Ken's feeling parts that can feel hurt by it. Since you are such a good thinker you can just make an intellectual decision about some of the things that might be hurtful to other parts of Ken. You can protect them, and this would be a great role for you. Would you be willing to help Ken in this way?

Thinker: Yes, I can do that. It sounds like a good job for me.

Therapist: I agree, Thinker. I'm really glad you are there, and you can help Ken out a lot. (Pause) Low, I think you have been hearing what we have been doing. You have some really good parts that can help you. Honor is there with you now appreciating the work that you do, and Thinker is willing to take care of any criticism or rejection so you can concentrate on work. Work is what you do best, Low. As a matter of fact, Low, I wonder if it would be okay with you if we change your name to Worker? Since that is what you do so well, it seems like 'Worker' would be a great name for you. What do you think?

Worker: I like that name.

Therapist: That's good, 'Worker'. From now on I will call you, 'Worker'. What do you think of Honor being there giving you praise and appreciation for the work that you do?

Worker: I like that. I like him too.

Therapist: That's great. Now that all you have to worry about is doing work, and that is something you are really good at, how do you feel about working to find another job? Honor will be there with you, appreciating the work that you do, and Thinker will also be there to assess any criticism or rejection. There is often rejection when a person is looking for work, so it is really good that Thinker will be there to think about everything and assess it properly. With the help of Honor and Thinker, how do you feel about starting again what you do so well, and that is work?

Worker: I would like to try.

Therapist: I want to say thank you to all the parts, Worker, Honor, and Thinker. You are all very important and useful parts of Ken. I look forward to hearing how you help each other. Ken, you can go ahead and allow your eyes to open so we can talk about this some more.

Sessions structured in this way can help a resource Vaded with Disappointment get a better understanding about what its purpose is, and can clarify a way that it can work to fulfill that purpose in the future. As stated earlier, often these negotiations can take a number of weeks, especially if the client is taking antidepressants.

Further work was done with Ken to help ensure that Thinker would be the part that was Conscious during job hunting, so he could better deal with any rejection. We did this work using the imagery of Ken going for an interview and seeing that the job was obviously going to someone else. Ken had helpful Resources that he had not been using, and he had the useful Resource, Worker, that had been given responsibility beyond its ability to deal.

It is important, when the client returns for the next session, to ask how the client has done during the past week. Do not ask the general question, "How are you doing?" Often, when asked this question the client will think back to how life was before the last intervention. It is important to know exactly how the client has been doing since the last intervention so the therapy can be aimed at resolving any residual issues.

I find using these techniques in working with clients who present with depression facilitates change, often within a few weeks. Clients who are psychologically depressed also have a physiological component to the depression that takes some time to alter. It is positive, though, that even after the first session most clients are able to begin re-engaging in life in a positive way to a limited extent. This appears to help shift their physiology, which makes it easier to access and work with useful Resources.

Variations to treatment by Classification

Relationship blame

Relationship partner blame can come in two forms. The client can blame their ex-partner if a relationship has failed to continue, and the client can blame their current partner if they feel that person has let them down in some way.

Blaming the ex-partner

It is not unusual for clients to feel a need to blame the ex-partner when a relationship has not worked. Blame is a negative, heavy, emotion that prevents the client from moving forward and taking advantage of opportunities that present themselves. Blame holds the client in the past relationship. As long as the client blames his or her partner, extends that negative emotion to their past partner, he or she is still connected to their past partner. Their emotions and thoughts have to be focused on their partner in order to blame their partner.

It is often necessary for the client to intellectually decide that it is okay to stop blaming before they can have internal permission to do this. This does not mean they need to condone the behavior of their ex-partner. They can continue with an intellectual understanding that the ex-partners negative behavior brought an end to the relationship, but when the emotional component of blame continues to connect the client to their ex-partner a pathological element is introduced.

There is a difference between intellectually knowing something was wrong, and feeling blame. A parent can easily intellectually know that something their child does is wrong without holding on to blame toward that child. A person can intellectually know the neighbor's fence is higher than counsel regulations without holding onto an emotional blame toward the neighbor. In the same way, at the end of a relationship it is possible to intellectually understand that the other person did not do everything right, and may be did some things very wrong, but at the same time not maintain an emotional connection to that person through active blame.

Blame is a reflection of a Resource Vaded with Disappointment. The disappointment the blaming Resource feels can be pointed toward another person, or it can be pointed toward self. In order to be free from a past relationship and in order to be ready to move on in life the Vaded State that is holding blame needs to gain resolution.

When a client has decided it is time to let go of blame, the Separation Sieve (Action 14) is a useful technique to help align intent with change. A benefit of this Action is that it can be introduced as an experiment to help the client determine if he or she actually wants to stop blaming.

Blaming the current partner

Relationship blame can also destroy a relationship that the client would like to continue. If the client's partner has done something that the client continues to hold blame about, it will be difficult for either partner to experience a positive relationship.

For example, if one partner in a relationship has an affair it can be difficult for the relationship to continue. Trust is obviously something that will need to be re-established. While this must be earned by the offending partner, it is impossible to be earned while blame is still being held.

In some relationships, following an affair, one partner will hold so much blame toward the other that no positive aspects of the relationship can be enjoyed. The Resource Vaded with Disappointment can be so overwhelmingly upset at what the other partner has done that it will prevent any other Resource from enjoying the relationship. Some clients report that they catch themselves enjoying the relationship, then remember what the other partner did, and immediately stop the enjoyment.

Of course, it is legitimate for one partner to leave a relationship that has been found to be untrustworthy, but it is detrimental to both parties if blame continues to create a bad relationship when both parties would like a good one. It is possible here for both parties to have an intellectual understanding that some behavior was wrong, without maintaining the blame that comes from a Resource Vaded with Disappointment.

So how does a client learn to stop blaming? This is almost impossible to do unless the Resource Vaded with Disappointment achieves resolution. The Resource Vaded with Disappointment is upset because its reality does not match what it hoped or expected. That Resource needs to be negotiated with in order to make sure that it still has purpose, and that it has meaning within the client's current life.

The seven steps to help Resources Vaded with Disappointment are outlined at the beginning of this chapter. These steps include finding two Resources that are able to return to past activities in order to enjoy the present. Permission will have to be granted from the disappointed Vaded Resource for these two Resources to begin their positive activities.

These positive activities, in a relationship that the client will continue, might include permission to enjoy morning coffee with a partner, and permission to enjoy going to a movie or a show with a partner. If the client is blaming an ex-partner, two positive activities for the client might include enjoying surfing on the Internet, or enjoying going for walks.

Blaming Resources, like Depressed Resources, can keep the individual from engaging in life or in a relationship, so having two Resources that will cooperate in enjoying activities that the blaming Resource can give them permission to enjoy re-engages the client.

The other major step in helping a client who is stuck in blame is to work directly with the Resource that is disappointed. There will need to be a determination while talking with this Resource about what its purpose is in the family of states. Every Resource has a purpose. That is why they are here. They were created when coping skills were practiced over and over again, therefore, they have a purpose.

A good question for a Blaming Resource is, "What is your role? How do you help 'client's name'? By getting a role or a purpose for the Blaming Resource it will be easier to find something for it to do and feel positive about. It is important for the Blaming Resource to have something that it likes to do, and can do, so it can look forward in life, rather than backward. When the Resource that was Vaded by Disappointment has a positive new role it will no longer hang onto its disappointment of the past, and it will be able to focus on the future.

It is important to distinguish between a State Vaded with Disappointment and a State Vaded with Confusion, because the treatment for these states is different. A State Vaded with Disappointment feels upset and blocks the positive engagement of other states. A state Vaded with Confusion cannot internalize something that has happened and ruminates on it to the extent that it interferes with the person's life. If a state is ruminating, rather than blocking, then for a resolution refer to the next chapter. Blame is often associated with ruminating, especially self-blame.

Chapter 8
Treatment of states Vaded with Confusion

This chapter covers the types of presentations that are caused by states Vaded with Confusion and their treatment.

Resources Vaded with Confusion have experienced an initial sensitizing event that they cannot incorporate into their understanding. This Resource is left with a fundamental and profound level of confusion, and its response to this lack of ability to understand, is a profoundly uncomfortable unknowing. While Resources Vaded with Disappointment hold a distinctly negative emotion, Resources Vaded with Confusion appear to exhibit angst about what is not known. Like Resources Vaded with Disappointment, they may affect the energy of other Resources, but when they do, this is at a much lower level. They may exhibit symptoms of rumination, existential angst, complicated bereavement, or withdrawal following a breakdown of the relationship, loss of job, or other losses. Clients with these types of Resources report being unable to stop ruminating about what they do not know.

A Resource Vaded with Confusion is characterized by:

---

1. Rumination.
2. Feelings of Guilt or Shame.
3. Feelings that something was not handled properly by the client or by someone else.
4. An inability to let go of concern about another person.
5. An inability to understand another's action.

Common to Resources Vaded with Confusion is an unfinished yearning for understanding. While a resource Vaded with Disappointment suffers because reality is not what was expected, a resource Vaded with Confusion suffers because it cannot make sense of what has happened or suffers because it does not know something that it has a great need to understand. Like all Vaded States, it suffers emotionally.

Related Pathologies

Below is a list of issues that can be caused by Resources Vaded with Confusion. Where further elucidation may be beneficial items in the list will be described in more detail to explain the dynamic that is occurring within the personality.

Resources Vaded with Confusion can cause these Pathologies

- Complicated Bereavement
- Rumination (over the welfare of others, death, or an event)
- Guilt or Shame
- Existential angst
- Deep confusion over the breakdown of a relationship

Treatment Process

Table 26: RT Actions used to bring states Vaded with Confusion to Normality

Action 1: Diagnosis of Resource Pathology
Action 2: Vivify Specific   see page 88
Action 3: Bridging
Action 4: Expression
Action 5: Introject Speak
Action 6: Removal
Action 7: Relief
Action 8: Find Resource
Action 9: Changing Chairs Introject Action   see page 116
Action 10: Retro State Negotiation
Action 11: Conflicted State Negotiation
Action 12: Imagery Check   see page 131

- **Recognize a confused Resource exists:** There must be a determination that the Vaded State suffers from confusion, as characterized by it experiencing overwhelming feelings of confusion with an out of control anxiety or a lack of ability to understand something of profound significance. (Action 1 – Identify Pathology)
- **Bring the confused Resource into the Conscious:** The Resource suffering confusion should be brought into the Conscious, allowed to describe **what** it is confused about, and a name for it should be negotiated. (Action 2 – Vivify Specific)
- **Complete** Action 9: Changing Chairs Introject Action, see page 116.
- **Action 12: Imagery Check**, see page 131.

Case Example with Transcript

Leah discovered her sister had slept with her husband*

Leah was a 55-year-old client who presented with a very distraught affect. She had found, after the death of her sister, "Sophia," that Sophia had slept with her husband. She related that she had not been able to sleep properly for the three years since the discovery, and that there was never an hour in the day that she did not think about what her sister had done. She said she was tired, rundown, and did not know what to do. She said she had loved Sophia, and she thought Sophia had loved her, and she could not imagine how she could have done this.

Leah had a Resource that could not make sense of what had happened, that was overwhelmingly confused. It was keeping her from being able to have an inner peace, or even a good sleep.

Given Leah's presentation, it was clear that her Vaded Resource was often in the Conscious. It would not be difficult to speak with it. Just asking Leah to describe the upset feelings she had been experiencing was enough to bring her Resource Vaded with Confusion into the Conscious.

RT Action 2, Vivify Specific

Therapist: Leah, I get a sense you are already feeling upset, just from telling me about what happened. Tell me more about this feeling you are having right now, this feeling of confusion about what your sister did.

Leah: (Showing affect) I just don't get it. How could she do that? I really thought I could trust her more than anyone on earth.

Leah's Confused Vaded State was obviously in the Conscious. I placed an empty chair in front of her, facing her, at a conversational distance.

RT Action 9, Changing Chairs Introject Action

Therapist: Leah, I want you to imagine the presence of your sister sitting in that chair right now. Tell me when you have done this.

Leah: Yes, Okay.

Therapist: We know she is not really here so it is safe to say anything, so just imagining her presence in that chair, speak directly to her in the chair and tell her exactly how you feel about what she did.

It was important to make sure that Leah spoke directly to Sophia's Introject. For example, if Leah had said, "I want her to know that. ... ," I would have told her, "No, I want you to speak directly to Sophia, say, I want you to know that…"When a Vaded State speaks directly to an Introject, this helps hold the Vaded Resource in the Conscious, otherwise an intellectual state may come into the Conscious and think about what might have been a good thing to say. It is imperative that the Resource speak directly to the Introject.

Leah: Sophia, I can't believe what you did. How could you sleep with my husband? I trusted you above all others. I thought you would be the last person on earth to do something like that. How could you do that?

Therapist: Leah, stand up. Now, move over to the other chair. Turn around. Now, sit down. (As Leah was in the process of sitting down I called out clearly the name of her sister to engage with Leah's Introject of her sister. Sophia! Sophia, thanks for joining us. Sophia, she is really upset with you. How does that make you feel?

While the client is in the process of sitting, calling out loudly and clearly the name of the Introject you want to engage with is a good way of helping the client connect with that Introject. Immediately after calling the name, the name should be used repeatedly and a question should be asked about the feelings of that Introject. I, also, find that this is a good technique for calling out different alters in clients who suffer from DID. There appears to be something about the process of a disorienting motion that better facilitates switching.

The emotional change clients receive from this Action has more to do with what they feel while speaking as the Introject, than with what they learn from what the Introject says. When the client returns to their chair they carry back with them the feelings they experienced while sitting in the chair of the Introject.

Sophia: I just hate what I did. She was always better than me at everything. I had an opportunity to have something that she had and I took it. I know I shouldn't have and I wish I hadn't, but I did. It's just that I looked up to her so much, and I knew I wasn't as good as her, and then I had an opportunity to have something that she had. I'm so stupid. I want to be here waiting, I want to meet her when she dies, and she is not going to want to see me. I'm really sorry for what I did.

Something about Leah's belief is evident here with the statement, "I want to meet her when she dies." This comes from the client's belief and there is no reason to focus on it in therapy.

Therapist: I can hear that you're really sorry.

Sophia: I would give anything if I hadn't done it.

Therapist: It sounds like you would like to apologize to Leah. If that's true go ahead and apologize to her now. Just call her by name as you look at her chair, and apologize.

Sophia: Leah, I know you can never forgive me, but I'm really, really sorry. I don't know what came over me. Just stupidity, I guess. I want to meet you when you die, and you're not going to want to see me. I'm really sorry.

Therapist: Thank you, Sophia. Leah, stand up. Move back to the other chair, and sit down. (As Leah sat down I called out her name.) Leah, Sophia seems to be really sorry. What do you want to say to her?

Leah: I forgive you. I want you to be there for me when I die too. I know it was a mistake. I just want to say I love you, and I forgive you.

Therapist: That was really powerful. I could feel you meant that. Would you like to see if Sophia would like an internal hug?

Leah: Yes, I would.

Therapist: Just allow your eyes to close for a moment, and see if Sophia wants to share an internal hug with you. (pause) What happened?

Leah: (Leah opened her eyes) That was really something. I love her so much. And she does love me.

RT Action 12, Imagery Check

Therapist: Thank you for sharing this experience with me. I can tell that you and Sophia do care a lot about each other. Right now, Leah, I want you to do a little mental survey. Tell me how your body feels, and imagine going to bed tonight, and tell me how you feel about your ability to rest peacefully.

Leah: I feel amazing. It is really amazing. I just feel full of love right now. What was upset is now just full of love. I can't believe this feeling.

Following this interchange, Leah said she felt much better, much more at peace. She said she no longer carried negative confused feelings about her sister. Later feedback revealed she was able to sleep well again, and that only very occasionally she would think about what had happened. Her Resource that had been Vaded with Confusion no longer felt confused.

There appears to be a benefit for the client to sit in the chair of the Introject, and speak as the Introject. Once clients have experienced feelings from the perspective of the Introject, and returned to their own chair a deeper level of understanding is achieved. Upon returning to their own chair, clients carry with them the feelings they had while sitting in the chair of the Introject. I find the changes that come from this procedure go far beyond any conversation I can have with the client.

This work with a state Vaded with Confusion is a variation from Bridging and working to resolve states Vaded with Fear or Rejection. The main difference is that **Introjects** are used to bring clarity to the confused Resources. Clarity is the goal rather than empowerment.

Variations to treatment for Resources Vaded with Confusion

Complicated Bereavement

Complicated bereavement covers a wide area and is somewhat difficult to define. Grieving is a natural process that occurs after loss, and it is only considered complicated if the level of psychological distress and/or the length of the grieving process goes beyond a normal range. Grieving, of course, does not have to just be about the death of a loved one. Grieving can be in relation to loss of a relationship, a parent, a job, body function, beauty, and other things.

In order to distinguish between normal healthy grieving and complicated bereavement, I think in terms of the types of emotions that are healthy and normal in grieving, and those that are more associated with complicated grieving. A deep sense of sadness and loss, a sense of yearning for what was lost to be present, and a concern about the future without what was lost are all normal and healthy aspects of grieving. It is not pathological for a client to sense the presence of a lost love one near them. Some clients worry about themselves when they have these experiences, so part of working with grieving clients is an educational process about normal experiences.

Healthy grieving should be a bittersweet experience. It is a mix of love and sadness. Without the feeling of missing something there would be no grieving so it is obvious that something worth missing has been lost when grieving occurs. There can be a level of celebration in having had something worth missing, even at the same time that deep sadness is experienced. This sadness can be erratic, with tears coming on their own timetable, and with some clients crying without tears.

The length of time people grieve will vary greatly. It is good for the client to understand that the length of the time that is grieved does not have a direct association with the amount of care. While it is okay to indicate ballpark figures on the average length of time it takes to get through stages of grieving, it should be made clear to clients that everyone is on their own timetable. What is more important in grieving is not the length of time that it takes, but how it is experienced.

Emotions that are experienced as 'I, or someone, did something wrong' will prevent the client from moving through the grieving process. If, after the first few weeks, the client experiences guilt, blame, shame, anger, rumination, debilitating confusion, or a sense of wishing something had been said that wasn't, then there is a level of complicated bereavement. While sadness (a part of healthy grieving) is a reflection of love, these are heavy (someone did something wrong) emotions that can prevent the client from progressing through a normal grieving process.

It is not unusual for a person to have some of these negative feelings during the first days of the grieving process, but if they continue the client will become unable to allow the feelings of sadness and reorientation to progress normally. Below is some elucidation of these emotional responses.

- Guilt: Guilt is a negative emotion consisting of the feeling, "I did something wrong." It is sometimes experienced when a person feels he or she may have done something to cause a death, a loss, or clients may have feelings of guilt because they were tired of taking care of a loved one and wished them to pass quickly.

- Blame: A client can blame a drunk driver, God, or really anyone or anything for their loss. The feeling of blame keeps clients from moving forward in their feelings of sadness and their natural process of moving through grieving.

- Shame: Shame is guilt in higher intensity. It is a very negative emotion, and it stops the normal progression through the grieving experience.

- Anger: While blame has more of an intellectual component to the emotion, anger is a higher intensity feeling, directed at another person, unfairness, or even at God.

- Rumination: Rumination is the inability to keep from thinking about something, over and over again. The case of Leah is an example of a client caught in rumination.

- Debilitating confusion: Debilitating confusion is what a client experiences who cannot make sense of their loss. The loss goes so far outside their boundaries of understanding that they are stuck in confusion.
- A sense of wishing something had been said that wasn't: One of the most common types of complicated bereavement is when the person feels that something was left unsaid, or undone. A common statement is, "I did not tell her that I loved her."

While these aspects of complicated bereavement differ greatly, the therapeutic techniques for helping Resources Vaded with Confusion apply to all of them. Clients with these emotions, in relation to a loss, need clarity, need to be able to express themselves and feel understood, and need to understand the **Introjects** they hold within them.

RT Action 9: Changing Chairs Introject Action, page 116, provides a way for the sense of confusion to gain resolution. After having the client sit in the chair of the Introject, then return to their original chair, clients return with a deeper level of understanding. There seems to be something about having taken on the emotions of the Introject that the confused Resource State is able to use in processing.

Rumination (over the welfare of others, death, or an event)

Rumination is a common aspect of complicated bereavement. I have given some examples of this, including Hannah ruminating over the suicide death of her husband, the example of Leah ruminating over her sister having slept with her husband, and the example of Elizabeth ruminating over the murder of her son.

Rumination is the inability of the client to keep from thinking about something over and over again. Rumination keeps the client from being able to proceed through the normal grieving process. Clarity assists clients to stop ruminating, and they can get clarity with the use of the Changing Chairs Introject activity, page 116.

Existential angst

Occasionally a client presents with the need to understand, "Why am I here?" These clients sometimes wonder what they should be doing with their life, and sometimes they are more generally in a state of confusion about their meaning. They often appear to be doing average, or above average, in their work and in their relationships.

Sometimes this questioning follows exposure to the death of a friend, but it can also follow exposure to a number of other factors such as world poverty, religious philosophical confusion, the unfairness of the distribution of pain and suffering, or just a search for meaning.

It is probably the case that everyone experiences some of these questions at some time in life, but when they become profound enough to seek therapy a Vaded State is involved. This confused Resource in search of meaning needs some resolution, some clarity.

While the changing chairs Introject activity is useful for these clients it is necessary to make sure that the right Resource, and Introject, communicate. My process for working with people who have this existential angst about their meaning is to make sure I bring the confused Resource into the Conscious, then assist that Resource in achieving a level of meaning from one of their Resources they consider a 'higher state', and from whatever concept they hold of a higher power or God.

- I have the Confused Vaded State first express to the higher state in the opposite chair, then
- I have the client move to that chair and express back as their higher state. Then,
- I do the same process again having the Confused Vaded State express to that client's concept of a higher being, then
- I ask the client to move to the other chair and express back as the higher being in the way described in the changing chairs Introject activity.

It is not unusual for a client having existential angst to report having no belief in a God or a higher power. When that is the case I asked the client if there is anything they consider a higher force. One client described Mother Nature as being her higher force. Therefore, we used Mother Nature as the Introject for the other chair.

When the client has no concept of any higher force, I tell the client that that is fine, but that for this technique it would be helpful if he or she imagines a concept of a higher force, and describes the hypothetical imagining. I tell the client that it is not at all necessary for them to consider this real, but for the purpose of this activity for them just to describe 'if there was a higher force' how they would like to imagine it being. I ask them to give me a name for it. Then whatever name they give is used in this process.

When the client has the opportunity to sit in the chair of their Introject of a 'higher being' they are often able to become more clear about the meaning they seek. It is interesting that this clarity does not come as easily from merely questioning the client about ideals. The clarity appears to be present when they sit back in their original chair, still feeling the message they received from their Introject of a higher force.

Case Illustrations of Resources Vaded with Confusion

Hannah: Complicated Bereavement

A few years ago I had a client, Hannah, whose husband committed suicide. She did not understand why he had done this. He left no note. She felt guilty, felt that she should have known that he was feeling such psychological distress, and she was ruminating about his loss. While it had been six years since his suicide, she still did not feel an ability to move forward.

I had worked with her for a number of weeks with little success in helping her to feel resolution to her feelings of guilt and her experience of rumination. The technique that helped her is one that I would use much more quickly now. I asked her what she would like to say to her husband, if she could talk with him now. I also asked her what she would like to learn from her husband, if she could talk with him now.

Then, I placed an empty chair in front of Hannah and told her that although we know her husband is not here, just to imagine the essence of her husband in the chair right now. I told her to let me know when she felt that. She did.

I then told her to just go ahead and tell her husband, sitting in the chair, exactly what she would like him to know. I instructed her to speak to him directly. In other words, I did not want her to say, "I want him to know that...." I wanted her to say, "I want you to know that...." When clients are speaking to **Introjects**, it is very important that they speak directly to the Introject.

Hannah became very emotional and told him the things that she had already told me she would want him to know. I encouraged her to say everything that she wanted to say (by looking at the notes I had taken). I encouraged her to ask him questions that she would like answers to.

Then, I asked her to stand and move over to the other chair, and as she was in the process of sitting down, I called her husband by name, "Ted, thank you for talking with me. It's clear to me, Ted, that Hanna loves you a lot and that she is very confused. How does that make you feel, Ted?"

By calling Ted's name while Hannah was sitting down and by immediately asking him direct questions about his feelings, Hannah was better able to speak from the Introject of her husband. This is most helpful to assist the client in gaining an experience of feeling the emotions they attribute to the Introject, and it often results in 'Aha' experiences for the client.

Ted said that he did not want Hannah to be upset. He said he wished he had written a note to explain things, and that it was selfish for him not to do that. He said that his killing himself had nothing to do with her, that he was upset that he was never able to hold a job and do the things that normal people are able to do.

I asked him what he wanted Hannah to know, and he said he wanted her to know that he was sorry, that he never meant to hurt her, and that she was a great wife to him. He said he wanted her to be happy, and he said he wanted her to be able to move on. He said he loved her.

I thanked Ted for talking with me and said, "Hannah, I want you to stand up now, stand up, and move back over to the other chair and sit down." As Hannah was sitting down I called her by name saying, "Hannah, Ted really had a lot of things to say. He said he loves you, that he is sorry, and that you had nothing to do with his decision to kill himself. He said you were a good wife. How does that make you feel?"

Hannah said she felt a lot more relieved. I asked her if there is anything else that she wanted to say to Ted. She wanted to tell him again that she loved him and that she wished he had not killed himself. I allowed her to do this, and since she had no more questions for Ted, and since she was not indicating any further need to gain more information from him, I did not ask her to move back to the other chair.

When Hannah came in for the next session, she said that the week that she had just experienced was unlike any that she had had since Ted had committed suicide. She said she still missed him, and she felt a loss about what he had done, but she said that when she was Ted she was able to understand his feelings. She said that she now knows that he loves her and that his death had nothing to do with anything that she had done. She said that her week had been very peaceful.

It is interesting that clients who participate in these changing chairs Introject activities report gaining an emotional understanding that they previously did not have. I have experimented with hundreds of changing chair Introject activities and I have found the important components to be that the individual is able to speak clearly and directly to the Introject, then when moved to the chair of the Introject speak clearly and directly back (directly to the client) as the Introject. After this occurs, the client feels a guttural understanding that was previously missing.

One would think that the client would merely feel like they were role-playing and not walk away with a cathartic experience, but when these changing chair Introject activities are exercised properly, the experience for the client is often cathartic and lasting.

When clients experience guilt, blame, shame, anger, rumination, debilitating confusion, or a sense of wishing something had been said that wasn't, it is possible for them to talk to the associated Introject, express themselves fully, then hear directly back from that Introject to gain clarity, rather than maintaining confusion.

When the client is angry at God, I invite God into the other chair. I thank God for his or her presence, and after the client has expressed completely to God I ask the client to stand up and move to the other chair. As the client is in the process of sitting down, I say, "God, she really has a lot of feelings that she expressed to you. How does that make you feel, God?" As you can imagine, given the concept most clients have of a god, the replies from God are loving and understanding. I ask God what gift he or she would like to give the client, and then say to just go ahead and do it now.

So far, following this experience, I have not had a client who continues with an anger at God. Obviously, the client who is angry at God believes in God.

Jacob needed to find meaning in his life

Jacob was a client who reported being bothered by any sense of meaning in his life. He said he did not know why he was here, and he said he did not know how to focus his life.

I asked him to describe for me the feelings of frustration experienced in relation to this. This was to help him bring this confused, Vaded State, into the Conscious.

He said he just really wanted to know what life is about. He said that his life was not difficult, but that it had no real meaning. He said he often thought, "Why am I here?"

I asked him what I could call this part of him that wondered, "Why am I here?" He said I could call it, "Drifting."

I asked him to close his eyes and tell me where he experienced this drifting feeling in his body. He said it was above the stomach and below the chest area, and with further questioning he said that it was about the size of a tennis ball.

I said, "Thank you for talking with me, Drifting. I will want to talk to you again, but right now I want to talk to another part, a part that has always been there, a part that if you really want to know what is right to do in a given situation and you want to think in a non-selfish way, what should I really do, the part that is there to answer that question. I said I want to talk to the higher part, that noble part, that selfless part, and for that part just to say, I'm here, when it's ready to speak."

That Resource State of Jacob said, "I'm here." I said to just open your eyes enough to move over to the other chair so you will more easily be able to talk back to Drifting. Jacob changed chairs. Then, I said to that part to go ahead and allow the eyes to close again.

I said, "Thank you for being here. What can I call you? What can I call this part that feels non-selfish and knowing? What name or term fits you? The answer I received was, "Center."

I said, "Center, did you hear what Drifting was just saying? Did you hear how confused Drifting is?"

The response I got was, "Yes, I heard." I questioned if Center felt the same way as Drifting did about this, and I was told that, "No, I don't feel that way at all." Center said that he felt quite peaceful, and that everything was unfolding as it should.

I asked Center if he knew what Drifting needed to feel more peaceful, and I was told that he needed time to learn what was important in life. I said that sounded very wise, and I asked Center, "What is important in life?"

Center said that it was important to learn to accept everyone, so I asked Center if he would be willing to communicate directly with Drifting and share that information with him. Center said that he would do that.

I said thank you to Center, and asked my client to open his eyes and return to his original chair. Then, I asked Jacob if he believed in any kind of higher power. He said he did not. He said that he believed that we evolve, then we die, and that is it.

I said that that was fine, and that I had no need for him to believe in any higher power, but that if he were to imagine a higher power, for him to describe to me the nature of that power. He said that it would be loving, understanding and accepting, watchful and not interfering.

I said, "Right now, just imagine that imaginary loving, understanding, accepting, watchful and not interfering being to be sitting in the other chair. Then I said, go ahead and tell him or her exactly what you would like to say, and ask him or her any question you would like to ask.

Jacob said some interesting things to his imaginary power about something that did not make sense to him, and he asked, "What's it all about?"

I then asked Jacob to stand up and move to the chair, and as he sat down I said, "Power, Jacob appears to be a little confused and he would like some answers. How does that make you feel?" Interestingly, Jacob's imaginary power said that he was sad that Jacob was unhappy, and that he loved him.

I asked Jacob's imaginary power what gift it would like to give Jacob, and he said," Peace and patience." I told him just to go ahead and use his power right now to make sure the that gift was transmitted to Jacob. I then said, thank you, and I said to stand up and move over to the other chair. As Jacob sat down, I said, "Drifting, it is good to speak with you again. Drifting, I have just spoken with Center, and with your imaginary power. Did you hear what they had to say?

Drifting said that he did. I asked him to focus on the area at the top of his stomach and lower chest and tell me how that area felt. He said it felt better.

I ask him if he still wanted to be called Drifting, or if he would prefer another name. He said he still liked the name Drifting.

He said the name made him feel like he was still learning.

I told him just to go ahead and allow his eyes to open so we could debrief.

Jacob said he did not feel he got any answers, but he said he did feel more peaceful. He said his body felt much more relaxed. In a follow-up Jacob said he was still curious about the meaning of life, but that it was a more intellectual curiosity and that it was something that did not cause him concern. He said that it was somewhat hard to relate to the concern that he had felt about it previously.

Chapter 9
Treatment of Retro Original States

This chapter covers the types of presentations that are caused by Retro Original States and their treatment.

The Retro State is a part of the personality that conducts behavior that other parts of the personality dislike. By definition, a Retro State is in conflict with other states, because other states do not like its behavior, but the Retro State is willing to sacrifice being liked because it believes its behavior is necessary.

A Retro Original State is characterized by:

1. Statements by a personality Resource State indicating a disapproval of this state's behavior.
2. An indication that during this behavior the client is dismissive of attempts to cease the behavior, even though after the behavior the client is regretful.
3. An indication that this behavior has been evident since childhood.
4. No indication that this behavior relates to an Addiction.

Related Pathologies

These states all share in common that they were vaded in childhood, when the personality was forming. The client will have conducted these behaviors for as long as he or she can remember. Often others find the behavior of a Retro Original State more problematic then does the client. Some clients will only decide to change these behaviors when they see that they are so disliked by others that their ability to have good relationships is threatened.

Retro Original States can cause these Pathologies

- Anti-Social Behavior
- Withdrawal
- Pouting
- Rage
- Personality Disorders
- Passive Aggressive Behavior

Treatment Process

The best way to begin work with a Retro State is to praise it and show gratitude for its efforts and sacrifice. This approach can result in a willingness to take on a different, more preferred, type of behavior that the other parts of the personality will appreciate. A Retro State may be praised without praising its past behavior.

Table 27: RT Actions used to bring Retro Original States to Normality

---

Action 1: Diagnosis of Resource Pathology
Action 2: Vivify Specific   see page 88
Action 3: Bridging
Action 4: Expression
Action 5: Introject Speak
Action 6: Removal
Action 7: Relief
Action 8: Find Resource   see page 113
Action 9: Changing Chairs Introject Action
Action 10: Retro State Negotiation   see page 123
Action 11: Conflicted State Negotiation
Action 12: Imagery Check   see page 131

Case Illustration of a Retro Original State

Case Example with Transcript

Grant could not control his RAGE*

I had a client, Grant, who could not control his behavior when he felt that his manhood was compromised in social settings. He reported that when he was with friends at a pub, if someone insulted him, a member of his family, or someone he cared about, he could not control his behavior. He would physically attack the person and sometimes beat that person unconscious. Grant would later feel remorseful, and also fear he might kill someone, or at minimum wind up in jail for assault.

In this example, Grant had a Retro State that was coming into the Conscious and fighting. It was a Retro State because other states did not like its behavior.

Grant reported that when he entered his rage state he was totally out of control. He even said he would often not remember everything he did while in this state. This was scary for him and he wanted to regain control.

I asked him to describe in detail a time this had happened. He explained that he had been at the pub and his sister came in wearing less than he felt she should be wearing in a public place. This made him feel nervous and on edge, and he felt it was his responsibility to defend his sister and her honor. When he saw a man he described as 'drunken' coming close to her and making disrespectful remarks, Grant said he got out of his chair and flung it behind him, then he came up to the drunken man and told him he would take back what he had said, if he knew what was good for him. The man, who Grant described as being quite a lot bigger than he was, had said, "Sit down, boy."

Grant reported feeling a surge of adrenalin, then the next thing he could remember was that his friends were pulling him off the drunken man. The man was unconscious. At this point, Grant was sitting on top of him on the floor of the pub repeatedly hitting him. He said that he might have killed him if his friends had not pulled him off.

RT Action 2, Vivify Specific

Therapist: Grant, I want you to do something to help us understand this better. Just allow your eyes to close right now. That's right. Now, return to the point where you flung your chair behind you, and approached the man. What is the noise like in the pub, and exactly what are you feeling as you approach him?

Grant: It is a loud pub. There is a part of me that doesn't really want to go over there, but he has insulted my sister and it is my duty. I am pretty upset, but he still has a chance to get out of this, if he apologises.

Therapist: So you are angry walking across the loud pub, but you still have some control.

Grant: That's right. I don't really care what he says. It is OK with me if he apologises and it is OK if I beat the hell out of him. I guess I'm pretty full of adrenalin.

Therapist: Sounds like it. But, he doesn't apologise. What is it he says?

Grant: Sit down, boy.

Therapist: I can see you are really close to rage now. What are you feeling?

Grant: This is where I click off and do what has to be done.

Therapist: It sounds like there is a really strong and powerful part of you here that is able to 'Do what has to be done. ' What can I call you now as you are feeling this strength?

It is very important, no matter what the behavior of the Retro State, to speak to it in a positive way. Here, I bragged about its strength. This does not mean I approved of its behavior, but saying something positive about it will help the Retro State feel understood and want to be cooperative.

Grant: 'Rage'.

Therapist: I just want to speak directly with you, 'Rage'. Rage, you are a very strong part, aren't you.

Rage: I am really strong.

Therapist: I understand that. Rage, you sound like a good Resource to have. It would be good if everyone had a really strong Resource like you. At the right time you can be very protecting. Rage, you work really hard and it would be good if the other parts of Grant appreciated you. There are parts of Grant that don't appreciate some of the things you do. I bet if you were to only come out when Grant is physically in danger, and during other times if you were to allow Grant's other parts to handle situations, then I bet all the parts would appreciate you and always pat you on the back for being there.

When Rage is the issue, normally this approach works very quickly. The Rage part can be there with a role to protect the person only when the body is physically in danger (**for most people, never**) and an assertive part can take care of other situations. Grant did not respond in the way most clients do. Another Resource State that did not agree with this arrangement spoke up.

Grant: But, I'm supposed to defend the honor of my sister, and my own.

Therapist: I think I just heard from a different part. You are not the Rage part, are you?

Grant: No, I guess not.

Therapist: What can I call this part that cares about honor?

Grant: 'Honor', I guess.

Therapist: 'Honor', thanks for speaking up. Tell me what you mean when you say that you are supposed to defend the honor of your sister. Does that mean you feel you are supposed to fight?

Honor: Yes, I am supposed to fight.

I told him I understood that he thought at that time it was a good idea to defend her honor using violence, and I asked him how he feels about that now. He said he still felt that way. He said the guy deserved a lesson. The conversation revealed that he just wanted to 'make the guy hurt', but he did not want to lose control, and possibly kill him. I remember thinking at the time, "My work is cut out for me here."

A rage state can be out of control when it is in the Conscious, but there is always a decision to bring this state into the Conscious. A person may go into rage at home, but not at work. A person may go into rage against one kind of person, but not against another kind of person. There is always a point internally where the rage state is called into the Conscious. I could see that he was actually quite proud of his rage state. He said it did not make any difference how big the other person was. He said that when he lost control he could take on anyone. He said he always won.

I found that from a young age Grant had been taught by his father that, "You don't take crap off anyone." He had been taught that it was his responsibility to fight. In order to be able to fight he had developed Rage. Rage was useful to him, because it allowed him to fulfill what he saw as his responsibilities. It became a Retro State when other parts of Grant became frightened of what it did.

Grant had come to therapy for help. He had conflict between his Rage part and other parts, and the only way he could gain peace was to find a way that all his Resource States could be at peace with each other.

Grant needed to be educated on assertiveness. Although he was positively gregarious and a pleasure to work with, he did not appear to have a concept of being assertive without anger or violence. He needed this so his behavior could be appreciated by other states. Over a few sessions we talked about the difference between assertive behavior and violent behavior, and he was able to build an image of how he could defend his honor, and that of his sister's and friends' without resorting to violent behavior.

I told him that it was great that he had a rage state that could protect him if he were ever physically in danger. I told him that if he were attacked by wild dogs, or by a group of thugs down an alleyway it would be great to have that rage state that he could use to protect himself, but at other times it was much more mature and wise to use an assertive state in order to take care of most situations in a nonviolent way. I wanted him to understand the concept of assertiveness, and to have a resource that could be assertive so he would be able to use that resource at the appropriate time.

This work needed to be done because one Resource can call out another Resource when it feels it is needed. As long as Grant's Resource, Honor, felt that it was appropriate for Grant to fight it would call out Rage. 'Honor' needed education so it would be happy to call out an assertive part of Grant to take care of most situations. In order for this to happen Grant needed to have an Assertive Resource State.

RT Action 8, Find Resource

Therapist: Grant, when in the past have you been assertive? When have you been able to be firm without being angry?

Grant: I don't think I've ever done that. If someone doesn't listen to me, I get a bit angry, then they listen.

Therapist: And, from our conversations I now understand you would like to handle things differently. Is there a time in the past, when talking with a child, when talking with a family member, or when talking with someone at work, you can remember being firm without being angry?

Grant: Not really. I'm not very good at that sort of thing.

Therapist: Tell me what it would be like if you were good at it. If you were good at being assertive, at expressing yourself firmly without anger, tell me what that would be like.

Grant: I would just tell the person what I have to say. I would be very clear, but I would not be angry.

Therapist: What can I call this strong part of you that just said that? The part of you that just said that really seems to have an understanding of assertiveness.

Grant: I don't know. 'Strong', I guess.

RT Action 10, Retro State Negotiation

Therapist: That's a good name. I just want to talk with you, 'Strong', right now. You seem to have a good understanding of assertiveness, Strong. I realize you may not have done this behavior before, but you really do have a good understanding and it seems to me like you would be an excellent part of Grant to be assertive for him. You have such a good handle on assertiveness you could take on this role and really help Grant out. In the future, Strong, would you be willing to be Grant's assertive part? Would you be willing to help Grant out by saying things firmly and clearly, when Grant really needs you? This would be a big help to Grant. Would you be willing to help him out in this way, Strong?

Strong: Yes, I could do that.

When Resource States are offered a role that they feel they can do, especially a role that is presented as important, they normally jump at the opportunity. Resource States like to be needed and they like to do things that are helpful for the person. If they are offered a role they do not feel they can do, then they will either not do it, or they will not continue to do it. Therefore, by asking Grant what it would be like to be assertive I was able to engage with a part that could understand that behavior, a strong part that would be able to take that behavior on.

Therapist: That's good. The more practice you get at being assertive, Strong, the better you will get at it. Grant, I want to speak directly with that part of you that decided to come to therapy, that part that was upset with the rage behavior. Part, now that Rage is only going to come out when there is a real physical danger, it is good that he is there, isn't it? He can protect if he is ever needed, but Strong will take care of every other challenging situation. That is OK with you isn't it?

Grant: Yes, that sounds good to me.

Therapist: Did you hear that, Rage? You are appreciated, and the parts are now glad you are there. They are there to pat you on the back for being there. Thank you for being there, in case the body is in any real danger. How does that feel to be appreciated?

Rage: Good. Did not really think that would happen.

This is confirming to the Rage part. Parts like to feel they are liked by other parts. Sometimes Resource States are not willing to change until they learn how they will be liked by other parts, and they need to hear that directly from the other parts. After another Resource part has held the Conscious (and confirmed, 'I like you now in your new role'), the previously Retro part can easily remember the feeling of being appreciated when it regains the Conscious. This feeling of being liked is compelling to it. Parts like to be liked.

RT Action 12, Imagery Check

Therapist: Let's just practice for a bit what we have learned. Grant, allow your eyes to close, and imagine being in the pub where the drunken man made an inappropriate remark to your sister. You know you have Rage there if he is needed, if you or your sister are really physically in danger, but you also now have Strong. Strong can say things clearly, and appropriately. The drunken man has just made a stupid comment about your sister. How are you feeling, and what do you want to do?

Grant: He's an idiot. I can see that. It's really sort of sad. I just want to say, 'Hey Mate …', No actually I don't want to do anything. As long as nothing else happens, I just want to let him walk on by.

Therapist: That sounds really wise. Honor, you now have two resources and more wisdom about which one you want to use. You know you have Rage if there is ever a really dangerous situation, but you also have Strong to handle other situations. How do you feel about that, Honor?

Honor: Good. That makes sense to me.

Therapist: And, Strong, are you happy to be there when needed?

Strong: Yes, I'm here.

Therapist: Good. Grant, survey your feelings and tell me how you feel now. There were parts of you that were upset about times that Rage used to be out, and there was confusion about when it was appropriate for Rage to be out. Rage is a great part of you, but you now know you have Strong to handle most situations. How does all that feel to all parts of you, Grant?

Grant: It feels really good.

Therapist: Very Good. You can just go ahead and allow your eyes to open.

The key to this intervention is for the Resource States that have been directly involved in the behavior to be directly involved in the resolution. If I had only worked with the part of Grant that brought him into therapy, the part that was unhappy with what he had done, it would've been easy to get an agreement from that part in terms of Grant's behavior. But, Grant's behavior would probably not have changed.

A permanent, and a more comfortable resolution is obtained by making sure that all Resource States involved in the problem are also involved in the resolution. All Resource States need to feel appreciated, and they need to feel that they have a positive role. Therefore, it is important to find a positive role for Retro Original States so they can move to a state of normality.

Chapter 10
Treatment of Retro Avoiding States

This chapter covers the types of presentations that are caused by Retro Avoiding States and their treatment.

While a Vaded State holds unwanted feelings, Retro States conduct unwanted behaviors. When a Vaded State is Conscious the person feels fragile and not in control. When a Retro State is Conscious the person feels, "This is what I do. Don't bother me."

A Retro Avoiding State is characterized by:

---

1. Statements by a personality Resource State indicating a disapproval of this state's behavior.
2. An indication that during this behavior the client is dismissive of attempts to cease the behavior, even though after the behavior the client is regretful.
3. No indication that this behavior has been evident since childhood.
4. An indication that without this behavior anxiety is consistently experienced (usually with a feeling of fear or low self-esteem).
5. An indication that sincere efforts to cease this behavior are met with frustration and failure.
6. An indication that this behavior relates to an addiction, OCD, or Self-Harm.

Related Pathologies

These states all have in common (with the exception of drug behavior) an experience of feeling 'focused or zoned out'. The person experiencing OCD behavior will be highly focused, and even the person who has an eating disorder will be highly focused during the unwanted behavior. These states know they are not liked by other states, but they feel their behavior is important.

The Retro State that gambles knows other states detest its behavior, but when a Vaded Avoided State begins to surface with its negative feelings and a sense of not being able to cope, it is the Retro State that steps up to the plate to save the psyche with gambling behavior. The personality is more at ease gambling than experiencing the negative feelings of the Vaded State. Later the Retro State may promise not to gamble again, but when the psyche needs saving it will gamble, until this dynamic is broken.

Retro Avoiding States can cause Pathologies

• Addictions	• Anger or Rage as a means to act out
• OCD	• Eating Disorders
• Self-harming behavior	• Work/relationship avoidance
• Obsessive behavior (shopping, eating, work)	• Shopping Addiction
	• 'Perfectionistic' behavior
• Drug Taking	• Self-Harming behavior

Treatment Process

As with all Retro States it is important to thank them for their behavior. They feel what they do is important and feel that their sacrifice is not understood or appreciated. When they are thanked and appreciated they feel much better and become ready to hear what the therapist has to say. They will then be more ready to compromise and take on new behavior that is acceptable to the client.

Table 28: RT Actions used to bring Retro Avoiding States to Normality

Action 1: Diagnosis of Resource Pathology	
Action 2: Vivify Specific	see page 88
Action 3: Bridging	see page 94
Action 4: Expression	see page 101
Action 5: Introject Speak	see page 104
Action 6: Removal	see page 106
Action 7: Relief	see page 108
Action 8: Find Resource	
Action 9: Changing Chairs Introject Action	
Action 10: Retro State Negotiation	see page 123
Action 11: Conflicted State Negotiation	
Action 12: Imagery Check	see page 131

Case Illustration of a Retro Avoiding Resource

Case Example with Transcript

Meagan could not stop buying clothes*

Meagan was a 28-year-old client who presented with the problem that she obsessively bought clothes. Her closet and drawers were full of clothes that she had not even worn, and she could not afford to do many of the things she really wanted to because of the amount of money she was spending on clothes. It seemed to her that if she had money, it would just go to clothes that she did not need.

This is an example of a helping Resource, A Retro Avoiding State helping in a way that is problematic to the client. Her clothes buying state was helping by preventing her from feeling the hurtful feelings of a Vaded State. The first step in therapy to stop the unwanted behavior of a Retro Avoiding State is to resolve the Vaded State so the bad feelings do not surface.

The painful feeling of the Vaded State coming to the Conscious, in Meagan's case, was avoided when her clothes buying Retro Avoiding Resource took over the Conscious. This can be seen as a form of addiction. Psychological addictions are caused by the need to escape from the uncomfortable feelings of Vaded States. In order to assist Meagan with her problem it was necessary to locate a time when the Vaded State would come to the Conscious. I asked Meagan to tell me when the last time was that she felt compelled to buy clothes.

Therapist: "Meagan, I want you to recall the last time you went clothes shopping when you did not really want to."

Meagan: "It was actually last Saturday."

RT Action 2, Vivify Specific

Therapist: "Please describe that day to me, starting at a point just before you decided to go shopping. What, exactly, were you doing?"

Meagan: "I got out of bed and I can remember feeling good that I would not have to go to work. I fixed my breakfast, and thought about what I might do during the day. I decided that I would clean the house and then possibly call my sister to see if she wanted to do something together. Then, I started cleaning my house, and sometime while I was cleaning it I felt compelled to stop cleaning and go shopping."

The conversation is now directed to present tense to help with the Vivify Specific Process.

Therapist: Ok, I understand, you are cleaning the house. Allow your eyes to close. Tell me more about what you are feeling and thinking as you are cleaning, including exactly where and how you are cleaning, what is the lighting like, and what are you physically doing to clean?

Meagan: I'm attempting to get a stubborn spot off my couch. I remember now, I was thinking how my sister had a much nicer couch than mine. I don't really want her to see this spot. It looks awful.

Therapist: What is happening now?

Meagan: I just have to get out of the house. I am going shopping.

Therapist: Before you go, right now tell me what that spot looks like. What are you doing trying to remove it?

When responding to this question she began to show emotional distress. Her voice changed to sound more like that of a little girl, and a tear came to her eye. This was evidence that the Vaded Avoided State had come into the Conscious.

Meagan: It looks so bad. No matter what I do it just looks worse.

RT Action 3, Bridging

Therapist: Tell me exactly where you are feeling this upset feeling in your body right now.

Meagan: I am feeling it around my middle, between my chest and tummy

Therapist: What is the size of the area it covers right there between your chest and tummy?

Meagan: (Gesturing to the area with her hand) It's all over here.

Therapist: Let's just explore that area. Are the edges of that area distinct and clear or do they muffle out?

Meagan: They're not clear.

Therapist: On the inside of that area, is there a tint? Is it more light, or more dark?

Meagan: It's sort of grey.

Therapist: And does it have a color, or is it just grey?

Meagan: No. It's just grey.

Therapist: Is there the same amount of greyness all the way across that area, or is it more grey in the middle?

Meagan: It's more grey in the middle.

Therapist: Is that grey stuff more thick, or thin. Would it be hard or easy to move around in it?

Meagan: It is more thick.

Therapist: I see. And right now if you are sitting on the edge dangling your feet down inside that thick grey stuff, what do they feel like?

Meagan: It is hard to move them.

Therapist: Notice what they look like and tell me.

Meagan: They look small.

Therapist: Watching them dangle there looking small, how old would those feet be?

Meagan: They look like about six-year-old feet.

Therapist: I see. Just let those feet be yours right now and let that six-year-old body be you, and you are having these same feelings as a six-year-old. Being six right now with these feelings, are you more inside a building or outside a building?

Meagan: I am feeling more like I am inside a building.

Therapist: Does it feel like you are alone or with someone else?

Meagan: Like I am with someone else.

Therapist: Who are you with?

Meagan: My father.

Therapist: Tell me what is happening right here, being six, with your father.

Meagan: He does not have time for me. (Meagan started to cry)

Context

When doing this kind of work, it is not necessary for clients to give any real detail in what experience they were having. It is only necessary for them to give enough detail so that they can become empowered and feel supported within the experience. In Meagan's case there was no abuse, verbal, physical, or sexual, but when there is, there is no necessity for the client to describe anything in detail.

There is only a need for clients to be able to fully express themselves, decide whether or not they want the other person in their space, and then for the Vaded State to get support from a helping Resource. For example, if the client bridges to an original sensitizing event and it becomes evident from his or her body language or voice tone that some kind of abuse is occurring in the ISE, there is no need for the therapist to inquire at all about what is occurring. It is appropriate to make a statement such as, "We know this is not really happening right now, so we have the power to say and do anything we want. Right now let's just shrink him down to 1 inch tall, with a squeaky little voice. Please don't step on him, because I want you to be able to tell him exactly what you want to say."

The necessary component of the resolution is the empowerment of the Vaded State so that it can be left feeling safe supported and cared for. Therefore, there is no value in going into the detail of what actually occurred, but there is value in helping the Vaded State realize that what happened in the past is not happening now, and that now it has the power, it can speak and say anything it wants, it can decide to clear the space from what was upsetting previously, and it can gain safety support and care.

A therapist should not revisit a traumatic experience and then leave the client in that experience. That would be re-traumatizing. For example, after bridging to a traumatic experience, if the client were to show emotion or abreact, it would not be good to try to calm the client down by having them think of something pleasant. This would have just brought up a traumatic experience without bringing a resolution to it. But, when a client is bridged to a traumatic event, if the Vaded State gains a sense of safety and resolution, then the client is not re-traumatized, the client is de-traumatized.

Meagan's father was not good at showing love

Therapist: I can see you are upset. Can I call you 'Upset' right now?

Meagan: (Nods tearfully)

Therapist: 'Upset', thank you for talking with me. I really appreciate it. I can see that you're not happy right now. What do you need?

Upset: (Sobbing) I brought my dad my grapes and he told me to go away and stop bothering him. I really wanted the grapes myself but I thought it would make my dad happy if I gave them to him. I really love him but I don't think he feels the same way about me.

RT Action 4, Expression

Therapist: I know you are really upset right now, Upset, but we know he is not really here right now, so it is safe to tell him exactly how you feel. You can tell your dad exactly how you feel about bringing him those grapes. Tell him how you feel about what he said to you. Tell him out loud so I can hear you.

Upset: I really wanted those grapes, and you didn't even care.

Therapist: Go ahead and tell him that he should have treated you nicer.

Upset: You should treat me nicer.

RT Action 5, Introject Speak

Therapist: I want to speak directly with your dad, and I want you to be like a great actress who is able to really be him right there where he is. Dad, thank you for talking with me. Your daughter has just offered you her grapes and you just asked her to leave. What are you feeling right now, Dad?

Meagan's Introject of Dad: I am very busy. I am trying to get some work done, and she is just far too demanding. She is always wanting something.

Therapist: Do you love your daughter, Dad?

Meagan's Introject of Dad: Of course I do! I work all the time for my family, and I never get the appreciation that I really deserve.

Therapist: Dad, Meagan doesn't really understand that you love her. Would you like to tell her?

Meagan's Introject of Dad: She knows it already.

Therapist: Thank you for talking with me and being honest. I want to speak to Upset again. Upset, you mentioned earlier that you love your dad. Is that right?

Upset: Yes, I love my dad.

Therapist: Just go ahead and tell him that right now, out loud so I can hear you.

Upset: Daddy, I love you.

RT Action 6, Removal

Therapist: Upset, I can see that you're really good at loving. You are actually much better at it than your dad is. He seems very busy, but when I heard you tell him that you love him you did that much better than he was able to do it. I'm impressed at how good you are at loving, and I'm sorry that you dad isn't as good. I hope that sometime in the future he learns to be better, but right now I don't think he's able to give you what you really need and deserve. Every little girl deserves to get unconditional love no matter what. When she's good, and even when she makes mistakes, every little girl deserves to get unconditional love and I want to make sure you get what every girl deserves. In the meantime, do you want your dad in this space right now or do you want this space to be clear?

This is another example of allowing the Vaded State to express itself, telling dad exactly what she needed, and for that state to have the opportunity to decide whether or not she wanted the introjected dad to be in her inner space. The answer to this question does not affect other states and their relationship to the father. It does allow the Vaded State empowerment to make that decision.

There was an important clarification here made to the client about what had happened. The Vaded State had felt unlovable, and it has been shown that this upset part is very good at loving. It was dad at that time who was not as good at showing love.

Upset: He can stay in my space.

Therapist: That is fine.

It does not matter how the Removal question is answered (go or stay), what matters is that the Resource State has the empowerment of being able to make the choice.

RT Action 7, Relief

Therapist: I want to speak with a mature part of Meagan now. Meagan, if you saw a six-year-old girl upset and feeling like she may not be loved, someone you know and care about, what would you do?

Client: I would put my arm around her.

Therapist: What can I call you, the part that would put your arm around her?

Client: Carer.

Therapist: Thank you Carer. Go to Upset right now and put your arm around her and let her know that she will never, ever be alone again.

You can do this and everything else you do, Carer, the more you do the more powerful you become.

Therapist: Upset, just allow yourself to feel that love flowing in, into every cell and fibre, and to know that Carer will always be there for you, right there on the inside. (Short pause) Upset, how are you feeling now?

Upset: I'm feeling much better.

Therapist: That sounds good. I can see you are feeling better. It must feel very nice to have Carer there with you. It seems like Upset is not the best name for you now, because that is not how you are feeling. What would you like to be called now?

Upset: Happy.

Therapist: That is a wonderful name. From now on I will call you Happy. Is that okay with you?

Happy: Yes.

At this stage of the session the state that had been vaded was resolved. The Retro Avoiding state would no longer need to save the personality from this Vaded State. Still, one more step was needed, otherwise this helpful Retro Avoiding State might offer similar services sometime in the future if another Vaded State were to begin coming into the Conscious with anxiety. This often happens.

A person who has had a problem with gambling or even with smoking may be able to stop, but if the Retro Avoiding State does not gain a new way to help the person cope in the future, the unwanted behavior may return when the person experiences heightened anxiety at a later time.

RT Action 10, Retro State Negotiation

Therapist: Thank you, Happy. Now, Meagan, I want you to think again about last Saturday. You are shopping for clothes, and you are seeing things you might want to buy. Describe where you are.

Meagan: Well, I'm in one of my favourite shops.

Therapist: How are you feeling?

Meagan: I really like being here.

Therapist: I understand this is a shopping part of you, and I understand this part has in the past helped distract attention away from the part that is now Happy, when that part felt upset. Is it okay if I call you, Helper?

Meagan: Yes, you can do that.

Therapist: 'Helper', thank you for helping in the past. Are you aware that in the past, sometimes when you were helping, there were other parts that were upset with what you did? There are other parts that felt you spend too much money.

Helper: Yes, I guess so.

Therapist: I think it is great that you have been available to help Meagan. You may be needed in the future to help again. You work hard and I think it is appropriate that the other parts of Meagan appreciate you. In the future, if Meagan needs your help again, it would be good if the other parts could appreciate you, rather than wish you did not do what you do.

Helper: I don't think they will ever appreciate me.

Therapist: We can see about that. Helper, other than shopping, do you like to go out for a cup of coffee and read?

Helper: Yes, I do like that.

Therapist: Meagan, I have a question for the part of you that came in the therapy feeling that too much money was being spent on clothes. Your bank account was suffering. What can I call this part of you that came in the therapy for change?

Meagan: 'Concerned'.

Therapist: 'Concerned', I think Helper is a very good part, a part that has helped in the past, and a part that may need to help in the future. Concerned, if in the future Helper is needed it would be good if she helped by going out and having a cup of coffee while reading a newspaper or book, wouldn't it? It would be okay with you if she helped in that way, wouldn't it?

Concerned: Yes, that would be okay.

Therapist: Concerned, just say out loud to Helper that you would appreciate it if she is needed in the future, if she were to help by getting a cup of coffee and reading. Say it directly to Helper, so I can hear it too.

Concerned: Helper, in the future if you need to help I would like it if you get a cup of coffee and read.

Therapist: Concerned, tell Helper that you will like her if she will do this.

Concerned: Helper, I will like you if you help me in this way, rather than shopping.

Therapist: Thank you, Concerned. Helper, did you hear what concerned said? She said that she would appreciate you if in the future you help by getting a coffee and reading. She will like you, if you do this. Helper, you can be liked by Concerned and all the other parts, and you can still help. Does this sound like something you would like to do, Helper?

Helper: Yes, I can do that.

It is very compelling to a part to learn that it can be liked when it thought that it would never be. We are our Resources and we like to be liked. If a Resource can accomplish its mission and be liked at the same time it will be happy to do that.

Therapist: I want to thank you for helping, Helper. And I want to thank you for being there in the future to help again if you are needed. I'm glad that you have a way that you can help and still be liked by all the other parts. They will all be patting you on the back for helping in the way they appreciate. Thank you Helper.

Helper: That's okay.

RT Action 12, Imagery Check

Therapist: Meagan, right now I want you to once more imagine being near your couch. You see the same spot as before. Look at it. As you look at it how are you feeling now?

Meagan: Yes, I can see it. It just looks like a dark spot.

Therapist: How are you feeling, as you look at it?

Meagan: Like I said. It just looks like a dark spot. It seems strange I got so upset before.

Therapist: That's great. You have done really well. Meagan, you can go ahead and allow your eyes to open so we can talk about the session.

Analysis

A part of Meagan's personality had been vaded and upset. That state felt overwhelmed with feelings of rejection because it felt incapable of winning her father's love no matter what she did. It felt that there was something wrong with it, that it was unlovable. Using Resource Therapy, this Vaded State came to realize that it was the father who was not good at loving, and that she was actually good at loving, better than her father. It also gained a feeling of being loved from an internal loving state (Carer). It was left feeling fulfilled and loved, no longer holding on to the overwhelming feeling of being unlovable.

When Meagan was cleaning the spot on her couch, and was unable to be successful, and while thinking at the same time how her sister had a nicer couch, Meagan's Vaded State, filled with the painful feelings of rejection, took over the Conscious.

Meagan had subconsciously learned a way to get the state out of those upset feelings. She could go shopping and buy clothes that would momentarily cause her to feel special. She could bring these clothes home, admire them, and feel better for a period of time. Other busy Resources might hold the Conscious for hours or days afterward, but at some point her Vaded State would return.

Following the resolution of this Vaded State, there was no need for a helping state to assist Meagan's desire to get away from it. She would be able to attempt to clean spots on her couch, feel a reasonable level of frustration at not being able to do so, and get on with their day without feeling a need to escape.

It is interesting that following the resolution of Vaded States clients almost forget that they have had them. When reminded of the Vaded State issues they had brought into therapy, they look reflective and recall that, yes, they used to do that, but they don't anymore. It feels so natural to them that their mature adult states are now able to do what they want to do; it is easy for clients to not focus on the way it used to be.

It is imperative, when helping clients with addictive behavior, to focus on the Vaded State that is experienced immediately prior to the addictive behavior, and not on the behavior itself.

When I first started to work with Resources, I focused on the addictive behavior, or the OCD behavior, and I found little ability to help clients change. Then, I discovered that the behavior is merely a coping mechanism to help the client move away from the pain of the Vaded State. It is the Vaded State that causes psychological addictive behavior, and it is the Vaded State that needs resolution in order to stop that behavior.

The helping states (Retro Avoiding States) that help move the client away from the painful Vaded State cannot normally stop their behavior, because it is how they help. If no more therapy is done the Retro State will normally not continue (in this case over-shopping), but at a later time the unwanted behavior may return when the Client feels upset by something else.

Therefore, it is important to do Retro State Negotiation to make sure the Retro State is able to take on behavior that will be appreciated by other states. When it agrees to do this it is no longer Retro, because a Retro State is one that carries out behavior that other states do not like.

Chapter 11
Treatment of Conflicted States

This chapter covers the types of presentations that are caused by Conflicted States and their treatment.

Conflicted States that are ready to benefit from a therapeutic intervention would be in a Normal Condition if not for the conflict they experience. That is, they are neither vaded nor Retro. The conflict experienced by Vaded and Retro States is most normally resolved once an intervention brings them from their Vaded or Retro Condition to a Normal Condition. States that can benefit from conflicted state negotiation are most normally states where both have a positive role, but they do not understand or appreciate the importance of the role of the other state.

The other type of states that can benefit from conflicted state negotiation are states that disagree on something important to the client, such as, Should I stay in this relationship?, or, Should I leave this relationship?

Conflicted States are characterized by at least one of the following:

---

1. Two states wanting to be out at the same time.
2. One state disliking or disrespecting another state.
3. The client may report being bothered by an unhappy voice, e.g., You should be working.
4. Procrastination.
5. Inability to decide on a major life decision.
6. Lack of ability to rest or sleep.

Related Pathologies

These states will all have in common a feeling of a level of conflict that is anxiety producing for the client. They do not respect each other.

Conflicted States can cause these Pathologies

- Procrastination
- Sleep Disturbance
- Chronic Fatigue
- Cognitive Dissonance

Treatment Process

Conflicted State negotiation is a process that is only necessary when two states that are not either Retro or Vaded are in conflict. The processes for working with Retro and Vaded States resolves the conflict between those states.

	Two Conflicted States want the Conscious at the same time	Two Conflicted States cannot agree on a major decision	A Retro State is doing behavior that causes conflict	A Vaded State is not liked by other states because it becomes emotional
Example	Work and Rest	Leave job or stay	Passive Aggressive	Fear or High Anxiety
Therapeutic Response	Conflicted State Negotiation	Conflicted State Negotiation	Retro State Negotiation	Vaded State Resolution

When two states in a Normal condition are in conflict the following procedures should be followed.

Table 29: RT Actions used to bring Conflicted States to Normality

---

Action 1: Diagnosis of Resource Pathology
Action 2: Vivify Specific   see page 88
Action 3: Bridging
Action 4: Expression
Action 5: Introject Speak
Action 6: Removal
Action 7: Relief
Action 8: Find Resource
Action 9: Changing Chairs Introject Action
Action 10: Retro State Negotiation
Action 11: Conflicted State Negotiation   see page 128
Action 12: Imagery Check   see page 131

Conflicted State Negotiation (RT Action 11) helps bring states out of conflict.

A Case Illustration of Conflicted State Negotiation

When working with conflicted states there is no need to have clients close their eyes. Therefore, it is easy to use two chairs to facilitate the Resource States' negotiation.

Stewart came in because he was having difficulty sleeping. Sleep problems can be caused by many different things (Emmerson, 2012), but I find they most often relate to Conflicted States. One state is tired and wants to sleep and one or more other states want to spend the time thinking, communicating with someone over an electronic device, playing a game, or surfing the net. In Stewart's case the state that was keeping him from sleeping was a thinking state. It wanted to review the day and plan for the next day. This state was not Vaded or Retro, it just wanted time for reviewing and planning.

RT Action 11, Conflicted State Negotiation has 10 steps to resolve the conflict between two Conflicted States. While all steps are merely guidelines, I will list each step as I illustrate my work with Stewart.

Some things to notice while reading this example of working with conflicted states is a continued emphasis on the positive value of each state. It is important to continue to highlight the importance of each state both while speaking with it and while speaking with the state it has been conflicted with. Imagine speaking with two people. If one person heard you saying negative things about him or her, that would make that person uncooperative. We want the states to want to cooperate.

Case Example with Transcript

Stewart could not sleep*

Therapist: Stewart, I think I understand that when you are trying to go to sleep your head keeps going. You keep thinking about the day you had, and you keep planning the next day. Is that right?

Stewart: I would say that's exactly right.

---

1. Situate two facing chairs with the client in one looking toward the other.

Therapist: (Reaches over and pulls an empty chair a safe talking distance from Stewart, facing him) As you are sitting in the chair you're sitting in right now, do you relate more to wanting to sleep, or wanting to think? Right now, are you feeling more like the tired part, or the thinking part?

Stewart: The tired part.

RT Action 2, Vivify Specific:

2. With the client in one of the chairs use the Vivify Specific Action to ensure one of the **Conflicted States** is in the Conscious, and then get a name for that state.

Therapist: That's good. I want this part of you that just said that, the tired part, to think about being in bed right now, possibly feeling a bit frustrated because you're not going to sleep, but you're very tired. Tell me exactly what it is like where you are right now. Is it dark?

Stewart: Actually it's totally dark.

Therapist: What are you feeling like, laying there in the dark, wishing to go to sleep?

Stewart: I'm feeling really tired and really frustrated. I get so tired of being tired all day and not being able to sleep at night.

Therapist: I can hear your frustration. (Because it is clear that Stewart's tired part is Conscious it can be asked for a name.) What can I call you? What term fits you as you are tired and frustrated?

Stewart: 'Tired'.

RT Action 11, Conflicted State Negotiation

3. Call it by name and ask it what it feels about the other state that it has been conflicted with in the past. Take notes detailing what it says.

> **Therapist:** Tired, thank you for talking with me. I can understand that you would be tired and frustrated. You want to sleep and that has not been happening. Tired, I want you to imagine that thinking part over in the other chair right now. How do you feel about that part?

> **Tired:** I just wish he would leave me alone and let me sleep. I just want to sleep, and I think my health would be better if I could.

4. **Show understanding for its feelings, but make a case to it how important and useful the other state can be**.

> **Therapist:** I can hear you really want to sleep. That makes sense to me. I also expect that that part in the other chair is important too. I know you are very important, Tired, because you recharge the body and get ready for the next day. I can see you need more time to be able to do that.

5. **Ask the client to stand and switch chairs then speak directly with the other conflicted state, making sure you get a name from it for itself.**

> **Therapist:** Right now, Stewart, I want you to stand up (pause while client stands), move over to the other chair (pause while client moves to

other chair) and sit down (as client is in the process of sitting call out the other part). THINKING PART, thank you for joining us. Thinking part, Tired has been telling me about wanting to sleep. I'm sure you are a good part also, and I'm sure you have a reason for wanting to think when Stewart goes to bed. Tell me about yourself. How do you help Stewart?

Stewart: I think about what has been done during the day, and plan the next day.

Therapist: That sounds very important. What term fits you? What can I call you?

Stewart: 'Planner'.

---

6. **Call it by name and ask it what it feels about the other state that it has been conflicted with in the past. Take notes detailing what it says.**

Therapist: Planner, thank you for talking with me. What do you think about what Tired just said? He wants more time to sleep.

Planner: Yes, I guess he does. But that's the only time I get to plan.

---

7. **Show understanding for its feelings, but make a case to it how important and useful the other state can be.**

Therapist: I believe you do need time to think, to review, and plan. Do you also understand how important sleep is? He needs to sleep to stay healthy and be able to function well during the day. Unless he gets enough rest he is not going to do very well in the day that you plan.

You can even do a better job planning if you have a healthy, rested body. Do you understand that?

Planner: Yes, I guess that's right but I still need time to plan.

---

8. **Continue making a case until the conflicted state begins to understand the utility of the other state, then ask it to speak directly with the other state, saying how it understands its importance and how it wants to work together with it in the future with a specified plan of compromise.**

Therapist: Yes you do, Planner. I want to make sure you get that time. If I can find some time for you to plan, would it be okay with you if Tired gets the night to rest. If Tired has the night to sleep, rest, and recharge the body then the body will be healthier and you will do a better job planning. Is it okay with you if I look for some other time for you to plan?

Planner: Yes, as long as I get time to plan.

Therapist: Thank you. You are very cooperative. About how much time do you think you need to plan? I understand this time may vary, but generally about how much time do you need to think about your planning?

Planner: Probably 45 min. would do it

Therapist: Thank you, Planner. Stewart, when would be a good time, either before bed or in the morning after you get up, for Planner to have about 45 min. in order to plan? This needs to be uninterrupted time, so Planner can plan.

Stewart: I think I could have a bit longer coffee in the morning and plan during that time. I would actually rather enjoy that.

Therapist: Thank you Stewart. That sounds perfect. Planner, how would that be for you? You can have 45 min. to plan in the morning while having a cup of coffee. That will be your time and you will be able to plan with the rested body because Tired will have been able to get some good sleep. How does that sound to you?

Planner: That sounds good.

Therapist: Planner, what do you want to say to Tired now? It would be good if you could show some appreciation for how Tired restores the body, and let Tired know that you're going to give him the night to sleep. You are both very important parts. Can you say that now directly to Tired? Just call him by name, start out by saying Tired, and tell him.

Planner: Tired, you can have the night to sleep and I will plan when I have coffee in the morning. Thank you for resting the body.

Therapist: That was very good, Planner. Now, Stewart, stand up and move back over to the other chair.

---

9. **Again, have the client switch chairs and make sure the other state is able to respond in the same way, saying how it understands the other's importance and how it wants to work together with it in the future with a specified plan of compromise.**

Therapist: (As the client sits down call out the name of the other Resource State clearly.) TIRED, did you hear that? Planner understands that you are important, and he is willing to give you the night to rest and sleep. He is happy to plan during his coffee time in the morning. I think Planner is a very important part. What would you like to say to Planner about how important he is, and about thanking him for allowing you to have the night? Call him by name, start out by saying Planner, and then tell him what you want to say.

Tired: Planner, thank you for letting me have the night. Thank you for planning in the morning. I understand that you are important.

---

10. **Show appreciation to both states for working together and suggest that in the future as circumstances change they will be able to continue to work together and compromise.**

Therapist: That was very good, Tired. It is good that both of you, Tired and Planner, understand and respect each other. It is good that you are both able to communicate directly together with each other now. There may be times in the future when Tired needs some extra time, or there may be times in the future when Planner needs some extra time. Now that you can communicate together you can work that out between you.

RT Action 12, Imagery Check

Therapist: Now, Stewart, I want you to imagine yourself tired, and laying down at the end of the day to sleep. Planner is happily giving permission for Tired to rest. How are you feeling?

Stewart: Peaceful. I don't hear anything in my head.

Therapist: That's very good. I want to say thank you again to all those great Resources. They each have an important job, and it is good when they have their own time.

It may sound like the Resource States are being spoken with in a simplistic language. I find this is a good way for them to hear and understand clearly. I also speak in a rather loud voice so it can easily be heard. Anything that makes it hard for a Resource State of the client to hear or understand can cause another Resource State to take over the Conscious in an attempt to help it understand. We want to be able to finish work with the Resource States that need the work. If you do notice that a different Resource State is talking, politely indicate to it that you want to continue to speak with the state you were addressing, e.g., "This isn't Planner that just said that, is it?"

No.

I didn't think so. Right now I want to speak directly with Planner. Planner, I know you work hard to plan the day. (Then, the next question is for Planner) It helps to call states by name continuously. That keeps away any question of who you may be speaking with, or who should be answering.

In this example no Vaded State was involved. Sometimes during Conflicted State negotiation a Vaded State becomes evident. This is noticed when one of the states shows affect that does not correspond with the moment. A state may begin to cry, or show other affect. When this occurs the client may be told, "Just allow your eyes to close." Then the RT Actions for Bridging and Vaded State resolution can follow. It is not necessary to do the Vivify Specific Action, as the affect reveals that a Vaded State is already holding the Conscious.

Chronic Fatigue

I have found a high correlation between Chronic Fatigue Syndrome and clients who have Resources that resent rest. It appears that when clients resent rest, and do not allow Resources that want to rest, the body can become depleted of energy and run down and chronic fatigue syndrome can ensue. When Resources can be negotiated with to understand and appreciate the importance of rest than a balanced work rest regimen can help keep the body healthy.

This kind of negotiation requires Work States to be able to speak directly to Resources that would like to rest in order to give them respect and to let them know that they will be given an amount of time so the body can be kept healthy. Here, again, empty chairs may be used where the client can move back and forth during these negotiations. It is imperative that the Rest State and the Work States speak directly with each other indicating that a compromise has been made and will continue to be honored.

With clients who have suffered from Workaholism, or clients who suffer from Chronic Fatigue Syndrome, it can at first be difficult to find a state that is good at, and enjoys, rest. A good way to do this is to ask the client to allow his or her eyes to close and begin resting right now. Ask the client to relax, to let the muscles go, to allow the chair or couch they are sitting on to hold the body completely. As the client begins to relax you can ask, "What can I call you, right now, as you are resting?"

When you get a name for this part, you can say something like, 'Rest', I think you are a very important part of this person. I'm not sure if, in the past, you have gotten enough time to keep the body rested and recharged. Do you get enough time to do this?

By finding, and engaging with a rest state, the conversation can be started to negotiate a proper amount of time to have a Work/Rest balance. This negotiation cannot possibly work prior to the resolution of any Vaded Avoided State, otherwise those negative emotions would continue to compel the person to work.

Chapter 12
Treatment for Dissonant States

This chapter covers the types of presentations that are caused by Dissonant States and their treatment.

A Dissonant State is characterized by:

1. A feeling of discomfort when doing an activity.
2. Performance that is below normal for the person.
3. Feelings of frustration with self in the way a situation is being handled.
4. A feeling of frustration that an activity has to be done.

Dissonant States are merely the wrong Resource for the moment. They do not want to be Conscious, and feel uncomfortable or inept in dealing with the moment. Where two Conflicted States both want to be out, a Dissonant State does not want to hold the Conscious. It feels uncomfortable, incapable, or restless.

Related Pathologies

These states all have in common the client reporting a feeling of not being able to be as good as they know they can be. Clients will sometimes actually use the phrase, I just feel like I am in the wrong skin.

Dissonant States can cause these Pathologies

- Frustration in coping ability
- Feelings of ineptitude
- Inability to be real self
- Writer's block
- Sporting slumps
- Below par performance

Treatment Process

Treatment of Dissonant States is straightforward. It is important for the clients to find their best Resources to handle difficult situations. There is a negotiation with the state that had been Conscious to give permission for the preferred state to take over during specified times. The Dissonant state is most normally very happy for another capable state to take over.

Table 30: RT Actions used to ensure the Best Resource is Conscious

---

Action 1: Diagnosis of Resource Pathology
Action 2: Vivify Specific   see page 88
Action 3: Bridging
Action 4: Expression
Action 5: Introject Speak
Action 6: Removal
Action 7: Relief
Action 8: Find Resource   see page 113
Action 9: Changing Chairs Introject Action
Action 10: Retro State Negotiation
Action 11: Conflicted State Negotiation
Action 12: Imagery Check   see page 131

Case Illustrations of a Dissonant Conscious State

Case Example with Transcript

Ramona: Argued with her teenage son*

Ramona came to therapy highly stressed. She did not feel good about how she was responding in the relationship she had with her son. He was showing her disrespect, slamming doors, and leaving and staying out later that she wanted. Her response to him was to yell louder and louder. She had felt that raising her voice originally worked, but she had found that it worked less and less, and she had become embarrassed by the way she was talking with him.

This was a situational concern that would either relate to a Vaded State or a Dissonant State. If the amount of emotion that Ramona was experiencing was in line with the situation at hand, then the probability would be that a Vaded State would not be involved.

It appeared that the amount of emotion that Ramona was experiencing was in line with the situation. It would be frustrating to almost any parent of a teenage child, to be yelled at, shown disrespect, have doors slammed, or have to deal with their being out very late. If the amount of emotion that Ramona was experiencing did not fit the situation then a Vaded State would have been the source of that emotion, and it would've been appropriate to follow the RT Actions for Vaded States.

A Dissonant State is not vaded with emotion from the past, therefore it merely feels anxiety in relation to the current situation. A Vaded State carries unresolved emotion from the past, so the level of emotion it experiences will go beyond what would be expected from a current situation. This is the way a Dissonant State is distinguished from a Vaded State.

Ramona was not pleased with the way she was handling her situation and this added to her amount of stress. She needed to access a more appropriate Resource State so she could respond in a way she could feel better about.

RT Action 2, Vivify Specific

Therapist: Ramona, I want you to tell me exactly what you are experiencing with your son. Just pick out one single incident and tell me about it.

Ramona: Where do I start? Two nights ago he came out of his room and down the stairs after hibernating in there for over an hour, and he told me he did not want any of my crap, that he was going out. I told him not to walk out that door, but he went straight out and slammed it behind him. He did not come back in until 11pm.

Ramona was obviously upset when she finished saying this. This is an indication that the disturbed Resource State was in the Conscious, so therapy could continue working with that distressed state.

Therapist: That sounds very difficult. It makes sense to me that you would be upset, and that you would want a different way of responding to him.

Ramona: I really do. I'm not sure how much longer I can take this. Sometimes I feel like kicking him out, but he's just 16

Therapist: Yes, I might have some of the same feelings too, if I were you. I have a question for you. Considering his behavior, considering and acting just exactly the way he is acting, how would you like to respond to him both externally and internally? That means even if he does not change, when he yells at you and shows disrespect, how would you like to respond? How would a person that you would see as the best parent in the world respond?

Ramona: I guess I wouldn't yell back at him. He yells at me and then I yell at him, and then he gets angrier and I get angrier and it just gets out of control.

Therapist: That sounds like a really good start. You don't want to yell back at him, even if he is not showing the kind of respect that he should. That is one aspect of how you want to respond externally. How do you want to feel, internally, when this is happening? It is important to us to know both how you want to respond and how you want to feel. When he is yelling at you and you are not yelling back how do you want to feel internally?

Ramona: I just want to remember how I love him and how he must be going through something that's hard, for him to be talking to me in the way that he is. I really do know that he loves me. It hurts me a lot that we have started having these yelling matches.

Therapist: I think I'm getting more clear on how you want to respond externally and internally. You want to stay calm internally and show him respect externally. Is that right?

Ramona: Yes, that's right.

RT Action 8, Find Resource

Therapist: Okay Ramona, when have you in the past been able to stay focused on how you feel about a person when they are disrespectful to you? When have you been able to see through the other person's anxiety to see how much you care? When have you been able to remain calm even when the other person is upset with you? When have you been able to do those things recently, a long time ago, at work, with a friend, or with a family member?

Ramona: I guess I could do that when Tommy was little. He would get upset and I could see that he was upset, and I wouldn't yell back. Yes, I was able to do it then.

Ramona was able to answer this question quite easily. It is not unusual for a client to have difficulty answering the question that defines the Resource they would like. If they do find difficulty in answering that question I merely ask them to describe what it would be like to have that Resource. When they are describing what it would be like to have the Resource, as they are explaining I stop them and ask them what I can call the part of them that is describing this Resource. Then I ask that part if it would be willing to take on this role that it is able to understand and explain so clearly.

Because Ramona was able to remember a time she was able to use the Resource that she needed, all I had to do was get a name for it and ask if it would be willing to help her.

Therapist: Ramona, just allow your eyes to close and tell me about a time when Tommy was young and you were able to see him upset and you were able to respond with love. Tell me exactly where you are. Are you in his room, the living room, or a kitchen? Tell me exactly where you are right now while in your mind's eye you are seeing him upset as a child.

Ramona: I'm in the kitchen.

Therapist: What is happening?

Ramona: He is just little. And he doesn't like what I gave him to eat. He actually flung it to the floor. I can see that he is upset, but I just think he's cute.

Therapist: Right now, as you look at him thinking he's cute, how are you feeling?

Ramona: I feel really proud to have him.

Therapist: What can I call you as you watch him, feeling really proud to have him? What term fits this part I'm talking with right now?

Ramona: Proud Mom.

Therapist: Proud Mom, thank you for talking with me. I can see you are a really good part of Ramona. Proud Mom, Ramona really needs you now. You are a part that can see through upset behavior, you are a part that can stay connected to life, and you are part that can help Ramona today. Proud Mom, would you be willing to be a Resource for Ramona when Tommy gets upset? Would you be willing to be Ramona's part that can see Tommy, see his upsetness, and remember the love?

Ramona: Yes.

Therapist: That's great. You can be very helpful. This will not only help Ramona, I'm sure it will help Tommy too.

RT Action 12, Imagery Check

Therapist: Now, Ramona, knowing you have this Proud Mom part, I want you to think again of Tommy coming down the stairs in one of his bad moods and yelling. Proud mom is here. How do you want to respond?

Ramona: I just want to see him as my baby. I want to have a smile for him and tell him what I need to tell him.

Therapist: What do you need to tell him?

Ramona: I need to tell him that I love him, and that my rules are because of my love for him. Maybe he will hear that.

Therapist: I expect that at some level he will, if not instantly, over time. How are you feeling right now responding to him in this way?

Ramona: I don't feel out of control. I feel like this is his problem and I'm not adding to it. I may have a chance to help him with it.

Therapist: You are very articulate, Ramona. I can imagine this is still going to be challenging, but it seems like you have found a Resource that you feel better about using.

Ramona: I hope so.

Therapist: You can just go ahead and allow your eyes to open now.

Ramona was a good client who responded well to this technique. The key to finding a preferred Resource is to make sure the client defines exactly how they want to respond externally and how they want to feel internally. Then find a time when they have been able to experience this, get a name for that Resource part and make sure it realizes that there is an important job waiting for it. Use imagery to take the client to the situation when that Resource will be needed so it can be tested.

Case Example with Transcript

Jane was nervous about talking with men*

The client, Jane, reported having difficulty often when she spoke with men, especially men who she did not know very well. This was one of the things she presented at the beginning of the session. Following work for another issue, a near drowning, which I have also described in this book, there was still time left in the session, so I decided to work with her on this issue.

At the beginning of the session Jane had mentioned that she was assertive when teaching assertiveness training, but that she was not assertive when speaking with people she did not know very well, especially with men.

RT Action 2, Vivify Specific

Because this was over half way through the session it was much easier to access Resource States. At this point in the session Jane already had her eyes closed and I had been talking with other Resource States, so all I needed to do to gain access to the states I wanted to speak with was to ask them to say, I'm here. Had this not worked, I would have returned to the process of Vivify Specific (see RT Action 2).

My purpose in the first part of this transcript was to locate a better state to be in the Conscious when Jane talks with men, and others who she does not know well. In order to do this I asked to speak with a state she had mentioned earlier in the session that could be assertive.

At this point I did not yet know if Jane might have a Vaded State that would cause her negative feelings when she talked with men, but as the session progressed I found that she did not have a Vaded State in regard to this issue.

The state that had attempted to speak with men ('Hidden One') was merely the wrong state for the occasion. It showed no emotion, other than a belief that girls don't really have a right to express themselves to men. This was a fragile part of Jane that might be a good part to view a rainbow or eat a treat, but not a good part to be in a conversation when Jane wanted to be assertive.

RT Action 8, Find Resource

Therapist: I want to talk with another part that can help teach people how to be assertive. That part is assertive itself and it can teach people how to be assertive. Just say, I'm here, when you are ready to speak.

Client: I'm here.

Therapist: Okay. What can I call you?

Client: 'Confident'.

Therapist: 'Confident', thank you for talking with me. 'Confident', I was talking with this person earlier and she said that she sometimes isn't very assertive with people she doesn't know very well. Especially with men. I wonder if there is some way you could help her with this?

Confident: (Nods head) Ahuh, I can do that.

Therapist: I can see you are very confident.

Confident: I am.

Therapist: And you have a lot of talents and that could help here because when she doesn't assert herself and when she doesn't talk with men, that causes her to take on things that she doesn't really need to carry around and if you are assertive with the people that she meets, that could help her feel really expressed and she doesn't have to be burdened by carrying things around.

Confident: (Nods head) Ahuh.

Therapist: I would really appreciate that. Thank you, Confident, and I want to talk with you again, but first I want to talk to a part that in the past hasn't been very assertive, especially sometimes talking with men she doesn't know very well. Just say, I'm here, when you are here.

Client: Yep.

Therapist: What can I call you?

Client: The 'Hidden One'.

Therapist: 'Hidden One'? Thank you for talking with me, Hidden One. Did you hear what Confident said, that she's willing to help you if you are willing to allow Confident to help you?

Hidden One: Yeah, I heard it.

Therapist: I get a sense that you are not too sure about that?

Hidden One: (Nods ambivalently) Yeah.

Therapist: Can you tell me something that might help me to understand this?

Hidden One: I didn't think that girls were allowed to be assertive.

Therapist: What do you think now, Hidden One?

Hidden One: I still think they're not really allowed.

Therapist: Ahuh. That they are not really allowed. When you're talking with men, even though you don't think they're allowed, can you… and I don't know this answer to this, but I would really like to hear it from you?. . . Can you give Confident One permission to come out and help you out?

Hidden One: She can do it if she wants! (laughs)

Therapist: You're really happy with that, aren't you? You're not too keen on sitting there and being nervous, are you?

Hidden One: (Nods and smiles approvingly) She can do it if she wants!

Therapist: Fantastic. Okay, I appreciate that, Hidden One, and I'm sure you've got things that you can do really well. You sound like a nice sensitive part and I'm sure you've got nice roles that you can play.

Hidden One: (Nods appreciatively).

Therapist: Is it okay if you tell Confident One now directly that she can help be assertive when you feel like it with men or with other people that you meet that you don't know very well?

Hidden One: (Nods and communicates with part silently for a little while)

Therapist: What happened?

Hidden One: She laughed. (Hidden One laughs as she speaks.) I said she can do it. I have no problems with that, and she just laughed.

Therapist: Okay. Thank you very much, Hidden One. Confident, can I speak with you one more time please?

Confident: Ahuh.

Therapist: Is that okay with you? That's okay with you too?

Confident: (Confident nods and laughs) Yes.

Therapist: It sounds like you and Hidden One really have worked this thing out.

Confident: Yes.

Therapist: I appreciate that a lot. Jane, how are you feeling right now?

Jane: Really good.

Therapist: You have done a very good job. Just go ahead and open your eyes so we can debrief.

(This therapy was done before I consistently did an imagery check at the end of the resolution stage. It would have been better had I done that. The imagery check helps the therapist and client understand the probably effectiveness of the intervention. If the imagery check indicates no improvement, then further intervention can follow.)

This therapy segment is a good example of a Dissonant State having a role it did not want. 'Hidden One' did not enjoy talking with men, and was not the best state to hold the Conscious while Jane was in those conversations. When Hidden One was in the Conscious during conversations with men, Jane had nervous feelings, and felt like a non-equal.

'Confident' felt totally equal and was really happy to take on the role of talking with men. Resource States like to be useful and they are happy to take on a role if they believe they have the ability.

The only times a Resource State is not happy to take on a helpful role is if it feels it cannot handle the role (I.e., a fragile state could not take on an assertive role), or if an emotional Vaded State has not been resolved (e.g., a fear filled Vaded State can prevent a communicative state from talking in front of a group, but once this state is resolved then the communicative state can take on that activity).

It is more often the case that two states want to control the Conscious at the same time (Conflicted States) than that no state wants to be out. We are our Resources, and we like to do things we feel we can do well.

It should be clear in this example that there was no Vaded State involved. Had there been a Vaded State more intervention would have been appropriate, depending on the type of Vaded State (See RT Action 1: Diagnosis of Resource Pathology). Vaded States are emotional. Hidden One was not emotional. There were no tears and there was no show of emotion. Hidden One merely felt girls were not allowed to talk with men.

There was no need to attempt to change this opinion. It was only the opinion of a young, fragile, Resource that was happy to have no future role in conversations. What was important was for it to feel positive about itself and its role. An attempt to age and educate it would merely have left it feeling criticized. Jane had other states that were happy to assert themselves, and a state that was happy to talk with men in an assertive way. Hidden One was happy with this arrangement also.

Case Example with Transcript

Samantha: Hated washing dishes*

During a workshop I asked for a volunteer who had something to change. No one was immediately forthcoming, until Samantha said she wished she did not hate washing dishes so much. I was really looking for something bigger than dishwashing for a demonstration, but it wound up being interesting. It was an example of a Dissonant Resource State that did not want to be out. It was not vaded.

Samantha came to the front of the room and sat in the demonstration chair.

RT Action 2, Vivify Specific

Therapist: Samantha, thank you for volunteering. Go ahead and tell me everything I need to know about your dislike of washing dishes. What happens?

Samantha: I just don't like it. I have a lot of things I want to do and standing in front of a sink with a bunch of dirty dishes is not one of them.

Therapist: Okay, just allow your eyes to close now. You are standing in front of your sink filled with dirty dishes. What do you see and what do you feel?

Samantha: I see dirty dishes. I feel like I don't want to be there.

Therapist: What time of day is it, and where is the light coming from, the window, or overhead?

Samantha: It is in the morning. I have just had breakfast. The light is coming from the window just in front of the sink.

Therapist: What term fits you now as you stand in front of the sink right now?

Samantha: 'Wistful'.

There was no expression of negative emotion other than not wanting to be washing dishes. Therefore, this was not a Vaded State. It was merely a state that did not want to be doing what it was doing.

RT Action 8, Find Resource

Therapist: 'Wistful', that sounds like a good name. Wistful, I have a promise for you. Wistful, you will never have to wash another dish for the rest of your life. (Samantha looked surprised) Wistful, you are not the best part to be washing dishes. I can see you have other things you would much rather be doing. Right now I want to find a part that would like some brain dead time, a part that might like to have some time out to do something crafty, a part that would like to feel her hands in warm water and see dirty things become clean. I want to talk with a part that may not have had much time out lately, a part that would like to be helpful. Right now I want a part that would like to have some time with her hands in warm water to say, I'm here.

Samantha: Yes, I'm here.

Therapist: Thank you part. What can I call you?

Samantha: 'Crafty'.

Therapist: 'Crafty', that is a good name. Tell me about yourself, Crafty. What kinds of things do you like to do?

Crafty: I used to like to play in the mud. I would make figurines out of the mud and let them dry. I have not really had much to do for a long time.

Therapist: Right now there is something that you could do that would help Samantha. She needs a Resource that would like to have her hands in warm water, and would like to watch dirt disappear. Would you be happy to help Samantha with this activity? It would be very helpful.

Crafty: I would like to do that, as long as I don't have to think about things.

Therapist: That sounds perfect. You won't have to think about things, and this will help out Samantha. Let me just make sure you have permission from Wistful. I want this to be easy for you. Wistful, I know you have not enjoyed washing dishes. Do you give permission for that time to be taken over by Crafty? You can take a well-deserved rest so that you will have more energy for things that you find important.

Wistful: I would love that. Of course I give permission as long as I don't have to wash the dishes.

Therapist: That sounds perfect. Wistful, would you just say out loud right now directly to Crafty that you give her permission to wash dishes.

Wistful: Crafty, you totally have my permission to wash the dishes.

Therapist: Thank you, Wistful. Did you hear that, Crafty? Wistful is extremely pleased that you are going to be helping out. So, next time Samantha has dishes to do, you can have some time out that you can enjoy, time to have your hands in warm water, and time to watch dirt disappear. Is that okay with you, Crafty?

Crafty: Yes.

RT Action 12, Imagery Check

Therapist: Thank you. Samantha, right now, while your eyes are still closed I want you to imagine having just had breakfast. There are dirty dishes that you want clean. Allow yourself to be standing in front of the sink, and allow Crafty the opportunity to have some time. (Pause) How are you feeling right now?

Samantha: I actually feel okay.

Therapist: Just go ahead and allow your eyes to open so we can talk about this a bit more.

Samantha: (Samantha opened her eyes)

Therapist: Samantha, how was that experience for you?

Samantha: That was strange. I really felt a difference. And right there at the end when I was standing in front of the sink I was actually happy to be there.

Therapist: That sounds really good. I just want to say thank you to both Wistful and Crafty, two really good resources that can each help in their own way. And thank you Samantha for volunteering. Samantha, if you ever notice that you have a part out that isn't the best part to be washing dishes, remember you have Crafty.

Resources may be called out when needed. I sometimes find myself getting frustrated when sitting in stalled traffic. It can feel like, if I will the traffic to move, it might actually make a difference. When I notice my frustration I offer that 'stalled time' to a part I have that likes to look around and notice things. It notices other drivers and notices things off the road that I normally would not be able to focus on. That changes my experience of waiting, from frustration, to enjoying the moment. I still want the traffic to get moving.

Chapter 13
Resource Mapping

Resource Mapping: Learning the Self

Resource mapping is the process of learning which Resources a person has, the roles of the states, which states know other states, the nature of their communication, and available states to call into the Conscious so they can be used at the best times (Emmerson, 2003).

The following are some benefits of conducting a Resource Mapping.

1. To learn the range of Resources that are available to the person.

2. To assess the connections of the Resource States to ensure they are cooperating and are not in conflict.

3. To discover if there are states that are Vaded or Retro that need intervention.

4. To assist in self-understanding and self-esteem.

Normal Resource Therapy interventions for presented issues will involve some degree of Resource Mapping, as good notes should be kept with information concerning all Resources contacted, but these interventions differ from Resource Mapping sessions, as they entail only contacting a limited number of Resources and only to achieve the goals of therapy. There is not an effort to produce a more complete map of the client's Resource structure. Resource Mapping is to provide the client with information that may be useful in achieving higher performance, more satisfaction, greater enjoyment, and a healthier psyche.

During the process of mapping, trauma and/or poor communication between states may become evident. At these times, clients who have asked specifically for mapping sessions should be asked if they wish to extend the scope of the sessions to therapeutic intervention. Most normally, clients want to attend to issues as they arise, therefore it is difficult to know the number of sessions a mapping may take.

It appears to be impossible to do a self-mapping. We need the assistance of another therapist to discover our states, at least our underlying states.

The client needs to decide how detailed a Resource mapping is preferred, and this decision can be amended at any time. This decision will entail a balancing between time and money, and the level of self-awareness and work on issues desired. The fee for mapping sessions is normally somewhat higher than a normal consultation fee, as a written map presentation needs to be prepared for the client.

Process

Discussion with each state is limited, mainly to 1) role, 2) name, 3) knowledge of other states, 4) attitude toward other states, and 5) willingness to help either in communication or role.

1. Select any Resource State

2. Vivify Specific when that Resource has come out, and then snowball from it to other States. This means ask it what other Resources it knows, and write down those States.

3. When the Resource is speaking, gather info on 1) Role, 2) Name 3) Knowledge of other states, 4) Attitudes toward other states, 5) willingness to help.

4. Then, move to one of the other states it knows and continue the mapping, gathering this info about each State.

5. Always move to a state from a state that has knowledge of it. This means that when moving to states you may need to return to a state you have already spoken with in order to get to a state that other states do not know.

(Select the first State) The first step in Resource Mapping is to gain access to any Resource States by using the Vivify Specific Action (2). It is helpful to have large, blank sheets of paper available. The name of each state can be circled during a mapping session. A line should be drawn from each state to the other states it knows.

(Role) When talking with a Resource State first ask about its function or role. This provides useful information for Resource naming.

(Name) Next ask the Resource what you can call it. It is a good idea to circle the name it prefers. This makes it easy to quickly locate the name on a page that will become full of words, lines, and arrows. It is not unusual for a state to have some difficulty choosing a name and it may be necessary to suggest a name yourself, but always check that the name you choose is acceptable with the state with which you are speaking. For example, if the role of the state is to tidy and clean, you might ask the state if you could call it "Cleaner." It is important to get a name for each of the states you speak with so that you can easily call the state out again whenever needed. This also provides a reference to the state for communication with other states. You will be able to ask other states if they know "Cleaner." Always give the state the first opportunity to name itself, and do not assign a name to a state without first checking that the state is happy to accept the name. Occasionally a state will give itself a negative name, such as "Dummy." When this happens I attempt to see if there is a less negative name that the state will be happy with, but if the state is reluctant to change the name, I will accept the negative name. In therapy it is often the case that a state that first gave itself a negative sounding name, later wants to change the name to something more positive, to reflect a change in how it feels. I do not accept negative behavior names for a state. For example, I would not accept the name 'Smoker'. I would ask the state what its, purpose is, how it helps the client. A state that currently smokes might help by being a 'Rebel', by being a 'Socializer', by helping 'Relax', or by helping the client to 'Escape'. Remember, do not let a different state name a Resource. The first state you speak with may say it knows a lazy state, but when that state is given an opportunity to name itself it may name itself, 'Recharger'.

(Knowledge of other states) Most Resources communicate frequently with one or more other states. It is useful in mapping Resources to discover which states each Resource knows and communicates with. "What other states do you know?" can be a revealing question. Another technique is to ask the Conscious state if it knows states you have already discovered. I like to draw a pencil line between the circled names of the states that they communicate with. There will often be clusters of states that know each other well, and work together, and they may be quite separate from other states or clusters of states. There are often surface and underlying states that have no knowledge of the existence of some underlying Resources. Sometimes even surface states do not know each other, as is the case when a person cannot remember the last few minutes of driving, or some other activity.

(Attitude toward other states) Along the pencil line that connects states that know or communicate together I write comments about how the states think and feel about each other. Above the line I put an arrow in one direction and below the line I put an arrow in the other direction. This allows me to know the feeling of each state toward the other. For example, if the state 'Protector' dislikes 'Hedonist,' above the line I would make a note of this with the arrow pointing from 'Protector' to 'Hedonist.' Below the line the arrow would point in the opposite direction with comments on the attitude 'Hedonist' holds toward 'Protector.'

(Willingness to help) An important part of mapping is discovering how the different states would like to be helpful. It is useful information for the client to learn about a state that has skills in assertiveness when that state is willing to interact with people when called upon. A wise state may be asked to call upon either the state that can be assertive or a state that can show more anger, depending on the situational need. Resource Mapping can inform clients of their potential and give them the information to reach toward that potential.

What to give the client

Following a Resource Mapping the notes should be typed so the client can have a copy of the information gained during the mapping. I use a hanging indent paragraph format where the name of the Resource is indented out followed by its role, the other states it knows, its attitude about those states, and how it may be able to be useful to the client. There is a paragraph for each Resource State that has been mapped.

Clients love the process of Resource Mapping and the information they receive from it. When Resource Mapping is used in couple's therapy, both individuals seem to enjoy seeing and talking about both their map and the map of their partner.

Advantages to a Resource Mapping

There are several advantages people gain from learning about their Resources. A number of my clients have said they feel much better in just knowing who they are and why they are the way they are. When we experience our own states and feel what each state feels it is a self-revelation. Some clients have said they thought they were crazy, the way their mood changed in a seemingly random fashion. When they learned their states, and the role of each state, it made sense to them. They felt empowered and better able to be in control in their lives. The following section will deal with how learning your Resources can increase personal development, and our ability to enjoy life.

Personal Development with Resource Therapy

Knowing our states can benefit our personal development in several ways. Some of the assets include:

1. We can safely experience the emotional depths of childhood, regardless of our age.

2. We can feel love.

3. We can become assertive at appropriate times.

4. We can be angry at appropriate times.

5. We can be confident in speaking.

6. We can face criticism without feeling abused.

7. We can be our logical self when it is appropriate.

8. We can be our party self when it is appropriate.

9. We can experience better physical health.

A hug while in a fragile, child state, is an extraordinary experience. It is felt and appreciated deeply. A hug while in an intellectual state feels cold and uneasy. Imagine what it would be like having to live in a single Resource. Consider Paul, who is stuck in a head/rational state. Paul responds to everything rationally. There is no evident confusion over choice, since there is only the rational choice. There are no evident feelings of joy, fear, love, or hate. There is no excitement or feelings of awe and wonder. There is just "getting down to business," just evenness, just a low level of emotion. There are some Paul's out there, who have learned to stay in one or two states almost all the time, to the detriment of their ability to enjoy living.

What defines us is our feelings, our ability to experience love, awe, wonder, fear, and even hate. We are emotional people in a wonderfully emotional world. Too often we lose the ability to be a child, or to think of what we want, rather than what we "should" have. We are made up of a large number of Resources with a wide variety of potentials. Our most enjoyable states are the child states. It takes a combination of courage and wisdom to be able to readily access them. While they are our most enjoyable states, they are also states that should only be called out when it is safe, otherwise they can feel over-exposed and may refuse to come out at all. Therefore, we need our assertive states too.

As we age, many of us learn that it is easier to stay away from some of the more fragile child states that have the capacity to really get excited, to love, and to be amazed, but also have the capacity to hurt, and fear. We not only have these fragile inner states, but we have states whose role it is to protect them; states that are a bit hard and crusty, with a shell. Learning our states allows us the ability to allow a fragile child state into the Conscious to experience the 'wow' of a hug, love, awe, taste, and more, when it is safe. A wise state can be called upon to act as the traffic director to see if the time is safe to allow the child state into the Conscious, and to decide when the child state should be protected by calling out a tougher, protector state. The goal is to experience powerful feelings, without feeling exposed, or overexposed.

We can learn that it is safe to call out a fragile child state (all child states are not fragile) when we are with someone who we can trust. It is important to learn to expose fragile states only when it is safe, and allow the protector states to do their job when it is not safe. It would not be good to expose a fragile state to someone who would likely hurt it. This would make it more difficult for that state to become Conscious the next time. The more a state is hurt, the less it is willing to come out. This is why it is useful to use a wise state to determine the safety of allowing a fragile child state to come out.

I, personally, have a state that is so fragile I have learned to call it out only when I am with someone I have great trust with, and then only when my eyes are closed. When I have great trust and get a loving hug I can call this state out, and the experience is incredible. It feels like a very young state (started when I was young), so I have named it "Infant." If I stay in "Infant" and open my eyes I can feel over exposed. My wise state understands this and only calls infant out when it is safe to feel that wonderful flow of love from someone I trust. If I am with people whose purpose and/or honesty are something I question, my wise state calls out a nice hard, crusty, assertive state that can handle hardship; a state with a nice thick crust that can keep the barbs from penetrating to my fragile parts.

How many States to know?

Resource mapping will probably never result in all Resources being mapped or known. It is up to the individual how extensive a mapping is desired. Most of the surface states, the states that often become Conscious, and some underlying states may be mapped in a single session. A single session of Resource Mapping will generally result in the client and the therapist becoming familiar with 5 to 15 states. Becoming familiar with this number of states, especially with common surface states, can be enriching for the client. We have a much larger number of states.

Some clients will wish to gain a more full understanding of their Resource structure, and learn about their underlying states. These underlying states affect us occasionally, and often possess assets that we seldom gain benefit from. These underlying states may be accessed by Vivifying Specific times when the client have feel young or fragile. Learning about these states will give the client a more full understanding of their personality, their strengths, and their resources. It will also provide the client with a rather detailed history of experiences, since allowing underlying states expression brings to the surface experiences of those childhood states. It is important to note that the memories of any Resource may not be totally accurate. This is true for both surface states and underlying states.

A more complete Resource Mapping will take several sessions, especially if issue processing is undertaken. It will result in the client gaining a keen understanding of self and history. It will allow the person to be more fully functioning, even when issue processing is not undertaken. This more complete mapping results in the same kind of awareness that psychoanalysts hope to achieve during the course of analysis. Resource mapping allows this result in a few sessions, while psychoanalysis requires many sessions over a few years.

It is not unusual for trauma to be uncovered during Resource mapping, regardless of the detail of the mapping. When this occurs it is incumbent upon the therapist to ask the client if he or she would like to process that trauma. When a client has come for mapping, and has not indicated a desire to work on issues, a verbal contract is needed before issue processing is undertaken. Often the mapping may proceed and the client can decide after the session about returning to work on the issues that may have become evident. Occasionally, a prime opportunity exists during the session to process issues. The client may be asked immediately if this is something that would be preferred. It should be noted that bringing forth a trauma and not processing it and will leave the client feeling closer to the experience of the trauma. It is preferred to process trauma, rather than to leave it unprocessed, although this should always be the decision of the client.

Chapter 14
Managing Pain and Somatic Symptoms

In 1990, with the article, "Dissociation and displacement: where goes the "ouch?", John and Helen Watkins demonstrated that when the hypnotized client receives a suggestion that a pain will not be felt, even though the surface state may report experiencing no pain, an underlying state does feel that pain. This underlying state can cause the client later psychological or physical issues. It can become Vaded. It is therefore important to understand appropriate techniques for dealing with pain and somatic symptoms when using therapeutic interventions.

Pain and Somatic symptoms may be organic or psychosomatically based. Therapeutic techniques are required to both assess 1) if a symptom is organic or psychosomatically based, and 2) how to safely intervene to moderate or eliminate the symptoms of each. Organic symptoms require the recruitment of a strong underlying state, while psychosomatic symptoms require Vaded State resolution.

It is important to clarify that psychosomatically based pain or somatic symptoms often become organic, and measurable. For example, merely being stressed brings about the release of epinephrine. This is the same neurotransmitter commonly called adrenaline, and its release brings about a number of physiologically measurable changes. Digestion slows, the production of antibodies slows, blood flow to the extremities of the hands and feet slows causing finger temperature to decrease, are just a few of the physiologically measurable reactions to psychological stress.

When determining the appropriate psychological intervention the important aspect to consider is whether symptoms are based in a psychological root cause, or a physiological root cause. Tension headache is a good example of a symptom that is based in a psychological root cause. The psychological tension results in constriction of muscles that in turn results in a headache.

A tooth being drilled is an example of an organic root cause. It is obvious that the pain is coming from the drill touching a nerve in the tooth.

It is possible for a psychological intervention to benefit clients who have pain or somatic symptoms that are both psychologically caused and organically caused. Still, there are obviously limits to the ability of psychological intervention in physiology. While a psychological intervention may help a person deal with a physiology that is purely organically based, it may not have any further benefit. For example, a person without an arm will not get a physiological benefit from a psychological intervention. A cavity cannot be removed with good therapy.

It is possible for a person who is suffering from an organically based symptom to gain some relief with a psychological intervention. For example, the production of antibodies is important in both fighting off disease and limiting the time that it is present. When a client is able to feel internally at peace, and when a client is able to have better access to their Resource State that can relax deeply the production of antibodies greatly increases. Psychological pressure can cause a person to become more prone to physiological disturbance.

The appropriate psychological intervention will differ depending on whether the symptom is organically based or psychologically-based. Therefore, it is important to understand how to tell if a symptom is somatically based or psychologically-based.

Ways to determine if pain or illness is Organic or Psychologically-based:

- If the pain or illness is situationally based, in other words if it happens during certain times but not other times (e.g., "It happens when I go to town but it doesn't happened when I am at home"), then it is most likely to be a pain or illness that is psychosomatically based.
- If the pain or illness happens randomly then it may be either organically based or psychosomatically based.

- Disturbances that are almost always organically based include schizophrenia, manic depression, ADHD, and obviously, injuries.
- Disturbances that are often, at least partially, psychosomatically-based include, both tension headaches and migraine headaches, irritable bowel syndrome, endometriosis, asthma, and any situationally based symptom.

Course of action for Organic and Psychosomatic Pains:

- **Prior to working with pain or somatic symptoms** it is important to ensure that the client has seen a medical doctor to make sure that the symptoms are not indications flagging necessary interventions.
- **If a pain or somatic symptom is psychosomatically-based** the best course of action is to ask the client to describe in great detail the exact sensations that are currently being experienced, and during that description, ask the client to describe what is being experienced emotionally. Bridging may then take place from the emotion to the ISE, and work may be done to resolve the Vaded State associated with the pain, or to resolve and negotiate with the Resource State that is creating the pain.
- **If the pain or somatic symptom is organically based,** it is important to ensure that enough of the pain is continued to be experienced to keep the client safe. We do not want to eliminate a pain that is an indicator for further medical attention.
- **When it is clear that an organically caused pain is not benefiting the client,** a good technique to reduce the sensation of that pain is to ask a brave underlying Resource State to take on the sensations so that the Conscious state does not have to. The underlying state that is willing to take on the pain may be trained to go through the Separation Sieve (Action 14) anytime it chooses to cleanse itself of any pain it has collected. This process may be used for the underlying state to take on only a portion of the pain so that the Conscious state can be aware of a smaller amount of pain, in order to react appropriately. It is best to make sure the client returns to therapy, so that this brave underlying state can be returned to in order to determine that

it is happy to continue with its important work of diverting pain sensations from reaching Conscious states.

Non-appropriate and appropriate pain interventions, and why:

- **It is inappropriate to merely suggest to a client that a sensation or pain will not be experienced:** When this is done the underlying state that takes on that pain may not be prepared, may feel traumatized, and may cause the client psychological or physical problems in the future.

- **Interventions for somatic illnesses:** Resource therapists can work with somatic illnesses in the same way that somatic pains are worked with. In order to find the state that is associated with the somatic illness the therapist can ask the patient to describe in great detail the symptoms and sensations of that illness, and in the midst of this description the therapist should ask the patient to describe the emotions that are being experienced at the moment. Those emotions can then be bridged to in order to find the Vaded State that is associated with the illness. When this state is resolved there is often a reduction or removal of the symptoms that had previously been associated with that state.

Working with psychologically based Pain or Somatic Presentations

1. Have the client close their eyes and go into detail about the current vivified sensations of the pain or complaint (Imagery Check, Action 2).
2. Ask what emotion is being felt in the middle of this detailing.
3. Vivify the location in the body where that emotion is experienced.
4. Bridge
5. Resolve the associated Vaded State using Expression (Action 4), If Vaded with Rejection, Introject Speak (Action 5), Removal (Action 6), and Relief (Action 7).

6. If pain or illness was situationally based, use Find Resource (Action 8) to locate a Resource for that situation in the future, then Imagery Check (Action 12).

Working with organically based Pain or Somatic Presentations

1. Have the client close their eyes and go into detail about the current vivified sensations of the pain or complaint. This should take a few minutes to ensure appropriate focus.
2. Ask for a name of the Resource State that is experiencing the unwanted symptoms or pain.
3. Thank that state for having taken on the symptoms so all other states would not have to.
4. Ask to speak with a brave and strong state that would be willing to volunteer to take on the sensations so the other states will not have to. This can be an underlying state or a surface state. If it is a surface state there will later be a dual awareness of the sensations, with the more Conscious state barely noticing them. If it is an underlying state there may be little awareness of the sensations. The amount of awareness can be negotiated with the brave state, as there may be a need for some awareness.
5. Get a name for this state and praise the brave state and thank it for taking on such an important job. Let it know that other states will greatly appreciate its important role.
6. Let it know that you will check on it to see how it is going. Teach it to go through the Separation Sieve (Action 14) anytime it chooses, and every night during sleep, in order to stay cleansed of any residue from the sensations.
7. Ask the client to return so you can check on the brave resource state to make sure it feels positive about its work, appreciated, and able to continue helping.

Resources are here to help us. When they are offered an opportunity to help, and it is something that they feel capable of doing it is in their nature to step up and help. In order to find a Resource that is willing to be brave and take on sensations that other states find daunting, a scenario may be given. For example, "John, if there were an innocent infant who you cared about, who you loved, and this infant was being hurt and terrified, John, even if you might receive the pain, what would you do? John's Resource state that answers that question is a brave state that is willing to take on sensations nobly. You can get a name for that state, praise it, and ask it if it would be willing to help the less strong states of John in a way that will gain it appreciation from all other states.

Glossary

Changing Chairs Introject Action: This is a resource activity designed to assist clients to hold less confusion in relation to an Introject. The client is instructed to imagine the essence of an Introject in an empty chair, to say everything that they would like to say to that Introject, then to move into that chair and speak as the Introject back to the client, expressing how what was just said made the Introject feel. It often results in a cathartic sense of understanding.

Conscious: The Conscious is held by the Resource State that is currently aware and behaving. When a different Resource State takes over the Conscious, sense of self, emotions, behavior and abilities, change. The Conscious awareness may change from intellectual and reflective to reactive and emotional with a change of Resource State.

Conflicted States: Resources in a conflicted condition are in a level of conflict with another Resource to the extent that the individual experiences psychological distress. While it is common and appropriate that Resources hold different opinions (I would really like the car, and there's no way I can afford a new car) Conflicted States achieve a level of conflict that becomes stressful to the client.

Dissonant States: A Resource State that is in the Conscious at the wrong time.

Resource (State): A personality part that was created by the repetition of returning over and over again to a coping skill. It is a physiological part of the nervous system created by axon and dendrite growth and trained synaptic firings. Each Resource manifests the traits of the coping skills that formed it. Each will have its own level of emotion, intellect, and abilities. Whenever a person is Conscious there is a Resource holding the Conscious.

Resource Personality Theory: A theory that assumes that personality is composed of separate parts, called Resources. Resource therapists assume that the most direct way to promote change is to work specifically with the Resource that is troubled, rather than with an intellectual state that can easily talk about the problem.

Imagery Check: At the beginning of the intervention the Vivify Specific Action is used to locate the Resource that requires change. Following the intervention, the Imagery Check is used to return to this initial image to test the effectiveness of the intervention, to give the client practice in a similar setting in the future, and to give the client confidence that the intervention has been effective. If the Imagery Check reveals no change, there is an indication that more therapeutic work is required relating to the issue.

Intellectual Memory: An Intellectual Memory is one that when recalling an occurrence the emotional experience is not relived. Intellectual memories may be held by states that did not experience the original event. Sensory Experience Memories differ from Intellectual memories in that the recalling process includes the emotional experience of the original event.

Intellectual Protector States: These are protector states that come to the Conscious to protect the personality from the emotional feelings of Vaded States. During therapy Intellectual Protector States may attempt to block the therapist from Bridging to the Vaded State that needs resolution. The client intellectualizes, rather than feels. The Intellectual Protector State normally dislikes the Vaded State, seeing it as a state that gets in the way.

Initial Sensitising Event: This is a difficult and emotional event that has overwhelmed a Normal Resource, causing it to become a Vaded State. Later, when this Vaded State comes to the Conscious it brings with it the same negative emotional feelings that it experienced during the initial sensitizing event.

Introject: A Resource's internalized impression of another person, an animal, or an inanimate. Most Introjects are experienced as emotionally positive, but Vaded States hold Introjects from which they have experienced negative emotion. Introjects have only the power given them by the Resource States that hold them.

Normal States: Resources in the Normal condition exhibit psychological health. They function well both externally and within the personality. They are not conflicted with other states and they do not hold psychological distress.

Protector States: Therapeutic resistance is caused by protector states. These are states that attempt to protect fragile Vaded States from coming to the Conscious where the personality would experience the overwhelming emotions they feel. Behavioral examples of protector states coming into the Conscious include anger, withdrawal, intellectualizing, and perseveration. Protector States merely deflect attention, while Retro Avoiding States conduct unwanted behavior to save the personality from the negative feelings of Vaded States.

Retro Avoiding States: Retro States that learn to hold the Conscious to avoid the experience of a Vaded State. In problem gambling, the state that gambles is a Retro Avoiding State. It has learned to protect the client from a painful Vaded emotion filled state by filling the Consciousness with gambling activity. Other Resources will dislike this gambling Resource, but the Retro State believes its role in saving the client from the negative emotions of the Vaded State is more important than the disapproval it endures. Other examples of Retro Avoiding States include the states that cause a client to feel numb, states that act out OCD behavior, self-harming states, and states that are involved with eating disorder activities. These states will hold a strong compulsion to maintain their helping behavior as long as the emotional state they protect the client from remains vaded.

Retro Original States: These are states that have learned a functional coping skill in childhood that is no longer wanted by the client. Much antisocial behavior is a result of Retro Original States and examples include passive aggressive behavior and rage. These Retro States will continue to see their role as important, until they can be negotiated with to take on an altered or lesser role.

Retro States: Resources that, when conscious, act in ways that other Resources (and usually other people) find problematic. There are two types of Retro States, Retro Original States and Retro Avoiding States. Antisocial behavior, gambling, OCD behavior, and Eating Disorder behavior are examples of Retro States assuming the Conscious.

Sensory Experience Memory: A Sensory Experience Memory is one that, when experienced, the person emotionally re-experiences the original event. A Sensory Experience Memory is most normally experienced only closer in time to the event. For example, immediately after experiencing something emotional, good or bad, it is common to relive the emotional experience during recall. As time passes, most Sensory Experience Memories are transformed into Intellectual Memories. Sensory Experience Memories may only be experienced in the longer term when the Resource State that had the original experience is holding the Conscious.

States Vaded with Confusion: Following an initial sensitizing event, this Resource is left with a fundamental and profound level of confusion, and its response to this lack of ability to understand is a profoundly uncomfortable unknowing. While Resources Vaded with Fear, Rejection, or Disappointment hold a distinctly negative emotion, Resources Vaded with Confusion exhibit anxiety about what is not known to a level that is problematic to the client. These states are often characterised by rumination.

States Vaded with Disappointment: This Resource takes on an overwhelming feeling of disappointment because of the gulf between what was desired or expected in life and the perceived reality. It is not the magnitude of what has happened that vades this Resource, it is the interpretation of what has happened that vades the state. These states cause psychological depression.

States Vaded with Fear: Resources Vaded with Fear are carrying internal fear everywhere they go and when they come to the Conscious they bring it to the surface with them. Resources Vaded with Fear prevent clients from feeling free to live their lives in a way that they choose, and they are the root of many psychological disturbances.

States Vaded with Rejection: Resources Vaded with Rejection feel unlovable. This feeling of not being good enough drives the client, when it comes to the Conscious, to experience emotions of disempowerment, and they sometimes create a need to be perfect, as expressed in over competitiveness, out-of-control purchasing, and eating disorders.

Surface Resources: Surface Resources, as opposed to Underlying Resources, are those that are used frequently. They normally share memories together, and often observe other surface states when one is in the Conscious. A Resource that is out at work, and a Resource that is out while travelling are examples of Surface States.

Underlying Resources: Underlying Resources, as opposed to Surface Resources, are those that have been out frequently in the past but currently seldom come into the Conscious. Most childhood states are underlying Resources, with memories not readily available to surface states. Vaded States are most commonly underlying states, which occasionally come to the Conscious harbouring feelings of angst.

Vaded Avoided States: Vaded States are problematic for a client in two ways, they can be Vaded Conscious States or Vaded Avoided States. Vaded Avoided States do not hold the Conscious, but when they come near or temporarily into the Conscious a 'helping state' (a Retro Avoiding State) uses an addictive behavior to force the Vaded State out of the Conscious, saving the client from having to re-experience the overwhelmingly bad feelings of the Vaded State.

Vaded Conscious States: Vaded States are problematic for a client in two ways; they can be Vaded Conscious States or Vaded Avoided States. Vaded Conscious States come into and hold the Conscious, causing the client to feel emotional and out-of-control while they do. When they come to the surface they bring with them their overwhelming negative emotions, and this is what the client experiences when they are in the Conscious.

Vaded States: Resources that were in a Normal Condition prior to experiencing an initial sensitising event that, because there was no form of crisis intervention, left them feeling chronically overwhelmed with the negative emotions. These Resources, while in a Vaded condition, are the cause of much pathology.

Vivify Specific: This refers to vivifying a specific instance when a Resource has been in the Conscious in order to bring it back into the Conscious during therapy for the purpose of intervention. Some clients attempt to give the therapist general times a Resource has been out, and this presentation will not bring the desired Resource into the Conscious. The Vivify Specific Action requires very specific detail relating to a time the state has been conscious. During this process present tense language is used.

Appendix 1: Comparison of RT with EST

Resource Personality Theory and Therapy compared with Ego State Personality Theory and Therapy

There are a number of distinct differences between Resource Personality Theory and the Theories of John and Helen Watkins (1997) and their Ego State movement. Both are excellent therapeutic approaches, and both are based on the assumption that the personality is composed of parts.

There are fundamental differences between them in how the personality is viewed, and in therapeutic techniques. Below are some of the major differences.

Table 31: Difference between Resource Therapy and Ego State Therapy

	Resource Therapy	Ego State Therapy
A Personality State is called	A Resource State	An Ego State
When out it is called	Conscious	Executive
Where do the different personality parts come from?	Resources are Developed by practicing coping skills, resulting in normal brain growth.	Ego States are Developed by the Personality Splitting.
Can a part be made instantly?	State formation takes months of training. An existing state may be traumatized, but it can later return to normality.	A state can develop instantly during a single trauma.
What are Introjects?	Introjects are merely impressions states hold. They hold no power of their own.	Introjects are not created by states and can become a personality part, an Ego State.
How Introjects are worked with?	States become empowered by gaining an understanding that Introjects are merely impressions.	Introjects are worked with directly to get them to change so they can be more positive.
Is hypnosis a requirement to use this therapy?	No. No Hypnotic inductions are necessary.	Yes. Hypnosis is almost always used.
Who can practice this therapy?	Same requirements as learning CBT or any other therapy.	Only people with hypnotic training
Diagnosis of States	Diagnosis categories that relate to DSM classifications	No accepted diagnostic categories
Techniques	12 Core Actions	Sometimes used with EMDR.

Personality Development

The Watkins saw personality parts developing from the personality splitting; split off from the core ego because of trauma (Watkins & Watkins, (1997) pp. 26).

Conversely, Resource States are seen to develop when coping skills are needed. These personality parts physically develop over a significant amount of time by the behavioral training of the axon/dendrite/synaptic connections. The brain grows according to the amount and type of stimulation it receives and this is how our distinct Resource States develop.

In Resource Personality Theory a personality part does not develop from a trauma, rather an existing personality part that had developed over time can be traumatized. When this part receives proper therapeutic intervention it will again return to its pre-trauma state and assume its original coping function.

Introjects

Most Ego State Therapists see **Introjects** as personality parts that may be worked with so they can change into better personality parts. They work with **Introjects** to change their nature. They believe **Introjects** sometimes become 'Ego States'.

Conversely, In Resource Theory, Resource States are the only actual personality parts. As evidenced for this, Bridging will never go to an Introject. **Introjects** are seen as the internalized impressions of others, held by Resource States. They can be person, animal or inanimate. For example, a separate internalized impression (Introject) of Father is held by each Resource State. The Father Introject of a child state may be seen as scary, but the Father Introject of an adult state may be seen as helpful.

Resource therapists do not attempt to work with **Introjects** to change them. Resource therapists work with the client's Resource States to empower the state and assist it to understand that the past is past, and the negative **Introjects** they hold of the past have no power in the present. Just like actors can pretend to be the roles they play, a Resource State can pretend to be one of its Introjects, but the Introject is still merely an impression. Using the RT Action 5, Introject Speak, a Resource State can speak as an Introject to attain a higher level of understanding about why the state was treated in the manner it was by the Introject.

An Ego State therapist might attempt to change a negative 'Mother' Introject into a positive 'Mother' Introject. Conversely, A Resource therapist would empower the Resource State to understand that it is not responsible for the negative behavior of someone else, and would bring to the Conscious other inner Resources of the client to ensure the state that had felt disempowered or rejected gains a feeling of empowerment, support and understanding. A state that remembers 'Mother' as detached can keep that impression, but becomes empowered by gaining the understanding that it has a value separate from the impression it holds of 'Mother'.

There are two types of Introjects, internalized impressions held by Resource States, and the much more rare, Other Personalized Introjects (OPIs). The personality is dynamic and fascinating, as evidenced by the occasional presentation of an OPI. OPIs are occasional personality expressions that, 1) claim not to be a part of the person and, 2) say they are not where they belong.

Some Ego State therapists will point to a person with an Introject that appears to act like a Personality Part as an indication that an Introject can become a real personality part. I call these Introjects OPIs. When spoken with directly they will claim not to be a part of the personality, and unlike Resource States they can permanently leave the personality. A therapist can ask a Resource State to leave (I do not recommend it, as all Resource States should gain a positive function within the personality) but it will always be there during following sessions, if it is asked to speak. An OPI can leave and it will not be present again.

OPIs will also often say they do not want to leave. While their etiology is unclear, I find when they are negotiated with to leave they can do so without any further indication of being present. Clients will show improvement and often say they feel physically lighter.

The precise negotiation process I use to achieve this improvement uses the imagery of the OPI going to a light. I chose the imagery of a light because most cultures have an archetypal conceptualization of 'the light' as being a positive destination. I suggest to the OPI that while I understand it may not feel it can go to the light, it actually can. It just cannot take anything heavy or negative with it. I suggest to the OPI that it does not have to do anything that it does not want to do, and that we can just explore what its possibilities are, so it can make up its own mind. I use the RT Action 14, The Separation Sieve, to allow the OPI to experience what it feels like when it leaves everything heavy or negative in the sieve. Then I invite the OPI to visit the light, so it can make up its own mind. I suggest to it that if it wants to help the client it can help much more from the light. This process is completely non-coercive, and upon visiting the light and hearing that it can help as much as it chooses from there, it wants to stay. After an OPI has left, regardless of timeframe, other Resource States will consistently report, 'It left.' This is normally a short negotiation, and one that can be very beneficial for the client.

In summary, Resource Therapy and Ego State Therapy have many similarities. They are both powerful therapies that focus on cause rather than symptoms, and they both work with personality parts, but they have some major, core, differences in theory, practice, and in who can be trained. Appendix 2 defines the need for Resource Therapy.

Appendix 2: Why start a new Therapy?

I called myself an Ego State Therapist for many years, and I have written a number of books and articles on my conception of the personality from an Ego State perspective. I spent a summer with John and Helen Watkins in Missoula Montana in 2000, which was very meaningful to me. I had just finished a draft of my first book, *Ego State Therapy* (2003, 2006, 2010). They were welcoming, generous and lovely, and very much in love. On a few occasions Jack would be praising Helen, she would stop him, and say to me, "The problem with Jack is, he just loves me too much."

Jack knew my work was moving away from his, and he said the therapy would evolve and he saw that as a good thing. He had been frustrated that the Psychoanalytic community had not adopted his improved techniques for change, and that is why he and Helen established Ego State Therapy. They saw it as the best way they could get their word out, and it needed to be heard.

It is for this same cause I am starting Resource Therapy. There are three core reasons I believe my ability to 'get the word out' is increased through Resource Therapy.

They are:

1. Resource Therapy uses no hypnotic inductions, therefore significantly more therapists can be trained, and more clients can benefit.
2. In Resource Therapy Introjects are viewed as non-personality parts, and a Resource State can become empowered with this understanding.
3. The term Resource is a positive and accurate description of a personality part. Clients and therapists can understand and relate to it.

I have been teaching and developing parts techniques for a number of years (see Table 32), and I find that hypnotic induction is not needed for clients to gain benefit from the approach. My second book, *Advanced Skills and Interventions in Therapeutic Counseling (2006)*, which I wrote as a text while teaching Masters' Counseling Classes in university, was dedicated to showing how states could be worked with when no hypnotic induction was used. John Watkins commented, Emmerson shows how to activate and work with covert states without inducing hypnosis. This is a significant contribution to the entire field of psychotherapy (inside cover, *Advanced Skills and Interventions in Therapeutic Counseling, (2007)*.

Table 32: Theoretical and Technique Developments by Gordon Emmerson

Personality Theory based on Personality Parts being physiological neural growth, formed by the repetition of coping skills.			2006
The Concept of Surface and Underlying States			2003
State Conditions: Normal, Retro, Vaded, Conflicted (coined the term Vaded)			2006
Other aspects of state conditions	Vaded with Fear Vaded with Rejection Vaded with Confusion Vaded with Disappointment	Vaded Conscious Vaded Avoided Retro Original Retro Avoiding Dissonant States	2013
Criteria for Diagnosis into state condition pathological category			2014
Therapy Process: ACAR – Aim, Classify, Actions, Review			2014
Specific intervention techniques including: Depression, OCD, Addictions, Couples Counseling, Eating Disorders, Crisis Intervention, Grief, DID, Rage, Anti-Social Behavior			2002-2014
Bridging process of Vivify Specific, Attain Age, Funnel			2006
Designated Detailed Therapeutic Actions, including:	Vivify Specific Expression, Introject Speak Removal, Relief Retro State Negotiation Conflicted State Negotiation	Find Resource Resistance Alliancing Separation Sieve	2004-2014

The technique regimens presented in *Resource Therapy* require no hypnotic inductions, and they show amazing results. I want the techniques I have developed to be readily available to all therapists, and not just for those who have studied hypnosis. The current Ego State Therapy movement requires hypnosis training prior to study.

Secondly, a core part of my techniques is the conception of Introjects as being, Internal impressions held by Resource States. They are owned by our states and they have only the power our states give them. E.g., I am in a Resource State now and if while in this state I meet a person, my state will introject an impression of that person and hold it. The introjection of that person by my current Resource State is an 'Introject'. It is merely an impression. It is not a real person, may not be an accurate representation of the real person, and consists only of the impression held by the state that introjected it. This is core to my whole process of Resource Therapy.

When Introjects are understood in this way, the Resource State is seen as having power over the Introject. The Resource State owns the Introject. A Resource State may carry fear of a 'Bad Guy' from the past. The understanding that the 'Bad Guy' really does not exist now, and is merely an impression from the past, allows the therapist and Resource State to 'shrink' the 'Bad Guy' Introject, and express to it fully, "You no longer exist, and you have no power here." In this manner, a Resource State that carried fear can change its internal impression of the 'Bad Guy' from big and scary to little and powerless. The state that carried fear becomes empowered and feels safe (see RT Actions 4-7).

Conversely, many Ego State therapists see Introjects as real personality parts that must be worked with to change. By establishing Resource Therapy, the definition of Introjects and the core associated therapeutic responses to them can be clarified.

Thirdly, the term, Resource Therapy, gives the correct connotation that our parts are our resources. Too often clients and therapists have thought that Ego State Therapy was a therapy about how big someone's ego was. A resource is something that can be useful. That is exactly what personality parts are. When they are healthy and when they are in the Conscious at the right time we function optimally. The title 'Resource Therapy' will allow the therapy to grow more easily and be better understood by both therapists and clients.

I have great respect for Ego State Therapy. I hope the therapy continues to grow and develop. There is an important place for it within the hypnosis community. Because I believe the theories and techniques I have developed can move forward better as Resource Therapy I have chosen to use that title.

I invite others, from any therapeutic orientation, to use the technique regimens that have been developed for Resource Therapy, including the diagnostic categories and the RT Actions.

Appendix 3: Training Sheets

The following sheets are for training. They are flash cards for use with each of the following techniques.

1. Vivify Specific,
2. Bridging
3. Conflicted State Negotiation
4. Practice and Debriefing: Dissonant State (Work with a past issue non-Vaded State, Vivify issue, Ask preferred internal/external experience, find a state that can do this, vivify, name, ask it for help, Imagery Check)
5. Working with an Introject using Empty Chairs: Vaded with Confusion: The Changing Chairs Introject Action
6. Working with a State Vaded with Rejection or Fear
7. Retro State Negotiation: for Retro States or states Vaded with Disappointment
8. Mapping
9. Working with Pain or Somatic Presentations
10. Using the Separation Sieve
11. Working with Dissonant States/Anchoring

Vivify Specific:

1. Find 1 single specific time the desired state was in the Conscious.

2. Ask the Client to allow their eyes to close.

3. Speak in the present tense and vivify a continuing number of aspects about being in this event.

4. Continue until you notice the state you want to speak with is obviously Conscious

5. Ask it, "What can I call you, right now, as you are having this experience?"

Bridging

1. Vivify Specific to make sure the state Vaded with Fear or Rejection is currently Conscious.

2. Continue to define the state with the feelings it has given, while getting the age this upset state feels.

   a. This can be done with the, **'It sounds like I am hearing the voice of a child. How old of a child has this voice.'**

   b. Or, after defining the feeling in the chest or stomach, **'Sit on the edge of that dangling your feet into the middle of that stuff. Look at your feet and tell me what they look like. How old would a person with feet like that be?'**

   c. Or, you can be creative to discover the age feeling of the state that feels little and out of control.

3. Funnel, using the age, the client to the ISE, with questions like:

   a. Being (for example) 5 right now, does it seem like you are more inside a building or outside?

   b. Is it more light or dark where you are having these feelings, being (5)?

   c. Are you alone or is there someone else there?

   d. Tell me what is happening.

Conflicted State Negotiation: Action 11

1. With the client in one of the chairs use the **Vivify Specific** Action **to ensure one of the Conflicted States is in the Conscious**, and then get a name for that state.

2. **Call it by name and ask it what it feels about the other state** that it has been conflicted with in the past. Take notes detailing what it says.

3. **Show understanding for its feelings**, but make a case to it how important and useful the other state can be.

4. **Ask the client to stand and switch chairs** then speak directly with the other Conflicted State, making sure you get a name from it for itself.

5. **Call it by name and ask it what it feels** about the other state that it has been conflicted with in the past. Take notes detailing what it says.

6. **Show understanding for its feelings**, but make a case to it how important and useful the other state can be.

7. **Continue making a case** until the Conflicted State begins to understand the utility of the other state, then ask it to speak directly with the other state, saying how it understands its importance and how it wants to work together with it in the future with a specified plan of compromise.

8. Again, **have the client switch chairs** and make sure the other state is able to respond in the same way, saying how it understands the other's importance and how it wants to work together with it in the future with a specified plan of compromise.

9. **Show appreciation to both states** for working together and suggest that in the future as circumstances change they will be able to continue to work together and compromise.

Working with Dissonant States

(Vivify Specific, Find Resource, Imagery Check)

Vivify Specific:

1. Find 1 single specific time the dissonant state was in the Conscious.
2. Ask the Client to allow his or her eyes to close.
3. Speak in the present tense and vivify a continuing number of aspects about being in this event.
4. Continue until you notice the state you want to speak with is obviously Conscious.
5. Ask it, "What can I call you, right now, as you are having this experience?"

Find Resource:

1. How do you want to respond to the other person, and how do you want to feel internally?"
2. When have you been able to respond like this (repeat the client's response) at any time in your past, with a friend, a child, a family member, or at work?
3. **Vivify Specific** the time that the client has mentioned.
4. Calling this state by its name, ask it if it will be willing to help the client in the future?
5. Ask the Dissonant state if it is happy for the preferred resource to handle situations like this in the future.

Imagery Check:

1. Return to the original problematic image given when the wrong state was Conscious.
2. Suggest that the preferred Resource State is currently present.
3. Ask the client to report how this state is feeling, as it handles the situation.
4. Thank both states you have worked with for their cooperation.

The Changing Chairs Introject Action (9)

1. Vivify Specific:

2. Determine what needs to be said and/or asked:

3. Create an understanding of the Introject in the other chair

4. Ensure complete expression and questions:

5. Direct the client to move to the Introject's chair:

6. Ask the Introject how it feels.

7. Speak directly with the Introject.

8. Direct the client back to the original chair:

9. Debrief with the Client:

Working with a State Vaded with Fear

1. Vivify Specific to make sure the fearful state is in the conscious.

2. Bridge to the ISE

3. Expression: Use shrink if you like and ensure all is expressed.

4. Removal: Make sure the Resource State has the choice for the Introject to stay or go.

5. Relief: Bring in nurturing state, and make sure the Resource State has a positive name.

6. Find Resource: If needed, find a preferred resource to use in the future at this time.

7. Imagery Check

Working with a State Vaded with Rejection

1. Vivify Specific to make sure the fearful state is in the conscious.
2. Bridge to the ISE
3. Expression: Use shrink if you like and ensure all is expressed.
4. Introject Speak: Speak to the rejecting Introject and then return to the Resource State showing understanding at why he or she would have felt rejected.
5. Removal: Make sure the Resource State has the choice for the Introject to stay or go.
6. Relief: Bring in nurturing state, and make sure the Resource State has a positive name.
7. Find Resource: If needed, find a preferred resource to use in the future at this time.
8. Imagery Check

Retro State Negotiation

1. If the Retro State is Retro Avoiding first complete the resolution for the state Vaded with Fear or Rejection. (If Retro Original skip this step)

    a. Locate the Vaded State by using imagery to withhold the Avoiding Behaviour until the anxiety of the Vaded State is present.

    b. Use all steps to resolve the State Vaded with Fear or Rejection.

2. Vivify Specific to bring the Retro State that has performed the unwanted behavior to the Conscious.

3. Show respect and appreciation,

4. Find its purpose and devise a preferred behavior that would fulfil the purpose,

5. Ask the state that did not like the behavior to say directly to the Retro State how it will like it with its new behavior,

6. And, if appropriate, find another state to help with times the old behavior was evident.

7. Do an Imagery Check (remember for Retro Avoiding to do the Vaded State work first).

Mapping

1. Vivify Specific any state and get a name for it.
2. Find its nature and purpose, name, what other states it knows, its relationship to those states, and how it may be helpful.
3. Move to another state it knows and repeat steps 1 and 2.
4. Continue with 1, 2, and 3, until states are mapped or time is exhausted.

Note: Make sure you always move from a state that knows a state to a state it knows, i.e., if you want to engage with a state that REST has mentioned, and you are talking with PLAYFUL, go back to REST to move to the state it had mentioned earlier.

Working with Pain or a Somatic Presentation
(Make a medical referral, if appropriate, prior to work)

Resolution Technique for Resource State caused Symptoms

1. Ask the client to close eyes and ask for vivifying detail for the sensation that is experienced. (do not call it a pain)
2. When it is evident the client is highly focused within the description of the sensation, ask, "What are you experiencing right now, emotionally?"
3. Ask where in the body this emotion is felt (It is almost always in a different location to the pain or the symptom.)
4. Bridge to the Vaded State with this emotion and use the steps to resolve states Vaded with Fear or Rejection.
5. Debrief with the client and suggest that it will be interesting to just continue focusing on living.

Moderation for Organically caused Symptoms

1. Gather detailed information about the symptoms.
2. Get a name for the state that is reporting on those symptoms.
3. Vivify specific any time the client has been emotional (this is centering and helps give the client access to underlying states). If this state needs bridging and resolution do that, otherwise continue to the next step.
4. Ask to speak with a, 'Strong, brave part that would like to have the important and helpful role of experiencing the sensation so the surface state (you can name this state) does not have to.
5. Tell it that it will be very appreciated by the other states, and ask it just to say, "I'm here".
6. Get a name for it and suggest that it can take on the 'sensation' so the other state does not have to, and that it can go through the separation sieve anytime it wants to separate itself from the sensations.
7. Have first reporting state to speak with it directly, saying how much it appreciates what it is doing.
8. Have the brave state respond directly to the reporting state.
9. Tell the brave state that you want to check on it later.
10. Thank all states and ask the client to open his or her eyes.
11. Arrange with the client to return so you can reengage with this state, to check and praise.

Using the Separation Sieve

1. Suggest there is a powerful sieve that cannot possibly let anything heavy or negative through.

2. Just as an experiment (everything can be returned to as it was, if wanted), let the state know that it can easily come through the sieve to 'where my voice is', dropping anything heavy and unwanted, just like a heavy coat sliding off.

3. Ask how that feels now.

4. Ask the state to look back up at the sieve and tell what that stuff looks like.

5. Ask if it wants any of that back.

6. Ask what colour of light or fluid would sizzle it into nothingness.

7. Make a sizzling noise and indicate it is all gone.

8. Ask how the state feels now.

Working with Dissonant States/Anchoring

Vivify Specific:

    1. Find 1 single specific time the dissonant state was in the Conscious.
2. Ask the Client to allow his or her eyes to close.
3. Speak in the present tense and vivify a continuing number of aspects about being in this event.
4. Continue until you notice the state you want to speak with is obviously Conscious.
    5. Ask it, "What can I call you, right now, as you are having this experience?

Find Resource:

1. How do you want to respond to the other person, and how do you want to feel internally?"
2. When have you been able to respond like this (repeat the client's response) at any time in your past, with a friend, a child, a family member, or at work?
3. **Vivify Specific** the time that the client has mentioned.
4. Calling this state by its name, ask it if it will be willing to help the client in the future?
6. Ask the Dissonant state if it is happy for the preferred resource to handle situations like this in the future.

Anchoring

1. Ask the preferred Resource State what animal it associates with itself.
2. Ask it to describe the animal in some detail,
3. To describe its breathing,
4. To describe the setting that it is in,
5. And to describe what it feels like being this animal, with its lungs and abilities.
7. Suggest to the client that any time he or she wants to use this resource, just to imagine begin this animal in this scene.

Imagery Check:

1. Return to the original problematic image given when the wrong state was Conscious.
2. Suggest that the preferred Resource State, the imagined animal, is currently present.
3. Ask the client to report how this state is feeling, as it handles the situation.
4. Thank both states you have worked with for their cooperation.

Appendix 4: Supervision

(Emmerson, 2014)

This section relates to some of the issues brought up during supervision sessions with Resource Therapists. I supervise a number of therapists who have studied Resource Therapy. There are some common issues they bring to supervision that may be beneficial to address here.

Bridging

Therapist: I am having trouble bridging. I'm not sure I'm getting to the initial sensitizing event.

Supervisor: Tell me exactly what you say during the bridging process. What exactly do you say to the client?

Therapist: I tell them to go to the first time they remember having this feeling.

Supervisor: When you use the word remember, you are asking the client to intellectually remember something. That is taking the client away from their Vaded State, into an intellectual state. The only way they will be able to bridge is by having their Vaded State in the Conscious. It is the feelings of the Vaded State that allows that state to connect with the event that caused those feelings. Make sure, while you are bridging, that you only ask about experiences and feelings. Never ask the client to remember, think back, or think about when was the first time you experienced this? It is impossible to bridge unless the client is in the Vaded State.

Therapist: When should I bridge?

Supervisor: You should bridge when the client has a State Vaded with Fear or Rejection. There are other techniques for helping clients with the other types of pathological Resource States.

Changing Chairs Introject Action

Therapist: I wanted to use the Changing Chairs Introject Action, and my client was not comfortable with that. She felt silly talking to an empty chair.

Supervisor: How did you introduce that Action to her?

Therapist: I told her there was an activity I would like to try. I asked her if she would be comfortable talking to an empty chair, pretending that her husband was there?

Supervisor: You are the professional therapist. The client has come to you for your professional understanding of techniques, and for you to select the techniques that will help her get to get the change that she desires. It will be easier for the client when you tell her clearly the steps you want her to follow. If a person goes to a medical doctor with a wound filled with dirt the doctor will not ask the client if the client thinks that wound should be cleaned out and scrubbed, or left the way it is. The medical doctor knows that the wound should be cleaned and gives the client clear instructions so that the wound can be cleaned. In the same way, if you see that the Changing Chairs Introject Activity will help your client become less confused, it is better not to put the responsibility of which technique to use on to the client. Merely pull an empty chair in front of the client, and clearly say, 'This is what I want you to do.' The client will follow your clear instructions, will not be stressed about having to make a therapeutic decision, and will benefit from your professional knowledge.

Holding a State in the Conscious

Therapist: I am having trouble holding the emotional state in the Conscious. I can get the state into the conscious using the Vivify Specific Action, but then it seems like another state takes over.

Supervisor: As soon as you get a Resource State into the Conscious it is important to get a name for it, and continue to call it by that name. If you use its name constantly, almost in every sentence, it will stay in the conscious. It is also helpful to think about talking directly to that state. When states are addressed directly they continue to stay in the Conscious. An example is, if someone sees you may be a bit emotional and if they make a statement recognizing your emotions, that will bring that emotional state into the Conscious. It has been spoken to.

Therapist: What is the best way to ask a Resource State to name itself?

Supervisor: It is better not to say, 'What can I call this part of you?' When you recognize the state that you want to speak with is in the Conscious, say, 'What can I call you, the part that (e.g., is feeling upset)'. Imagine being in a room full of people and wanting to know the person's name you are speaking with. You would not say to that person, 'What can I call this person I'm talking with?' You would say, 'What can I call you? It is always important to speak directly to a Resource State as if you are talking to an individual. That will help it stay in the Conscious, and that will help it feel respected.

Vivify Specific

Therapist: I'm not sure I'm getting the right Resource State into the Conscious in order to do therapeutic work. The Vivify Specific Action does not seem to be working for me.

Supervisor: Tell me exactly what you are saying to the client.

Therapist: I tell him to tell me about a time he felt upset.

Supervisor: That sounds good. Then what happens?

Therapist: He tells me he feels upset most at work. But it seems like he stays in an intellectual Resource State.

Supervisor: Are you making sure he tells you about one specific instance when he felt upset at work?

Therapist: Probably not. He just tells me he feels upset at work.

Supervisor: That is an intellectual state telling about the problem. That is not the state that actually experiences the problem. In order to gain access to the state that actually experiences the problem you have to get him to tell you about a specific instance, and then have him to tell more about that instance in detail, while you speak with him in the first person tense.

Therapist: What do you mean the first person tense?

Supervisor: It is not the first person tense if you say to him, 'What was the expression on your boss's face?' It is the first person tense if you say to him, 'Right now, sitting at your desk, in the middle of the afternoon, what is your boss looking like, as he is looking at you?' In order to Vivify Specific, you must first have the client describe in detail one specific incident, and you must begin to talk with the client about being inside that incident using first person tense. It is much easier to do this when you ask clients to allow their eyes to close, immediately prior to the Vivify Specific Action. Clients are better able to connect with an event with their eyes closed, because they are not having to process all the visual information in front of them.

Therapist: When do I know they are in the right Resource State?

Supervisor: You will be able to recognize that. There's a big difference between talking with an intellectual state about something, and with talking to the state that is emotional. It is clear when a nervous Resource State comes into the Conscious.

Duck Billed Platypus Therapy

Therapist: Sometimes it seems like this just isn't going to go anywhere. I get lost and I don't know what to do next.

Supervisor: Yes, that happens to me too. I practice what I called the Duck Billed Platypus form of therapy.

Therapist: What's that?

Supervisor: A Duck Billed Platypus swims underwater with its eyes closed. When it bumps into a rock it backs up, moves over to the side, and goes forward again. If it bumps into the rock a second time, it backs up moves over again, and goes forward. It continues to do this until he gets around the rock. If I try something in therapy and it doesn't work, I remember what the client is ready to change, I back up a bit, move over, and try something else. That does not mean I will get around every rock, but it does help me in working with clients.

Highly emotional clients

Therapist: When I bridged my client became so emotional she said she did not want to continue.

Supervisor: It is understandable that clients will become emotional. That is often why they are coming to therapy. When we work with the client to bridge to an emotional initial sensitizing event, it is especially understandable that they may feel unable to handle the situation. That is why it is still something that is bothering them currently. Because we know it is only an illusion, an Introject from the past, that is problematic for them we can show strength and understanding. This will help them become empowered. If, after bridging, the client says to me, 'I can't do this,' I will say something like, 'That's OK. We don't have to. Since we know this isn't happening now, if you could do this, what kind of thing would you have liked to have said?' Another thing I might say is, 'That's fine. We don't have to. Let's just shrink him down to 1 inch tall. He is tiny with a squeaky little voice. Please don't step on him, because I want you to be able to tell him what you want to say.' The key is to help the client feel comfortable. Do not say that we have to do something that you don't want to do. Tell the client it is fine not to continue, but then help the client understand that all the power is held by the Resource State. It is much better to leave a Resource State feeling empowered, expressed, understood, protected, and cared for, than to back out and leave the Resource State holding the same fear that it has felt for years.

Introducing Resource Therapy to Clients

Therapist: How do I introduce Resource Therapy to my clients?

Supervisor: When I have a new client, I merely say that the personality is composed of parts; part of me might want to do one thing while another part might like to do something else. I say that I work to make sure that I speak directly with the part that needs change. Then I ask if there are any questions. Actually, very few clients have questions following this introduction, but if they do I answer them.

Appendix 4: Supervision

References

Berne, E. (1957). Ego states in Psychotherapy. American Journal of Psychotherapy, 11, 293 -309. Transactional analysis in psychotherapy: A systematic individual and social psychiatry. New York: Grove Press.

Blakemore, C., and Price, D. J. (1987), The organization and post-natal development of area 18 of the cat's visual cortex, Journal of Physiology, 384, pp. 293–309.

Boswell, Louis K. (1987). The initial sensitizing event of emotional disorders. Medical Hypnoanalysis Journal, 2(4), Dec, pp. 155-160.

Bryck, Richard L.; Fisher, Philip A. (2011). Training the brain: Practical applications of neural plasticity from the intersection of cognitive neuroscience, developmental psychology, and prevention science. American Psychologist, Jul 25.

Buisseret, Pierre, Gary-Bobo, Elyane, and Imbert, Michel (1982).Plasticity in the kitten's visual cortex: Effects of the suppression of visual experience upon the orientational properties of visual cortical cells, Developmental Brain Research, 4 (4), pp. 417–26.

Emmerson, G. J. (1999). What lies within: Ego states and other internal personifications. Australian Journal of Clinical Hypnotherapy & Hypnosis, 20(1), pp. 13-22.

Emmerson, G. J. (2003, 2007, 2010). Ego state therapy. Carmarthen, Wales: Crown House Publishing

Emmerson, G. J. (2006). Advanced skills and interventions in therapeutic counseling. Carmarthen, Wales: Crown House Publishing

Emmerson, G. J. (2012). Healthy Parts Happy Self. Charleston, SC, CreateSpace.

Emmerson, G. J. (2011). Ego state personality theory. Australian Journal of Clinical Hypnotherapy and Hypnosis, 33(2), pp. 5-23.

Emmerson, G. J. (2013). Ego State Conditions. Australian Journal of Clinical Hypnotherapy and Hypnosis, 35(1), 2013. pp. 5-27.

Emmerson, G. J. (2014). Resource Therapy Primer. Blackwood Victoria, Australia: Old Golden Point Press.

Federn, P. (1953). Ego psychology and the psychosis. London: Image Publishers.

Guntrip, H. (1961). Personality structure and human interaction. London: Hogarth.

Holopainen, Debbi; Emmerson, Gordon J. (2002). Ego state therapy and the treatment of depression. Australian Journal of Clinical Hypnotherapy & Hypnosis, Vol 23(2), pp. 89-99.

Jacobson, E. (1964). The self and the object world. New York: International University Press.

Kernberg, O. (1976). Object relations theory and clinical psychoanalysis. New York: Jasonc Aronson.

Levin, Berry. (2010). Interaction of perinatal and pre-pubertal factors with genetic predisposition in the development of neural pathways involved in the regulation of energy homeostasis. Brain Research, Sep2010, Vol. 1350, p. 10-17

Muir, Darwin W., Dalhousie, U., and Mitchell, Donald E. (1973), Visual resolution and experience: Acuity deficits in cats following early selective visual deprivation, Science. 180 (4084), pp. 420–2.

Ritzman, Thomas A., (1992). Importance of identifying the initial sensitizing event. Medical Hypnoanalysis Journal, 7(3), Sep. pp. 98-104.

Schrott, L. M. (1997), Effect of training and environment on brain morphology and behavior, Acta Paediatrica, 422, pp. 45–7.

Wark, Robert C., and Peck, Carol K. (1982), Behavioral consequences of early visual exposure to contours of a single orientation, Developmental Brain Research, 5 (2), pp. 218–21.

Watkins, J. G. (1978). The therapeutic self. New York: Human Sciences.

Watkins, J. G., & Watkins, H. H. (1990). Dissociation and displacement: Where goes the "ouch?", American Journal of Clinical Hypnosis, 33, 1-10.

Watkins, J. G. & Watkins, H. H. (1997). Ego states: Theory and therapy. New York: W. W. Norton& Co.

Wilkinson, Frances, and McGill, U. (1995). Orientation, density and size as cues to texture segmentation in kittens, Vision Research, 35 (17), pp. 2463–78.

Winnicott, D. W. (1965). The maturational process and the facilitation environment. New York: International Universities Press.

Weiss, E. (1950). Principles of psychodynamics. New York: Grune & Stratton.

About the author

   Dr Gordon Emmerson is an Honorary Fellow in the School of Psychology at Victoria University, Melbourne. He is the author of the books 'Ego State Therapy' (2003, 2007, 2010), 'Advanced Techniques in Therapeutic Counseling (2006), Healthy Parts Happy Self (2012), and Resource Therapy Primer (2014). He developed Resource Personality Theory and Therapy and has developed techniques for working with many psychological conditions. As a registered psychologist and member of the Australian Psychological Society, he has published numerous refereed articles and has conducted and published experimental clinical research. Dr Emmerson has conducted workshops in Australia, South Africa, Germany, the UK, New Zealand, the US, and the Middle East. He makes keynote conference and convention addresses on his therapeutic approaches. He provides Foundation Training, a Clinical Qualification in Resource Therapy, Advanced Clinical Training in Resource Therapy, and Train the Trainer.

   Upcoming workshops can be found at the URL, http://www.resourcetherapy.com.

Gordon Emmerson

www.ingramcontent.com/pod-product-compliance
Lightning Source LLC
Chambersburg PA
CBHW080811280326
41926CB00091B/4142